ELEVEN BRAVO

ELEVEN BRAVO

A Skytrooper's Memoir of War in Vietnam

by E. TAYLOE WISE

McFarland & Company, Inc., Publishers

Jefferson, North Carolina, and London

LIBRARY OF CONGRESS CATALOGUING-IN-PUBLICATION DATA

Wise, E. Tayloe.
    Eleven bravo : a skytrooper's memoir of war in Vietnam / by
E. Tayloe Wise.
        p.   cm.
    Includes bibliographical references and index.

    ISBN 0-7864-1916-4 (softcover : 50# alkaline paper)

    1. Vietnamese Conflict, 1961–1975 — Personal narratives,
American. 2. Wise, E. Tayloe. I. Title: Skytrooper's
memoir of war in Vietnam. II. Title.
DS559.5.W58   2004
959.704'3'092 — dc22   2004013459

British Library cataloguing data are available

Cover photograph: Patrolling an area with elephant grass. Note the
defoliated trees from Agent Orange.

Manufactured in the United States of America

McFarland & Company, Inc., Publishers
   Box 611, Jefferson, North Carolina 28640
      www.mcfarlandpub.com

This book is dedicated to the Vietnam dead — those individuals who were so young and so full of life and hope and who perished so uselessly. They made the supreme sacrifice. May their deaths serve as a shining star for all to see in the future, so that our politicians and government never involve us in another useless war where our military might get kicked around the wasted, bomb-cratered lands of some worthless, godforsaken country. This book is also dedicated to those brave individuals, the members of Blackfoot Platoon, Company B, 2nd of the 8th Battalion, 1st Air Cavalry Division (Air Mobile) who served with me from May 1969 to October 1969 — in particular, Bobby C. Barrett of Dallas, GA; Robert Bruce of Fishkill, NY (KIA 9/13/69); Raymond "Chief" Clark of Gallup, NM (deceased); David L. Elia of Hilo, HI; Terrell Gibson of Garysburg, NC (KIA 6/7/69); Fredrick P. Gillen of Clairton, PA (KIA 8/12/69); Wyman D. "Deak" Hensley of Maysville, OK; Edwin J. Hill of Phoenix, AZ; John W. "Hillbilly" Kerns of Greenville, SC; Fred Knight of Miami, FL; Gerald Lachute of New Orleans, LA; Robert C. McClelland III of Laurel, MD; Sgt. Mackey from PA; David H. McNerney of Crosby, TX; Lawrence "Larry" Mendez from California; Joe Musgrove of Warrior, AL; Robert E. Patterson of Libertyville, IL; William P. "Bill" Raley of Gadsden, AL; Virgil Renfro of Richmond, KY; William D. "Red" Rohner of Matamoras, PA; John Sivick of Dearborn Heights, MI; Victor B. "Vic" Tenorio from Guam; Daniel L. Webster of Cedar City, UT; and John E. Williams of St. Pauls, NC.

This book is also dedicated to the following four men, who did not return: Thomas D. "Tam" Grinnell, III — KIA 9/3/66; John Kuulei Kauhaihao — KIA 9/5/69; Johnny D. Swann — KIA 9/5/69; and Erskine B. Wilde — KIA 7/27/66.

Acknowledgments

This book was originally written in 1979, but I was unable to get it published at that time because it was poorly written. After I attended several graduate schools in the late 1980s and early 1990s and studied Asian history, I learned how to write. Along the way many people encouraged me to rewrite this book and try to get it published. Many of them had a lot more faith than I did! After I retired in 2002 from teaching Asian history at the University of Richmond (UR) in Richmond, Virginia, I decided to give the book one more try at being published.

The following is only a partial list of those who have urged me, in one form or another, to publish this book. I owe them my heartfelt thanks for their encouragement and belief that this book would add, in some small way, to the history of the Vietnam War. My thanks goes out to the following: many of my former Asian history students at UR too numerous to mention individually; my good friend, Ernest C. Bolt, Jr., Professor of History (UR), who not only offered me encouragement but also told me on numerous occasions that I could accomplish this rewrite; Harry M. Ward, Professor Emeritus of History (UR), who gave me kind and encouraging words; Brian Kelly, who in 1980 believed that it was a worthwhile project and has sporadically urged me for 23 years to finish the job; Mary Garth Flood, a good friend who read the original draft and never lost the faith; Cindy Conte, a special friend and writer who cheered for and supported this project since 1979; Liz Hill, who made helpful suggestions; Marsha Jacob, who proofread the book four times; Doug Miles, a good friend who read the original draft and told me that this needed to be seen in print; Ed Page, a now-deceased Vietnam vet who read the original and urged me to rewrite it; Dan Webster, who served with me in Vietnam and has been supportive of this project for longer than I can remember; Jeff Wolff, who told me on numerous occasions to get the job done; Cynthia Bailey, a corporate lawyer who not only proofread the book and gave me numerous helpful comments (and free legal advice) but also helped me find some of the men that I served with in Vietnam so that I could secure permission to use their real names in this book; and Beth Pratt, who also proofread the book and offered up cogent commentary.

This project could not have been completed had it not been for the support and encouragement I received from my fellow comrades in arms—many of whom I had not been in touch with for over 34 years. Of all the people I searched for and located, only two were deceased. Sadly, there were men I was unable to find. They have disappeared into the fabric of America, perhaps still hiding from the inner demons that beset them over their role in the Vietnam War. Thus, regrettably, I was forced to change their names since I could not obtain their permission to use their actual names. Still, there were other individuals whom I did not want to find because I had nothing positive to say about them. Their names, along with others who played a small part in this memoir, have also been changed.

A special thanks to John Stubblefield, who worked meticulously to ensure that the photos contained herein, which were made from my original slides, came out in such rich detail.

Of course, any errors, or omissions, in this memoir are mine alone. The views presented herein are also mine and do not represent the views of anyone mentioned in this book.

Contents

How do you ask a man to be the last man to die in Vietnam?
How do you ask a man to be the last man to die for a mistake?

John Forbes Kerry (1943–)
(Testimony before the Senate Foreign
Relations Committee, April 22, 1971)

Military History of E. Tayloe Wise

E. Tayloe Wise is a direct descendant of Martha Dandridge Custis, whose second husband was George Washington. He is the great-great-grandson of Virginia Governor Henry A. Wise (1856–1860), who was also a Confederate general. He graduated from Texas Christian University on May 29, 1968, with a bachelor of arts in geography and sociology-anthropology. On June 25, 1968, he enlisted in the United States Army. He was sent to Fort Benning, GA, where he underwent Basic Training with Company B, 7th Battalion, 2nd Training Brigade. He graduated from Basic Training on August 30, 1968, and was promoted to Private Second Class (E-2). He was then assigned to Company B, 2nd Battalion, 5th Advanced Infantry Training (AIT) Brigade in Fort Polk, LA. He was trained to become an combat infantryman, or in military lingo, an Eleven Bravo, which was the job title code for his Military Occupation Specialty (MOS). Upon graduation from AIT in late 1968, he applied for, and was accepted into, the Infantry Non-Commissioned Officer Course (INCOC) School at Fort Benning, GA. He washed out of INCOC School in March 1969 and was immediately given orders to Vietnam. Upon arrival in Vietnam on May 2, 1969, he was promoted to Private First Class (PFC, or E-3) and was assigned to serve with the 1st Air Cavalry Division (Air Mobile). Undergoing several days of in-country training at the 1st Cav's training center at Bien Hoa, he was later assigned to B (Bravo) Company, 2nd of the 8th Battalion, 1st Air Cavalry Division (Air Mobile). While with Bravo Company, he operated in the jungles of Tay Ninh Province, South Vietnam. He earned the Army Commendation Medal for Heroism on August 12,

1969. He was promoted to Specialist 4 (E-4) on August 23, 1969. On August 31, 1969, he was awarded his first Bronze Star Medal for Heroism in Ground Combat. He earned his second Bronze Star Medal for Heroism in Ground Combat on September 13, 1969. On October 7, 1969, he was assigned to Headquarters Company, Division HQ of the 1st Air Cavalry Division (Air Mobile). He served as a waiter to Major General E. B. Roberts, the 1st Air Cav's Commanding General (CG) in the CG's Mess. On March 6, 1970, he was awarded his third Bronze Star Medal for Meritorious Achievement in Ground Operations Against Hostile Forces. On March 15, 1970, he was promoted to Sergeant (E-5). He was awarded the Air Medal for Meritorious Achievement While Participating in Aerial Flight on March 30, 1970. He left Vietnam on April 8, 1970, after serving 342 days in the war zone. He was honorably discharged from the U.S. Army in Oakland, CA, on April 9, 1970, and returned to his hometown of Charlottesville, VA. In addition to the medals mentioned above, he was also awarded the Combat Infantry Badge (CIB) and the Vietnamese Gallantry Cross.

Preface

I served in Vietnam from May 1969 through April 1970. In that time, I estimate that I wrote between 750 and 800 letters to family and friends. Fortunately, over 200 of those missives were saved.

The following narrative is based upon information contained in those letters that recounted the daily details of my life in Vietnam, so that my correspondents could grasp the horror that man calls war. The only way I could combat the terror, boredom, and tedium of Vietnam was to write copiously of every incident that occurred around and to me. Along the way, my fellow infantrymen nicknamed me "The Professor," an apt sobriquet, since I was later destined to become an Asian history professor for five years at the University of Richmond in Richmond, Virginia.

What can one say about the Vietnam War that probably has not already been said, in one way or another, before now? I hope that my experience, elucidated here, will serve as an education to future generations about the evils of conflict that a foot soldier — known as a "grunt" in Army lingo — sees and experiences. Most accounts of the conflict are written by officers, former officers, newsmen, and those in the upper echelons who think they know something about the spilling of blood and guts, and who believe they can detail the overall philosophy of certain campaigns as to the whys and wherefores of specific battles. Historians have a tendency to research and minutely dissect the events of such a war — but they all gloss over the fear, the blood, the cries for help, the moans of men in their death throes, and the stiffening of bodies in rigor mortis which, after a few hours, emit a nauseous stench and begin to crawl with maggots.

The events detailed herein took place just one year after the devastating 1968 Tet offensive. This is the war as I viewed it from the jungle, as

1

both a rifleman and combat medic, and then as a personal waiter in the private Mess Hall of Major General E. B. Roberts, the Commanding General of the 1st Cavalry Division (Air Mobile).

I returned from Vietnam a soured individual. I had been at war, seen men die, participated in killing enemy soldiers and knew all the time that we were fighting a hopeless battle. When Saigon fell on April 30, 1975, it heralded the end of a fruitless effort on the part of our government to prop up a corrupt and debauched regime. America had lost its first war. Some 58,193 American men and women had died in vain. Untold thousands more are crippled — physically and emotionally — for the rest of their lives, by their participation in a grotesque and unwholesome war that our less than honorable politicians, including presidents Johnson and Nixon, managed to maneuver us into fighting.

In the following pages, I do not attempt to point any fingers at who was to blame for getting us into this mess, or who is answerable for our losing it. We are all, in some way, responsible. So, all of us must, in our own way, shoulder the blame for this senseless tragedy. I am bitter at having been forced to participate in it, bitter at having lost it, and bitter at not being appreciated by my country for what I, and all of us infantrymen, did in fighting this war. Our country took the cream of its crop, used it, and then, like a whore who takes your money and then slams the door in your face, left us high and dry. There were no welcome home parades for the men of Vietnam. Many of us lost our lives, our youth, our innocence. The sacrifice was too great.

Many of us feel lost — robbed of an indeterminate part of our lives — and still we grasp to comprehend why. At times, I feel an inner call to return to Vietnam. Is it to locate something I lost and never will find? Not a day has gone by during these past 34 years that I don't think of Vietnam in one way or another. The war has left an indelible stain upon my mind and soul. I often find myself repeating Lady Macbeth's words, "Out damned spot! Out I say!" but there is no way to rid myself of that traumatic inkblot that is forever etched upon my psyche.*

I graduated from Texas Christian University (TCU) on May 29, 1968, with a bachelor of arts degree in geography and sociology-anthropology. Lyndon Baines Johnson spoke at my graduation. In his address to the graduating class he introduced his support for the rights of eighteen-year-old individuals to vote, which was the maiden speech for the conception of the 26th Amendment to the U.S. Constitution. Four weeks later, on June 25,

*The Rev. H. N. Hudson, A.M., ed., *The Works of Shakespeare — The Students' Handy Edition*, rev. ed., Vol. 4 (Boston: Estes and Lauriat, 1871), 328.

out of fear of being drafted, I joined the Army. I was so naive. Having acquired a college education, I believed that I would get a good job in the Army, and would not have to go to Vietnam. How wrong I was!

The military, in sending me to Vietnam, stole my innocence and robbed me of my youth. It took an immature young boy and left a bitter and hardened man. There was no transition stage. In that loss, I found maturity and common sense; but still, after Vietnam, there was an unexplainable void. This void has plagued me since the war. We all lost, or were robbed of, that nebulous, inner peace — that transition stage from boyhood to manhood was not in gradual stages but took place instantly. Overnight, our rites of passage into adulthood were stolen from us. While I was there, I experienced an intimate, almost prescient, realization that I was living my life outside of my body. It was as if I were not really there, yet I was walking on the razor's edge. The reality as to what was actually occurring around me was just too unbelievable. I was a part of something that was so mind boggling that I still have trouble assimilating the fact that I really was one of the players on the stage. Sometimes, the desire to return — the memories of being needed by people to be an integral part of the destructive machinations of mankind — is overwhelming. Nothing can compare to it. It was profoundly exhilarating, yet pathetically sad. So there will always be a part of me in Vietnam, as I am sure there will be for many others my age.

In May 1998 I returned to Vietnam almost exactly twenty-nine years after I first landed in that enigmatic country. Why had I returned? Partly to lay some ghosts to rest. Partly out of curiosity. Partly to return to the site of the August 1969 battle of LZ Becky, recounted in Chapter 5, that has held me in thrall since my departure in 1970 from that war-torn country. I found Vietnam quite changed. The Vietnamese were friendly and the country was even more beautiful than I had remembered. There were paved roads everywhere instead of the thin, dusty, red tracks of my youth. Electric lines followed the highways, giving energy to a multitude of villages where there had been none some thirty years ago. I was amazed by the change in the landscape. What had been jungle so many years ago was now productive farmland. Rice paddies dotted the countryside. Rubber plantations had sprung up all over Tay Ninh Province where I had fought, bled, and seen so many of my comrades fall. The battlefield I revisited, the site of LZ Becky, which had been destroyed by the NVA on August 12, 1969, is now a sugar cane plantation.

After my 1998 visit, I felt as if a heavy load had been lifted from my shoulders. Perhaps I had banished some of my ghosts. But my brief two-week return was not really enough to assuage my desire to understand that country as it was then in 1969–1970 and is today. I wanted to return again and live there. Vietnam is a magnet and it will always have an inexplicable hold on me. After reading the following pages, I hope the reader will understand my fascination for this country and its wonderful people who also suffered so much.

Prologue: War Is

War is a boring, bloody muddle, punctuated by moments of fear and disgust.

A Horseman Riding By— R. F. Delderfield

War is seeing your buddy with half of his face blown off, and watching in mesmerized horror as blood gushes like a flooding brook from what was once a face into a huge, sticky, red pool, and his eyes take on that dull, glassy look common to those who have entered the land of the dead. War is dragging your buddy from a bunker that has just been destroyed by an incoming rocket and realizing that his chest has been crushed. War is seeing your buddy writhing in pain from two blown-off legs and a bone, with no flesh attached, for an arm. War is listening to his dying, almost hoarse, moans of agony. War is watching your friend's brains flow out through a small hole in his skull, as a medic fruitlessly gives him heart massage. War is conversing with your wounded buddy as you bandage him up, and then watching his eyes grow empty as his body slowly twitches in its death throes. War is dead eyes that you cannot close, but that stare lifelessly up at you while you enshroud the body. War is pulling your buddy's head out of the chamber of an artillery piece where it wedged after taking a direct hit from an enemy mortar shell and knowing that it is all of what is left of his body to send back to the States. War is watching blood as it slowly seeps out from underneath the poncho covering the body of a good friend and watching it dissolve in the nearby puddles of muddy rain water. War is praying fervently for the medevac and hoping it shows up before your buddy dies. War is riding in a helicopter and taking enemy fire as your chopper hovers twenty-five feet off the ground and you watch, in fascinated

5

horror, as the green tracers from a hidden AK-47 zero in on the bird. War is the screams of "Medic! Medic!" War is hearing the cries for God and realizing God is nowhere to be found, or just doesn't care anymore. War is hearing the never-ending screams of "Mamma! Mamma!" and knowing that some mother will never see her little boy alive again in this godforsaken world. War is holding your buddy in your arms as he dies. War is standing over a dying gook and blowing his brains out, as you smile, chuckle, and laugh nervously. War is killing an NVA soldier who is desperately trying to surrender. War is seeing a gook sewing his hand back on as you blow his brains out. War is scalping an enemy, or cutting off his ear to keep for a trophy — or a good luck talisman. War is carrying the three-day-old dead, bloated, maggot-infested body of your buddy for two days, and sleeping next to the nauseating stench until you arrive at a place where a chopper can relieve you of what was once a human being but is now a rotten, decomposed nothing. War is spraying insect spray onto a dead buddy's head and into his mouth to kill the fat, white maggots that continuously pour forth from his nauseously putrefying body. War is digging up a decomposed enemy body to make sure it's really a grave and not an arms cache. War is never forgetting the smell of a decomposed body, whether friend or foe, which is indelibly imprinted upon your olfactory senses for your entire life. War is wrapping up your buddy's hand, which has lost two fingers, and knowing that your buddy is a commercial artist. War is walking eighth in line down an enemy trail and suddenly seeing all seven of the guys in front of you get mowed down by the blast of a booby trap. War is listening to the death rattle of a man, shot in the throat, who is now gurgling and dying in his own blood, not ten minutes after he said to you, "Man, this is a groovy war!" War is hiding in the grass as Navy jets drop two 700-pound bombs not fifty yards in front of your position and, when those bombs explode, the ground underneath you feels like it is going to pick you up and fling you five feet into the air. War is pronouncing a much-disliked platoon sergeant dead after he received two suspicious bullet wounds in the back of his neck and head during a firefight and realizing that the wounds probably did not come from the enemy. War is the acrid smell of cordite as you empty your eighteen-round magazine clip and suddenly realize that you only have one more clip left in your sweaty bandoleer with resupply maybe hours away and the enemy only a few yards distant.

War is digging a hole under a log to hide in because your position is about to be overrun and you're praying like hell that it won't be or that somehow, against all odds, you will survive. War is saving someone else's life, and as a combat medic — with little or no training — I saved a few. War is aiding your fellow man as he cries out for your help. War is kneeling over a broken body and bandaging it, as bullets whiz by you and tag the guy lying flat on the ground two feet away. War is humping 75 pounds on your back for 5–6 months when you only weigh 110 pounds. War is watching your arms and shoulders toughen up from the onerous weight you are carrying, even though the ruck's straps bite mercilessly into your flesh. War is learning how to dodge quickly, strike quietly, and how to hug the ground as if it were your girlfriend back home, who you probably weren't going to see again anyway, because she would never be able to comprehend what you had gone through. War is a constant prayer that you survive long enough to board the Freedom Bird home, even though you had just received a "Dear John" letter from your wife, who wrote to say she had run off with your best friend from high school. War is learning to smoke pot on the landing zones and beating the hell out of anyone who smoked it in the jungle.

Yes, all this is war. All this and more too painful to speak about I have watched, participated in, or experienced.

The blood — the gore — the smells. I have visited hell, and Satan was kind enough to let me climb back out. Most people cannot comprehend this insane business we call war. They think war is a pretty little game — like cowboys and Indians — that you played as a child. It is much, much more. You haven't heard the cries of agony and dying moans as I did. You haven't heard the whistle of enemy rifle fire as it cracked six inches overhead. The ones you didn't hear killed you. The pressures in Nam were so unbelievable that it's amazing we all didn't just go stark raving mad. There were times I wanted to scream and scream and scream, and just beat the hell out of someone, or something, from all the insanity I encountered. We had to smoke pot. It was the only way to take the edge off. It relieved the tension of knowing that the guy sitting next to you might be dead in ten minutes. More often than not, it didn't even take that long.

It's hard to imagine what it would be like to be given the last rites. At one time, in the jungle, we were scared to death because of an impending human wave attack. No food, no water. Weak and frightened. We had been given instructions on what to do if we were lucky enough to be alive after being overrun. Do you know what it's like to realize you probably won't see tomorrow's sun? That's the night I really found God, and He's never left me since that night.

Still, the ultimate name of the game was to stay alive just long enough not to go home in a pine box. Had I died in Nam, I would have died knowing I accomplished something worthwhile in my life by being a combat medic.

We lived to escape from the jungle, which was the grunt's prison. Good grunts were rewarded grunts. Duds—goofoffs—remained in the field for a full twelve months, but men who didn't mess up, who did their job and more, were rewarded with a rear echelon job. I was fortunate. I ended up as one of four or five private waiters for the Commanding General of the 1st Air Cavalry Division (Air Mobile), in his private mess hall, where staff officers ate on china, used real silverware, and had steaks every day while grunts in the rice paddies and jungle not two miles away ate food out of tin cans. That was war!

I was fighting, or so I thought, to uphold American ideals. I risked my life so people could sit back and watch their color TVs, drive their Cadillacs and live in a free land. It was all a sham. A farce. I was scared out of my mind—I was fighting to preserve my life and make the other guy die before his bullet tagged me. One thing I learned from Nam—in life, there is a bullet with your name on it, and when God decides to let you meet the bullet, whether it's in Vietnam, or on the highway, or in bed at an old age, nothing you can do will stop the inevitable conclusion. We all gave a little of our blood, sweat, and tears for the name of democracy, or was it only to postpone the inevitable march of Hanoi into Saigon in April 1975?

I became my own man in Nam and turned into more of a non-conformist and rebel than I ever would have been, had I not gone. I mistakenly learned (the hard way) that the only way to accomplish anything in life is to attack it, like we did the gooks, and step on everything in your way to get to the objective. Only that way didn't ultimately work in Nam, and I have since learned it sure doesn't work in real life back here in the world. Like Nam, if you follow that route, all you leave are a lot of dead bodies along the wayside.

It was indeed a journey to a far land as a 1st Cav Skytrooper, also known as a "grunt."

APRIL

Leaving the World

*War is at best barbarism.... It is only those who have neither fired a
shot nor heard the shrieks and groans of the wounded who cry aloud
for blood, more vengeance, more desolation. War is hell.*

William Tecumseh Sherman (1820–1891)
(Attributed to a graduation address at
Michigan Military Academy on June 19, 1879)

In 1969, the principal purpose of Infantry Non-Commissioned Officer
Course (INCOC) School at Fort Benning, Georgia, was to provide non-
commissioned officers (NCOs) for the enlisted men (grunts) who were
fighting in Vietnam. Upon graduation, the NCO candidate earned his
sergeant's stripes (E-5) and, after a short leave home, was quickly shipped
to Nam to join the fray. To stay away, for as long as possible, from being
shipped to Nam, I applied to and was accepted into NCO school after
completing my Advanced Infantry Training at Fort Polk, outside of Leesville, Louisiana. My experiences and training at Polk were pure, unadulterated hell, because I did not get along well with my training NCOs or
officers. This was due, in part, to the fact that I was both older and better
educated than most of my commanders, which they resented; so I, and a
few others in similar circumstances, were continuously harassed because
we had the temerity to question. At Polk it soon became evident to me that
the service frowned upon individuals who were educated and questioned
authority. At that time, the Army wanted its draftees and enlistees to be
nothing more than dumb cattle who would blindly obey all commands as
they were led forward to the inevitable slaughter in Vietnam. Those who
did not fit the mold soon felt the wrath of their training officers and NCOs.

9

Those people were real pricks and only confirmed the Army statement about Leesville and its surrounding area. It was said that if the world needed an enema, it would definitely be injected through Leesville, Louisiana. My stay at Polk confirmed this observation to the hilt.

So, I was relieved, and surprised, when I received orders to report to INCOC School at Fort Benning, Georgia. That meant a few more months in the States, away from having to face Nam, and the inevitable … combat. Maybe … just maybe, the war would end … soon! Alas, it was not to be, and indeed it would only be a few months before I came face to face with the reality that I could no longer postpone my trip to Nam.

On an overcast day in March 1969, I was ushered into the INCOC Company Commander's office. I knew what was coming. I was out of NCO School. I was, however, not prepared for the reasoning behind my being kicked out.

"Private Wise," the captain said, "as you know, we have a lot of intelligent men in NCO School."

Oh really? Since when? I thought to myself.

He droned on, "We have mostly college graduates in the NCO Company. [Out of the 200 men in the INCOC Company, I had met only 13 who claimed to have college degrees—the rest were mostly high school grads or college dropouts.] We have a lot of smart people here in NCO School. I'm afraid, since you're not a college graduate, that you just don't measure up. We're going to have to muster you out of NCO school."

I remember telling him something like this: "Thank you very much, Sir. I would like to correct you on one point, Sir. If you had looked at my 201 file [which contained our military records], Sir, you would have seen that I graduated from Texas Christian University in May 1968, with a degree in geography and sociology-anthropology."

His mouth dropped a mile. I saluted, turned, left his office, and packed. They made you leave quickly when you washed out of INCOC School. I was glad — relieved — to be out because I was beginning to make enemies. Perhaps that is why I washed out. I was assigned to a Headquarters Company (where all transients went) for a few days, and on March 29, 1969, received my orders to report to Fort Dix, New Jersey, no later than 1200 hours on April 25, 1969, for shipment to Vietnam.

I flew to Sarasota, Florida, where my parents had a winter home, and stayed with them for a few days. Then I flew to Fort Worth, Texas, for a week to visit a few old friends at TCU. On April 14, I flew to my hometown — Charlottesville, Virginia — for what could have been the last time. I had already seen one of my distant cousins, Erskine Wilde, buried in the Ivy, Virginia, cemetery of St. Paul's Episcopal Church, which is just six miles west of Charlottesville. Erskine and I had attended a boys' prep school together in Alexandria, Virginia, in the early 1960s. He was killed in Vietnam on July 27, 1966, when the jeep he was riding in ran over a land mine. Another friend from elementary school days, Thomas D. "Tam" Grinnell, III, had also been killed in September 1966. I knew that there was a real possibility that I might not return from Vietnam. I thought about going to Canada, but decided against it. I wasn't so much afraid of the Military Police, or the FBI, tracking me down as I was of my family getting their hands on me and what they might do, or say, to me. So, I chickened out and opted for a free trip, courtesy of the U.S. Government, across the Big Pond.

While I was on leave in Charlottesville, an old problem flared up. When I had been stationed at Fort Benning, the bottom row of my front teeth had acted up due to a high school wrestling injury, which, it turned out, had killed them. An Army dentist had begun preliminary root canal work, but had not told me I would have to return for more dental surgery. My teeth ached again, so I went to see a local root canal specialist whose name was Dr. Rice. He operated on me for five hours, and then another dental surgeon at the local hospital finished the root canal surgery. By the time they had finished doing the surgery, my jaw was black and blue. Those bruises were to cause some odd looks when I arrived at Fort Dix because, from a distance, I appeared to have a goatee.

On Thursday, April 24, 1969, my mom and I left home and drove to Baltimore, Maryland, to stay at the home of my brother, Henry A. "Sandy" Wise. The next day my mother, Elizabeth T. Wise, and sister-in-law, Joshan Wise, drove me to Fort Dix. We arrived at 1030 hours. I shook their hands and kissed them good-bye. It was a matter-of-fact parting, with little or no emotion. I was past emotion by this time. I checked in, got my bedding, and walked to the barracks. I was cheered by the arrival of John Sivick, a buddy of mine from Dearborn Heights, Michigan, who had washed out of INCOC School with me. We bullshitted a bit and then went drinking at the Enlisted Man's (EM) Club that evening and every night we were at Dix.

I learned that I could have the stitches from the dental surgery removed when I arrived in Nam. On the 28th, however, the Army decided to remove them while I was still in the States. Fort Dix was not such a bad place, but you sure felt lonely. Thank goodness, the officers and NCOs did not harass us. Instead, we were treated like sacrificial lambs before the slaughter. My stay at Dix was uneventful except when one sergeant, who was some distance away, yelled at me to break ranks from a formation and haul ass over to him. I knew it was because of the bruises. Breaking ranks, I had moved about halfway toward him before he realized his error and ordered me back into line. I smiled and returned to my place in the formation. The stares I continued to get while at Dix were amusing.

On the 26th, we were issued our jungle fatigues and boots. I was amazed by the number of HUGE pockets in the fatigues. I had no idea what would go into them, but I would soon find out — when I got to the hot, humid jungles of Nam. During the rest of my time at Dix, I read voraciously to kill time and keep my mind off Nam. On Wednesday evening, April 30, 1969, we were bussed to McGuire Air Force Base (which is adjacent to Dix) and loaded onto a Trans International Airways flight to Bien Hoa, South Vietnam, with intermediate stops in Anchorage, Alaska, and Japan. At the base, I telephoned my parents for what I thought would be the last time, and said good-bye. The only reason I boarded the plane was because I was too scared that I would end up in jail if I didn't get on the airliner. Knowing what I now know, I doubt I would have gone to prison and probably should have opted to stay, or flee to Canada.

Once on the plane, which carried 225 of us, we waited several hours until, finally, on May 1, 1969, at 0030 hours the jet was cleared for takeoff. The runway was so long I felt we were never going to get off the ground. The plane kept going and going and going. I firmly believe the airplane must have used up 99 percent of the runway before it lifted off. Then, magnificently, we were in the clouds, heading northwest towards our first stop in Anchorage. The stewardesses served us all a snack, which I devoured. Then, I slept for about four hours when the stews woke us and served a breakfast that made me feel like a condemned prisoner having his last meal. We were served waffles, applesauce and sausage. It was delicious.

IT WAS ...

We arrived in Anchorage at 0800 hours EST, which was 0200 hours Alaska time. All of us were ordered to disembark and go into the terminal. Wearing our thin jungle fatigues, we found the Alaskan air more than just a bit nippy. I called my parents from the terminal one last time and spoke to my mother, who sounded surprised to receive my call from Alaska. Inside the terminal, we could see immense snow-capped mountains in the distance that were so beautiful and stood, like silent sentinels, bidding us adieu.

From Anchorage, we were to fly to Yokota AFB in Japan. It was finally light when we readied for takeoff. I wanted to get some pictures while we were still on the ground but, as I was not by a window seat, I had to turn and ask the guy in the seat behind me to take them, as the grunt by the window in my row was asleep. The grunt behind me was in his forties and, as it was dark in the cabin, I could not tell what rank he held. So I said, "Hey buddy, would you please do me a favor and take a picture for me?" He said, "Sure," took the camera and clicked off a picture. A few minutes later, when we were airborne, he tapped me on the shoulder and said,

"Now that we're in the air, I can get a better picture." So I gave him the camera. By this time, I knew he was a sergeant, but I still could not discern his rank because the insignia consisted of small metal black stripes that were worn on one's collar. He took another picture of the mountains, which, from what I could see, were breathtaking. I also got my first view of glaciers along the Alaskan coastline. To view a picture of a glacier is one thing, but to see it in person is just indescribable. They were so majestic and full of beauty in their vast whiteness. Later on, when we were over Cook Inlet, he asked for my camera again and took a magnificent picture of the inlet, its adjacent mountains, and iced-over rivers. I said, "Thanks, buddy, I sure do appreciate your doing this for me." Then I slept for a few hours until it was light in the cabin. I was still curious to know his rank, so I turned to look and boy oh boy, was I embarrassed. He was a sergeant-major — an E-9, which was (as far as I knew at that time) the highest enlisted rank in the Army! I wanted to crawl under my seat. Here I was, a mere private, E-2, calling a sergeant-major "buddy"! I bet this would never happen again as long as I was in the Army. I figured that, since he was seven grades above me, he probably had more TIG (time in grade) than I had in pay line! I guess the only reason I could get away with calling him "buddy" was that now we were all involved in a common cause. We were going into a combat zone where things were more lax and informal. No spit and shine or harassment from now onward. The grim reality of war loomed before us. There was no time left for rinky-dink stuff.

IT WAS ONE ...

We landed in Japan at Yokota AFB. Since we all were required to exit the plane again, I went to the terminal, shaved, bought some postcards, and wrote to several people. While there, I changed $6.00 into MPC (Military Payment Certificates). Several other grunts committed the same mistake. We really goofed! No one told us the MPC in Japan would be no good in Nam! To this day, my scrapbook displays the useless $6.00 of MPC that I got in Japan. We took off, in daylight. I could see that Japan was both extremely mountainous and beautiful. I even saw Mt. Fuji, which, at an elevation of 12,388 feet, is an awe-inspiring mountain. I wanted to take more pictures, but was too embarrassed to ask the sergeant major.

Although our flight had taken close to twenty-four hours, we had crossed the international date line, so I landed in Vietnam on May 2, 1969. We were flying at an altitude of 35,000 feet when I got my first glimpse of the Vietnamese coastline. From that height it was difficult to tell that here was a country undergoing the agonies of warfare. My 365-day ordeal had begun.

Landing at Bien Hoa, outside of Saigon, we were bussed to Long Binh, seven miles away. The first blast of heat, which struck us as we disembarked from the plane, was unbearable. I thought I had experienced heat before, but was totally unprepared for the inferno that greeted us. One hour later, I was ready to pass out — until I got some salt tablets. The intense heat was stifling. It smothered one and made breathing difficult. Copious amounts of sweat poured out of me until I was completely drenched. It was hard adjusting to the heat. Salt pills became my friends— my saviors. You sweat constantly day and night, until you feel dirty all over. Dust crept into your pores, coated your mouth and infiltrated your clothing. It seemed that every South Vietnamese owned and rode a motorcycle that kicked fine dust particles up as they scooted past. They were all over the road, passing back and forth, oblivious to us as we slowly wound our way to Long Binh.

IT WAS ONE MORE ...

My buddy, John Sivick, had accompanied me on the same bird and was at Long Binh with me. We had hung together at Fort Dix not knowing anyone else. John and I became close friends in Nam and, thank God, he survived and returned to the world in one piece, although he did lose some of his hearing during an enemy attack on a base we were defending.

On our first night in Nam, we stayed at the 90th Replacement Battalion in Long Binh. The 90th was like a cattle holding pen. You were trucked in and then farmed out to whatever decimated unit needed cannon fodder the most. That night, John and I went to the EM Club and had a blast, which eased the tension of the long plane flight that had been both physically and mentally tiring. We listened to a South Viet (SV) band play popular American hits. The roof almost caved in when they played a popular tune by the Animals—"I Gotta Get Out of This Place." Everyone was screaming at the top of their lungs, singing the song. Grunts held their hands up in the air displaying the peace sign — spreading two fingers into a "V"—like Winston Churchill's "V" for victory sign. The place almost burst at the seams when the band played "San Francisco" because that is where the Freedom Bird took us, if we were lucky enough to survive our 365-day incarceration in Nam and return to the World (the States). Listening to that band, I found it so unreal to believe I was in Vietnam. But, sadly, I was.

Sleep, that first night, was extremely difficult. Nearby, jets and choppers took off at all hours. Artillery and mortars erupted sporadically with blasts at the unseen enemy. Or were they merely practicing on some local village for fun? The area around the 90th Replacement was relatively secure, making it difficult for us to conceptualize that we actually were in a war zone. Homelike scenes were as common as dirt. For instance, dogs were everywhere, and they were so loveable. When we had first landed at

Bien Hoa, I saw a grunt waiting to be shipped somewhere, holding a puppy on his shoulder like a baby. It sure did not seem like war, but we would get our first taste of war soon enough.

IT WAS ONE MORE STEP ...

On May 5, 1969, John and I both received orders assigning us to Company A, 2nd of the 8th Battalion of the 1st Air Cavalry Division (Air Mobile). From the 90th Replacement, we were bussed to the 1st Air Cavalry training center in Bien Hoa.

Bit by bit, I was beginning to feel at ease — if one could ever feel at ease in Nam. Sergeants allowed us to call them "Sarge"— something we would not dare during stateside service without doing at least 100 push-ups for using such a familiarity. Officers were more friendly and less formal. One did not have to address them as "Sir" a whole hell of a lot.

While at the Cav training center, we completed paperwork designating how we were to be paid. The Cav paid us on the 15th of each month; we had to decide how much of our wages we would receive in script (MPC again!) and what amount we wanted sent home. I decided to take $35.00 a month in MPC and have the rest of my meager pay, $247.00, sent home. At that time, I also was promoted to PFC (E-3). It was a nice surprise, even though I subsequently learned that, upon arrival in Nam, almost everyone got an automatic promotion. I am sure this was true only for low-ranking enlisted men, such as myself, and not for NCOs (E-5 and above) or officers. While we were filling out the pay designation forms we also had to complete a form indicating whether or not we wanted our next of kin notified if we were lightly wounded. Shrapnel scratches or minor wounds were considered "light wounds." I elected to have the Army notify my parents should I have the misfortune of being so wounded.

Shaving in Nam was certainly different. It did not take long to learn that I did not need shaving cream because my beard was made soft from my sweat and, since there were no mirrors at the training center, I could not see to shave anyway. John told me that my "goatee" bruise was almost gone, which relieved me, because I was getting tired of the stares.

During our first two days at the training center, when we were not standing in line for something, or filling out forms, we pulled detail duty while we waited for the next indoctrination training class to begin. The first day I pulled KP for eighteen long, hot hours. I was on my feet the entire time. My feet, especially my heels, ached and ached. After that stint at KP, I felt as if my feet would fall off. I always harbored a deep-seated resentment for Army KP. One of the cooks, a black man, was a real son of a bitch and harassed us every five minutes. We could not rest because he was so fucking picky. Army cooks were, by and large, little Napoleons. No matter what their rank, they let the power of being a cook go to their heads. I met few Army cooks who were not on an egotistical power trip. They all loved to treat the KPs as lower than bat shit. One never got to rest, or sit down, on KP. It was always—"Do this, do that, peel this, clean that, scrub this, mop here, mop there." No matter how clean something was, one always had to clean, scrub or mop it a second, third or even fourth time. They always appeared to be so unsure of themselves and their power that, to keep the KPs busy, they made them do something over and over again for fear of letting a KP rest. I hated and despised them all, except for a cook I was to meet near the end of my tour. KP was the most unjust and demeaning part of being in the Army. There was no excuse for treating men like dogs, especially in Nam.

We spent our second day at the center moving empty footlockers in the merciless sun. It was hell, but I loved salt tablets and took as many of them as possible. Later that day, we were issued our M-16s. I checked mine thoroughly to make sure it was in working condition. Back in the world, I had read several stories about the propensity of the M-16 to jam. I wanted to make damn good and sure that my weapon was in top-notch, A-Number 1 condition. It was, and it never failed me.

Our training class occupied us during May 6–8. The Cav was priming us for the hell that was to come. The helpful hints that we were to learn were only the tip of the iceberg. One of the training exercises involved repelling out of a chopper. I had always hated heights so I sneaked off, found a safe place, curled up and read a book—one of the innumerable ones I found time to read in Nam. I never did have to repel out of a chopper. On our last training day, we had a fire and movement exercise which, incidentally, I never used in Nam. This was a process of moving a squad (approximately 10–12 men) in sections by fire teams (approximately 5–6 men). "A" fire team moves first into a position as "B" lays down a covering fire for them; and then "A" lays down covering fire as "B" fire team moves up and past "A." I volunteered to be a squad leader and found out that I had only two men on my squad with an 11 Bravo MOS—the Army's numerical job description for an infantryman. The rest were clerks, mechanics, or rear echelon types. Upon completion of the exercise, the E-7 in charge complimented me by saying that I had done extremely well. I had managed to keep all my men separated and on line so no one would shoot his buddy in the back by mistake (yes, we were using real bullets). Considering not one of them had more than basic combat training, I think I did rather well holding them together.

IT WAS ONE MORE STEP CLOSER …

I soon learned that our water, which the Army purified, tasted god-awful. Its taste was so bad that I immediately wrote home and begged my parents and friends to send as much pre-sweetened Kool-Aid as possible. I grew up disliking the taste of water and, to this day, still do not like it. I knew I had to get some Kool-Aid fast, or I would die of thirst because the tepid, foul-smelling and nauseous-tasting water was enough to turn my stomach. Oddly enough, it would take me eight years after returning from Nam before I could stand the taste of Kool-Aid again.

I got my first haircut in Nam at the Cav training center. It was one of the most pleasant and relaxing experiences I ever had in Nam. The South Vietnamese operated the barbershops in Nam. Although at first I was timorous to patronize the shop, I finally threw caution to the winds. After all, the only thing they could do to me was cut my throat with a razor, right? For $1.50 I not only got a haircut, but also received a back, chest, arm, leg, head (scalp) and facial massage that relaxed me so much that I did not want to leave. I just loved it. Massages were about the only endeavors in which the South Viets excelled.

On our last day at the training center, John and I learned where we were going. Two nights before, Charlie had attacked the 2nd of the 8th Cav at LZ Caroline. The NVA had managed to infiltrate the perimeter and take seven bunkers. Before the enemy was pushed out, there were 10 KIA (killed in action) and 53 WIA (wounded in action). One of the wounded, I was later to learn, had been found in a bunker under 14 dead NVA. He was damn lucky. There were over 200 enemy dead. We were flying to Caroline where the going would definitely be hot. Really hot. But first, unknown to us, we had an intermediate stop in Quan Loi with destiny.

IT WAS ONE MORE STEP CLOSER TO ...

We also learned that day that South Vietnam was divided into four corps, or combat tactical zones. The Cav was located in III Corps, which covered the area from the northern Mekong River delta to the southern Central Highlands of Vietnam. LZ Caroline, which was not far from Cambodia, was located near an oddly shaped border configuration that looked like, and was called, the Fish Hook.

On May 9, after waiting long, hot hours under the tin-roofed airport terminal at Bien Hoa, John and I boarded a C-130 for Quan Loi.

IT WAS ONE MORE STEP CLOSER TO DEATH.

MAY

Baptism

...this strategy would involve us in the wrong war, at the wrong place, at the wrong time, and with the wrong enemy.

Omar Bradley (1893–1981)
(Testimony to the Committee on Armed Services and
Committee on Foreign Affairs, U.S. Senate, on May 15, 1951)

Quan Loi, located northeast of Saigon, was one step closer to combat. Each new day in Nam was like coming out of the womb — the farther along we traveled, the more terrified we became of reaching the end, because, instead of light at the end of the tunnel, we were faced with blood, gore, and death. The C-130 touched down on the Quan Loi airstrip, which was located on top of the mesa-like plateau. It was a hot, dusty Saturday evening when John and I finally arrived. One more step nearer to combat. One more step closer to death. I wondered if I would ever return to the world, or whether my body would go out on the same C-130 that brought us.

That evening John and I pulled guard duty on the Green Line, which was a ring of bunkers, each one about fifty yards apart, surrounding both the airstrip and the military base at Quan Loi. In front of us were rows and rows of concertina wire. Deadly claymore mines had also been placed in front of each bunker. We checked to make sure that the detonator wires leading from them to the bunker were properly connected. A claymore is an innocuous-looking piece of death and destruction. It was about one inch thick, five inches high, and twelve inches long, curved in a 40° arc. The front, marked "FRONT — FACE TOWARD ENEMY" in big raised block letters on the outside of the arc, held 600 mini steel balls. The back, marked

18

"BACK," held about two pounds of dynamite (C-4). In training, we were taught to pick up the claymore and hold it against our stomach so that it curved around our midriff. That way, if one could not read (and there were a lot of people in the Army who could not read) he would know which way to face the claymore when he placed it in the ground. Otherwise, one could easily blow himself away. When you blew one, any living thing within 100 feet would be mincemeat. That first night, in the bunker, I was scared shitless. We had hardly any ammo— only six clips each (an M-16 clip held 18–20 rounds) and one or two grenades. When we had asked why we didn't need more ammo, the company staff sergeant simply told us, "Look guys, this is a

E. Tayloe Wise — my first week in country.

rear area. We haven't been attacked for eighteen months. This area's safe, so don't sweat the small stuff."

So we trudged off to pull our first guard duty on the Green Line. Our confidence and fear assuaged, we made it through that first night without a problem. After all, Charlie (the NVA or VC) was miles away. So, there was nothing to worry about. We were in a "safe" area.

They call a grunt who has not seen combat a cherry. This sobriquet was applied to all new grunts because we were like a girl who had not lost her virginity. A girl who had her first experience in sexual intercourse was considered to have had her cherry plucked. Instead of getting screwed for the first time, we grunts were instead introduced to combat and Charlie wasn't plucking no cherry — he was trying to kill your ass. A cherry was also called an FNG (fucking new guy). There were not a lot of experienced grunts who were willing to show an FNG the ropes. Guys who had been in the jungle for more than six months (and survived that ordeal) were somewhat leery of getting close to an FNG. About 40 percent of the infantrymen who got killed in Vietnam had been there three months or less. Only about 6 percent of the deaths were in the last three months of the one-year tour.*

On Sunday, May 11, 1969, John Sivick, I, and a black corporal named Tobler were assigned to a bunker on the western perimeter of the Green Line. I am thoroughly convinced that I owe my life to Tobler. Had it not been for his quick thinking and experience, I would probably be dead today — there is no doubt in my mind about that fact. Fortunately for John and me, Tobler had served in Korea prior to being assigned to Nam and knew the ropes. Somehow (I later learned how easy it really was), Tobler had scrounged 18 extra M-16 clips for himself and about 12–15 grenades. Without that extra ammo, I doubt we would have survived that night.

Good ol' safe Quan Loi. Great place to be! Safe as the U.S. dollar. Safe, my ass! Eighteen months of placidity had made everyone cocky and brazenly over-confident. Eighteen months of peace had lulled everyone to sleep — and, only eleven days after arriving in Nam, I got my baptism of fire.

All three of us were cherries. The only difference was that Tobler had his shit together, while John and I did not. At 0100 hours, Charlie started passing out business cards. The first few rockets whistled by overhead, landing to the rear of the Green Line in supply areas and on the airstrip. We heard them screaming by as their yellow tails streaked across the pitch-black sky like comets, and we prayed our bunker would withstand a direct hit since the attack had been launched from the west — the sector we were guarding! He hit us with everything he had — rockets, mortars, grenade launchers. It was the most fantastic thing that had ever occurred to me. I had never been so scared — or terrified — in my entire life. NVA and VC mortars and rockets rained death down upon us. Sappers (VC or NVA who stripped to their underwear, camouflaged their bodies with grease, and carried dynamite satchel charges and handheld rocket launchers) over-ran part of the perimeter 250 yards to the left of our bunker and 150 yards to the right of us.

The sappers must have caught some grunts sleeping in one bunker. What occurred I will never forget as long as I live. Every bunker crew had been issued a radio to communicate not only with each other but also with the CP (Command Post). The enemy hurled satchel charges into a bunker, blowing it up. We listened to the dying words of a grunt over our radio, as he screamed — "Help! Help! We're all wounded, someone ... help us!" No one came. We later learned that everyone in that bunker had died.

The sappers who penetrated our perimeter were suicide squads. Their

---

*James F. Dunnigan and Albert A. Nofi, *Dirty Little Secrets of the Vietnam War* (New York: St. Martin's Press, 1999), 77–78. [Henceforth, Dunnigan & Nofi].

whole purpose was to inflict the maximum amount of damage and die, if need be, doing it. Their objective was the airstrip and the chopper pads. They penetrated the barbed wire fences, slipped past the bunkers, and were on the road behind our bunkers before we realized our precarious position. Having reached the road, they could strike at the rear of every bunker, where the entrances were, before any defenders realized what was happening. Our asses were definitely hanging in the wind.

The situation was absolute hell. I found myself shaking uncontrollably. My whole body shook and shook as if I were having an epileptic seizure. Later, I realized that, sometime during the initial stages of the attack, I had actually shit in my pants.

We were in an intolerably critical position. The nonchalant attitude of the base personnel, who regularly pulled Green Line duty, had caused them not to carry enough ammo. I am convinced that 90 percent of the grunts in the bunkers had little or no ammo after the initial attack. We begged for ammo resupply on our radio, but none was forthcoming. We were furious. Some bunkers had a lot less than we did. Ammo resupply would not arrive until three hours later.

Tobler did an incredible job of keeping up our flagging spirits. He had been in the Army for four years and knew how to keep a level head even though he had never seen combat. He bolstered our morale even though we could see him shaking at times. He was so damn brave. Because the NVA were on the road behind the Green Line, Tobler constantly slipped outside our bunker's rear entrance not only to make sure that the NVA did not sneak up on us, but also to prevent the enemy from throwing a satchel charge into the bunker. He did a great job. Every so often, when he thought he heard or saw movement out front, he would sneak out the back, hang next to the rear wall, and chuck a grenade over the top and out front of our bunker. He threw all the grenades we had, and blew three claymore mines. All John and I did was shoot at shadows.

It took about a half hour before we got air support from Cobra gunships. These were Bell AH-1G attack helicopters, which had 7.62-mm miniguns, a 40-mm grenade launcher, a 20-mm cannon, antitank missiles and various rockets. Cobras were only 3 feet wide and about 45 feet long and could fire 5,000–6,000 machine gun rounds per minute, plus their grenade launcher could fire 200 grenades/minute. They also carried 48 rockets located in pods on either side of the fuselage. Indeed, they could rain death and destruction. They were everywhere and continuously strafed within fifty yards of our positions. It was the first time I was to hear the hair-raising Thoomp! Thoomp! of the rockets leaving their tubes as they were launched from the gunships. It was a chilling sound that one day in the not so distant future I would hear directed against my own platoon when a Cobra mistook us for NVA during a firefight.

Within minutes of the attack, we received illumination (flares attached to parachutes that were fired from mortars), which continued non-stop until daylight five hours away. Keeping our M-16 on semi-automatic, we fired at anything that moved. Had we used rock and roll (full automatic), our paucity of ammo would have been long gone. Luckily, with Cobras, we had fire support for five and a half hours.

At 0415 hours, just after our ammo resupply finally arrived, we were reinforced by a machine gun reaction team from the 1st Division — known as the Big Red One.

At dawn, we were alerted by radio that there might be a possibility of another rocket attack. As we were being told this, the rockets swooshed by overhead and exploded behind our position. During that incredibly terrifying night, I believed our bunker would get hit. Three mortar explosions (ours or theirs?) close by had shaken the bunker. I thought for sure that I would be wounded, but somehow I was lucky. By a miracle, we all escaped without a scratch.

It was truly a night I shall never forget as long as I live. I would never forget those desperate cries for help transmitted on the radio; they would haunt me for many years. By morning, we were partially deaf from all the repercussions of firing. This condition made us all the more jumpy when we heard any strange, unidentifiable sounds. At dawn, killer squads of grunts swept the perimeter and gathered lots of rockets and satchel charges off the dead enemy bodies. I found it hard to believe that these sappers could carry so much. Sweeping searches of the base camp were also conducted to locate any NVA or VC who might have slipped by and hidden in a tent or under a hooch. We had no opportunity to sleep because we had to pull guard duty at our bunker all day. We had lost three KIA, but killed twenty or so NVA or VC. I saw some of the enemy bodies being dragged off. We, from our bunker, never saw or killed any sappers, but we certainly were ready to kill anyone who got close. I was exhausted — we all were — but we were relieved that evening, put on standby, and told to expect an attack of even greater intensity that night.

During the day following the attack (Monday, the 12th), John and I were transferred from A Company to B Company, for some unknown reason. We were supposed to ship out that day, but due to the fact that all the choppers heading out to B Company were full and we had to pull guard all day, we were stranded in Quan Loi — at least for one more night. That night, I collapsed in the Company sleeping tent. After twenty-four hours without sleep, I was dead to the world but my sleep was interrupted. The enemy struck again. We ran for nearby trenches and remained in them for about an hour before retiring to our beds. It was to be the last bed I would see for a long, long time.

The next day, we left Quan Loi by chopper. This was my first chopper ride and it thrilled me because it was an exhilarating and exciting experience. We were flown to LZ Caroline located somewhere near the Cambodian border. The LZ had a big landing strip for C-130s, so I figured it must have been a big resupply base. Whenever we landed somewhere, whether it was at a firebase, or in the jungle, that landing point was known as an LZ (landing zone). In the Cav, we usually referred to the firebases (like Caroline) as LZs; but we also referred to the areas where we landed in the jungle as LZs. Other people referred to places like Caroline as a firebase or an FSB (fire support base).*

Caroline was the next-to-last link in the chain. We were not cherries anymore, but we were one step closer to the jungle and combat. And ... death! Besides, Caroline had been hit in the last week and grunts had taken heavy casualties at the expense of at least 200 dead enemy soldiers.

Death waits for no one. It strikes quickly and permanently. There is no hope for those marked by it. It is ... the final solution. We had been on Caroline less than an hour when I heard the sound of an AK-47 for the first time, off in the jungle. The AK-47 was an assault rifle that the Soviets supplied to the NVA. AK is an acronym for Automat Kalashnikov, which is Russian for "automatic Kalashnikov," and it is named for its designer, Mikhail Kalashnikov. It had a distinctive sound — something like "Crack! Crack!" It was a sound we would learn to recognize rather easily.

A platoon-sized recon patrol had enemy contact and soon radioed in that they had a Line 1, which meant that a grunt had been KIA. An hour later the grunts emerged from the jungle's edge carrying the body of their fallen comrade in a poncho. It was one of the saddest sights I ever saw in Nam. The LZ medics went out with a plastic, olive green bag and nonchalantly zipped the body into it. I remember watching the body lie there in the dirt while flies lit on the bag and dust from choppers blew over it. There was a grunt who did not make it. I wondered — would I be next? How long would I make it? Finally, a chopper landed nearby and two grunts tossed the body onto it, as if it were nothing more than a bag of trash destined for the dump. The chopper blades whirled, lifting the Huey off Caroline to take its excess baggage to some distant morgue. Here was life — or what had been life. Now another set of parents would mourn. How many more would mourn this senseless tragedy that was Nam? Nothing made

---

*The terms are used interchangeably in this book.

An OH-1H Huey helicopter brings troops in on a combat assault in the jungle.

sense to me anymore. It was all a question of survival now. I had to make it. I had to dodge Charlie's bullets. I had to live. I was in some deep shit, but I was not going to give up. Not yet. But Nam would soon impress upon me the futility of being there.

The next day, May 14, almost two weeks after I arrived in Nam, I joined Company B, 2nd of the 8th Battalion, 1st Air Cavalry Division (Air Mobile) in the jungle. This was it. The last link in the chain was gone. Now I was on my own.

We CA'ed (combat assaulted or, in Army lingo, Charley Alpha) from LZ Caroline to LZ White. I believe that day, and the next, were the worst days of my entire life. I was wearing my rucksack for the first time and it, coupled with the intensely humid jungle heat, about killed me. I became dizzy from the stifling heat and was so sick I could not eat. From White we moved 1500 meters into the jungle, which was an open inferno. I staggered along, praying for rest. My ruck, with all its equipment, weighed 50–60 pounds, and its straps bit savagely into my shoulders. The excruciating pain that this produced was all that kept me conscious and alert. That night, we set up along a trotter (an enemy trail) and dug in. Having to walk so far my first day in such heat, combined with digging a foxhole, I felt sure I would never survive Nam. The sun had hammered away at me all day and sucked every last ounce of sweat from my body. I was so physically and mentally exhausted I could not sleep that night.

The next day, we broke camp and only humped (walked) 250 meters. Ah! Respite! We set up in ambush along another trotter. No VC or NVA. Then, just as I was counting my lucky stars, we got word to return to White. Moaning, groaning, cursing inwardly, and dead tired from no sleep during my first night in the jungle, we saddled up and humped 2000 meters back to White. I was ready to die. Thank God for salt tablets. I was popping them like crazy. At White, choppers picked us up and CA'ed us to some place in the jungle. Our landing met with no resistance. It was my first CA to a jungle LZ where no one had any idea if Charlie would be waiting or not. If he was waiting, it would be known as a hot LZ. It was late afternoon, and I was out of it. I prayed for rain to cool me off and one hour later, miraculously, my prayer was answered. Staying out in it, I collected water in my helmet to replenish my three two-quart canteens and gulped down a lot of the excess. (Initially, I had been issued four canteens but one had been stolen.) My body sucked up the liquid like a potted plant that is dying from lack of water.

We dug in at the edge of the jungle clearing, where we had landed. Not fifty yards away lay the skeletal remains of a chopper that had been shot down. It looked ominous. That night, soaked to the skin from the rain, I finally slept.

Bravo Company consisted of three platoons known as Aztec, Blackfoot, and Cheyenne. I was assigned to Blackfoot. I soon learned that there were about 90 men in Bravo Company, which was supposed to contain about 150 men to be at full strength. In Nam, however, we were never at full strength. Each platoon had two squads. Every squad had one machine gunner who carried the twenty-three-pound M-60 machine gun, and one person who carried a shotgun-like weapon known as an M-79, which was a grenade launcher. Each night, six or eight of us would set up in position and pull guard duty, which usually lasted two hours for each man — and for the weary, such as myself, fear was the motivating force in keeping us awake. Unfortunately exhaustion played a greater role, thus making it difficult to stay awake. Because I was mentally and physically exhausted most of the time, it was a miracle I never fell asleep. I knew the consequences of doing so — death. Perhaps it was the constant fear of getting my throat cut or facing a court-martial that kept me awake. I don't know. I remember my first night in the jungle — one of the guys in my squad, Bill "Red" Rohner, had said to me, "If you hear anything, wake me up." I know I probably pissed him off a lot because I woke him several times. Despite my experience at Quan Loi, I was still a cherry — an FNG — and jumpy. But I deeply appreciated his telling me not to hesitate in awakening him. Later, when I had time in country, I told other cherries the same thing and

An OH-1H Huey helicopter picks us up in the jungle.

did not mind when they woke me. It was all part of the game. Stay alive. CYA (cover your ass) and all that bullshit.

The next day (my third day out) was a little easier. We traveled through dense jungle that was wet and cool, and not much sun filtered down upon us. Before long, we ran across a small unoccupied bunker complex that had not been used in quite awhile. After quickly checking it out, we moved onward. I was beginning to adjust to my pack. We carried everything in our rucksacks. Combat loaded, I was supposed to carry the following: poncho (it made a great tent); poncho liner (nice for sleeping in on the cool jungle nights); 2–4 frags (grenades, two of which I hung from hooks on the pack straps in front of my chest); 15 fully loaded M-16 magazines in bandoleers, which we hung around our pack; 2 smoke bombs (to pop smoke when choppers needed to locate us in the jungle); a claymore mine (which we set up each night and disassembled each morning); a machete (which I did not carry); 3–4 two-quart canteens (which had C-rings so we could hang them from the rucksack frame); a stick of C4 (dynamite which

I learned to break off in small chunks, light, and heat my meals); plus at least 3–5 days of C-rations (one quickly learned which ones to ditch). I usually carried enough C's for two meals a day because, if you carried enough for three meals a day, they just weighed too damn much. On top of the above, almost all of us carried 200 rounds of M-60 machine gun bullets for the machine gunners which criss-crossed our chest and back.

The next day was one of hope. My platoon sergeant, an E-7, was a 44-year-old African American named Tyrone Gambill from Garysburg, North Carolina, who had been in the Army 27 years. He learned from talking to me that I could draw and read maps, and interpret aerial photos. He questioned me and found out (I did not volunteer the information) that I was a college graduate. He exploded, and could not believe why, with my talents, I was out in the boonies— which was short for boondocks, or out in the sticks (the jungle). He emphatically stated that I deserved a desk job with 2/8 brigade in Tay Ninh and swore he would do his level best to get me out of the field when we got to Tay Ninh in a week or so. This revelation really brightened up my whole day. While it was true that I could read maps and interpret aerial photographs, I had stretched the truth about drawing maps. That was one skill I could not do, but I had learned the rest at TCU, while I was majoring in geography, and never figured I would have the opportunity to put those dormant skills to use. So, I was not beyond stretching the truth for my own purposes. At this point, I was ready to do *anything* to get out of the horrid jungle.

That day, we received log for the first time. Log was our resupply of food, water, ammo and other materials. We each received two Miller beers. They were warm — but oh so damn good! After log, we sat around all day next to the jungle clearing where the log birds had landed. It was late afternoon, on full stomachs, when we saddled up and marched out. Before long, we not only found lots of trotters, but also a big bunker complex. Many of the bunkers were in the process of being built. No enemy. Thank God! We rested right in the middle of it, for 30–40 minutes. It was here I made a sad discovery when I pulled out my camera to take some pictures. Somehow, in all the tramping around, I had broken it. I decided that I would have to buy another if I ever got to a PX, and would have to make double damn sure I packed it properly in my rucksack.

Evidently the powers that be decided that we just might catch a few NVA, so we were told to set up in the bunker complex and prepare a small surprise for Charlie, if he returned. Four other guys and I were chosen to be on LP (listening post). This is a hairy assignment — also known as "suicide squad." On LP, whether it was in the jungle or on an LZ, we were placed about seventy-five meters in front of our lines. We did not dig in.

LZ Barbara.

We lay on the ground, out in the open, totally exposed, with no overhead cover or foxhole for protection. You listen for Charlie, who might try to slither in and toss satchel charges at a few positions. We took all our frags and set up our claymores. Claymores, in this situation, were our one and only front line of defense, if Charlie walked into us. But they could be equally as dangerous to us in this situation because we had no bunker or foxhole to shield us from the back blast. So, we had to place them about fifteen yards from our position because, when blown, the claymore's plastic casing blew off and traveled back towards us. One could definitely be injured from the flying plastic that encased the charges and disintegrated into minute slivers when the TNT exploded. After setting up, we settled down. It poured all night. We did not get any sleep, for fear of not being able to see or hear Charlie, who was capable of walking right up to our position, so we were drenched to the bone. After the rain moved on, the droplets of water falling from the tree leaves made listening for enemy movement extremely difficult. Every little "Kerplunk!" became an enemy footstep. Every swish of fronds was a Charlie creeping silently through the jungle. It was a long, wet, cold, nasty, sleepless night.

Nui Ba' Den (Black Virgin Mountain). We patrolled the jungles surrounding this mountain.

Finding no action, we moved the next day to the edge of a nearby jungle clearing and waited five hours for the choppers to arrive at the PZ (pickup zone). I was able to dry out completely before we CA'ed to Barbara for LZ duty on the 19th.

LZ Barbara was north of Nui Ba' Den, also known as the Black Virgin Mountain, which lay to the north of Tay Ninh. Nui Ba' Den was a lone mountain rising majestically some 986 meters high from the plain surrounding it. It commanded everything in sight and was a truly beautiful, awe-inspiring work of Nature's art. Standing like a lone sentinel on the plain, it guarded all the lands it overlooked. We controlled the top, Charlie controlled the bottom.

Barbara was a stronghold — a veritable fortress. High earthen berms encased it on all sides. Heavily sandbagged bunkers behind the berm guarded the approaches and were miniature forts in themselves. The LZ sat in the middle of a savannah-like terrain, with at least a mile of grassland, scrub brush, and a few lone trees on every side between it and the jungle. Surrounded by minefields, and many, many fences of barbed concertina wire, it had been built to withstand any and all attacks. It was here that I ate my first hot chow. It was delicious, and I consumed every last drop.

That night, everyone was placed on standby alert, because that day was Ho Chi Minh's birthday. Our leaders suspected fireworks, but none occurred. LZ Grant, about ten miles away, got plastered all night long. While on guard duty, I watched the battle rage in the distance and thanked God they were getting hit, instead of us. Little did I know or realize then that, in a few months, I would be part of one of the biggest LZ annihilations in the history of the Cav.

Slowly, I was drifting into the regimen that was Nam. I quickly learned, after only a day in the jungle, that underwear was unnecessary because it held your sweat and made you itch like hell. So, I discarded it. I soon learned to take my heavy jungle fatigue shirt off at night, roll it up, and use it as a pillow, while sleeping in my T-shirt. My arms were beginning to turn brown from the sun, but had many scratches from the jungle flora on them. On Barbara, I mused what it would be like to be back in the World, because we felt as if we were on another planet in Nam.

That there was a lot of waste in the Army soon became apparent to me while on Barbara. One day, 212 artillery rounds to the 105-mm howitzer that someone, either inadvertently or deliberately, had buried with a bulldozer were uncovered. Two other men and I had to separate the good rounds from the bad ones. Each round, we were told, cost $172.00, and we only found 75 good ones. We were forced to destroy 137 rounds.

On my last night at Barbara, I had little or no sleep. It was a tense night. Earlier, in the daytime, sappers had gotten into the perimeter of LZ Grant, and we had been warned the same thing might occur to Barbara. I was sent out on LP and got only two hours of sleep.

After four days on Barbara, we were CA'ed back to the jungle. The jungle, of course, was everywhere. It became our mother, father, sister, brother — enfolding us with its vines, its musky dampness, and keeping some of us forever. The sun, which filtered through the vine-covered trees, was merciless on us. We bathed in our own sweat. I slowly adjusted to my ruck as we walked — stumbled — through the ever damp, rotting vegetation that made up the jungle. Rarely did we follow paths — thus avoiding booby traps and ambushes. It was virtually impossible not to trip on many of the vines. The Armed Forces newspaper, *The Stars and Stripes*, had a cartoon character called Nguyen Charlie drawn by Corky Trinidad. The following strip typified our struggle for survival in the jungle:

N G U Y E N   C H A R L I E

Our CA from Barbara was somewhat frightening. I had never seen a jungle LZ prepped by artillery and, as we came in, the chopper's machine gunners sprayed the jungle with long bursts of sweeping fire. I thought that we were hitting a hot LZ and wondered why we had not been warned. As soon as the chopper got within three feet of the ground, we were waved off. I hit the ground running and fell, as the backwash from the chopper blades flattened the elephant grass. As I struggled up from under the weight of my ruck, I saw a two-man news crew filming our deplaning from the chopper. I labored up and started to run for cover, only to go about five steps and fall flat on my face again. Scrambling up a second time, I dashed and made it to the wood line, where we spread out in a semi-circle. When it came time to move, we slipped into the jungle and traveled over 100 meters before we discovered one of our men was missing. Five men were delegated to retrace our steps to search for him. They found him sound asleep at the clearing's edge. Needless to say, he caught holy hell. I am surprised one of our guys did not shoot him.

It was the rainy season in Nam. Every day, like clockwork, the rains descended around 1600 hours. Keeping dry was impossible. I had some Army issue plastic bags in which I kept my wallet, film, and other perishables. On our second day out from Barbara, we received a laundry drop. Why we did not get clean clothes when we were on Barbara is a mystery, but now we had some. I had not changed in two and a half weeks! Of course, getting a shower was rare. We bathed in the rain. I soon learned to wear only my boots, socks, pants and T-shirt. I had to dry my feet once a day and, since I had some sort of a fungus on both feet, I used lots of foot powder.

Not only did we have to fight Charlie and battle the elements, but we also fought a never-ending battle with the insects, which were everywhere. They loved to land on you and nibble away. The flying insects were most bothersome, but not as annoying as the ants. I had never been bitten by ants until Nam. But Nam's ants would walk away with chunks of your flesh.

Sometimes hundreds would be gathered on a plant leaf. The unsuspecting grunt would brush by, and, before he realized it, would have 15–20 of the fuckers crawling all over an arm or hand, biting, tearing, and ripping flesh out left and right. Or worse yet, a bunch of these carnivorous insect cannibals would be perched on an overhead leaf, when you walked along and brushed it with your helmet. The red devils would then fall on your face or neck and nail you. Once I sat down, right on top of some red ants. Not for long! God, my ass hurt. Anthills were everywhere — they permeated the jungle. Many anthills were 20 feet thick at the base, and 8–10 feet tall. You steered away from them for fear the little cannibals would definitely chew your ass up, if they got a good grasp on your flesh. I never got used to them. When we were not being attacked by flies drinking our sweat, or carnivorous ants, the mosquitoes took care of what was left of our bodies. I wondered at times how I was physically going to survive.

We ran out of food. Someone fucked up and we ran out of Cs. For twenty-four hours we awaited the arrival of the log bird. All we had left the night before log was hot chocolate and coffee mix. We brewed both together and passed a common cup among five of us in my squad. Others did the same. Everything was communal in the jungle. I brewed up some Kool-Aid and passed my canteen around to the guys. In the World, I had been repelled by the thought of someone else drinking out of my cup, but not there in Nam.

We finally got resupply on the 25th (we always knew the numerical date, but rarely knew the day of the week). It was a joyous day. I heard from my parents for the first time. I also shaved. We only shaved every four or five days, when we got log, because the log bird brought shaving cream and lots of water. Otherwise, no one would have shaved, as water was just too valuable to be wasted on shaving. The log bird brought not only food but also goodies— M & Ms, Hershey bars, gum, soap (though God knows why we needed soap because we could rarely bathe), assorted hard candies, and cigarettes. The log birds usually brought so much junk food that a lot was just left in the jungle. We did not have room for it in our rucks. Our C's came in boxes and we threw away the unopened tins of food that were of no use.

In my first batch of mail, my parents had written and told me to be proud. I guess they thought my letters home were too pessimistic. I replied that if they had to participate in what I was having to do, they would not be proud. There is no pride in killing. There can never be. There was no pride in knowing you are killing *not* to win, but only to contain. There was no pride in knowing you are helping freedom because there was really no freedom in Nam. The South Vietnamese could have cared less about freedom. It was called a war — but we were only one bunch of guys hired out to kill another bunch of guys. Is there pride in being a mercenary? I did not know, yet I felt like one. I was glad my parents were proud of me, but being proud of myself — no. I was not helping the South Vietnamese by fighting in Nam. With no real front, with no real territorial objectives, this was not a war. The VC and NVA could strike *anywhere*, and at *any time*, they damn well chose and there was little we could do or say about it. I was not helping humanity by being in Nam — I was hindering it. These were rather profound and sobering thoughts from one who could have had his ass blown off any minute. In Nam a grunt's purpose was to kill, so it was only later that I was able to take pride in being a medic. There is no pride in killing. Yet that was why I was sent to Nam — to kill. I never looked at it that way until many years later. Simply put, I was a hired gun-slinger. The NVA and VC were supposed to be the bad guys, and we, of course, were the good guys. Too bad someone forgot to tell the enemy that fact. Maybe ... just maybe, if someone had told Uncle Ho, a nickname for Ho Chi Minh, the Vietnamese leader, he would have laid back, enabling us to leave Nam sooner, and then they could have rolled over South Vietnam with less loss of human life.

Twenty-eight hours after receiving my first mail from home, I was sitting in the middle of another bunker complex. We stumbled on this complex (which was not all that difficult to do in Nam) and discovered a rather large arms cache. We uncovered 60 mortar rounds, 20 of our *own* claymore mines, AK-47 rounds, M-16 ammo, and about 20 U.S. Army smoke bombs. I was amazed by the amount of U.S.-manufactured military equipment that we found. To me, during those early days in Nam, it seemed so improbable that the enemy would have so much of our matériel. Later, I was to take all this in stride. Anything the enemy wanted, they could usually acquire. I (as were all the rest of us) was later to become guilty of throwing away U.S.-issued matériel. Basically, it all boiled down to a question of weight. We could only carry so much. The rest had to go. I harbored a fear of grenades. Hated carrying them. What I could not give away, I conveniently "lost." Included in the cache that we uncovered was a lot of rice. We could not call in choppers to haul it all off because we were nowhere near a clearing and the thick jungle canopy could not be penetrated. We could not blow it up for fear of giving our position away, so we buried it. At the time, this seemed incredibly ridiculous because the enemy would surely find the freshly turned earth and uncover the supplies. We probably should have spread the rice all over the place and booby-trapped the rest. But the Army had an answer to everything — and when it could not come up with one — we were simply told to bury the evidence.

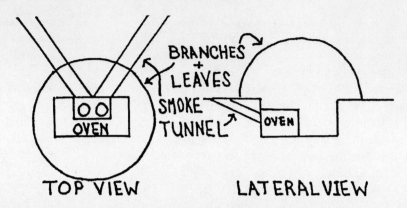

TOP VIEW   LATERAL VIEW

This diagram shows the earthen kitchen that I discovered in the NVA base camp. The first view (left side) shows an overhead view of the kitchen with two covered tunnels for dispersing smoke running out from the earthen kitchen oven in a "V" shape. The second view (right side) shows a side, or lateral, view of the kitchen. It is covered with branches and leaves and shows one exhaust tunnel running out from the earthen oven.

We also found a kitchen in the complex that I thought was somewhat interesting. The smoke outlets from the crude earthen oven, which I personally discovered, were small six-inch tunnels that had been covered by logs running behind the cooking area. The two tunnels ran in a "V" shape and the submerged cooking area was covered by a leaf hooch. Our enemy was most ingenious. This was a good example of his ability and innovativeness in adapting to his native habitat. See the diagram above for more detail.

Later that day, I heard and felt my first B-52 strike, which was about a mile away. The magnitude and force of the far-off explosions caused the trees to shake and the ground to vibrate. It was an eerie sensation. Imagine explosions so powerful that they could cause trees to shake miles away from the epicenter of the attack. There was another strike even closer that night. I thought for sure the bombs were going to walk right over our position. The earthquake-like shaking of the ground filled me with awe and made me extremely nervous.

We lingered for two days in the bunker complex — entrenched — hoping to catch Charlie. But he refused to take the bait. At noon on the third day, we saddled up and participated in the most grueling march I experienced while in Nam. We humped for five and a half hours. Not only was it an excruciatingly difficult march, but also it was pure hell. We only moved 1300 meters (or so we were told), but it was through some of the worst jungle I ever encountered. It turned out to be the toughest and most demanding day I had experienced since my arrival in country. We lost contact with the platoon behind us several times and had to send people out to get them. The jungle is an incredibly thick and dense environment. If you got ten meters ahead of someone, you could quickly lose sight of him. We were forced to stick even closer together; and that was bad, because the more we bunched up, the better our chances were of more grunts getting hurt if Charlie sprang an ambush. Never in my life had I seen so many vines and fallen trees. There were vines and then there were more vines, which stretched endlessly across our route of travel and impeded our progress. My shoulders became sore and raw from the pack straps, making me want to cry out in agony. Making things even worse, we ran out of water. I had only two sips all day. Thank God, when we stopped, choppers brought water to us.

The next day, the 28th, we humped to a clearing to receive log. Ten other men and I were helping to unload water cans from the log birds, about seventy-five meters from the wood line, so we were exposed when the birds took off. One bird had not gone far when a Charlie, somewhere nearby, opened up on it, or us, with his AK-47. I did not realize I could hit the ground so fast and found myself hiding behind the water cans. The shots, it turned out, were directed at the chopper. The waist-high elephant grass hid us in the clearing when the following conversation occurred.

"Oh, shit, they're only firing at the chopper."

Someone replied, "Then what the fuck are we doing on the ground?"

We all laughed, grabbed our stuff, and (I noticed) ran to the wood line.

Charlie had been a rather bad boy, so he had to be punished. We watched from the wood line as artillery from a nearby LZ pounded the area from which the shots had been fired. Cobras also came in and worked the area over with their ARA (aerial rocket artillery) and miniguns. Finally, to put the topping on the cake, jets strafed the area with bombs and napalm. It was all rather amusing because the culprit had probably been a lone VC or NVA who probably didi maued (Vietnamese for "go quickly," pronounced "dee dee mau") right after firing the shots. So, our fine American asses were protected and our honor avenged while some poor enemy soldier sat in a bunker miles away laughing his heart out at all the furor over one burst of AK-47 fire. After this fierce display of American military might, four more log birds came in with a Cobra firing cover. The Cobra didn't fuck around. They fired into the wood lines on both sides of the clearing directly over our heads. As the log birds came in, their door gunners opened up also. The Cav was determined to get resupply to us and make sure Charlie stayed away from the party.

Knowing that we had all this military might at our disposal was comforting. I felt, however, that this dazzling display of flexing our muscles was a bit overdone. It was overkill and probably proved to be a good exercise for some bored jet fighter and Cobra pilots who had nothing better to do. It was extremely doubtful that an enemy force of major size had perpetrated this attack. Our massive retaliation, however, was a waste of taxpayers' money. The flyboys could afford to show off because the likelihood of their being hurt was minimal. At any rate, this awesome backup power was always appreciated by the grunts in the field.

I was slowly adjusting to Charlie's world — the jungle — and I hated it. My pack felt as if it were burning a hole in each shoulder. I cringed whenever I picked it up. After a few hundred meters each day, I was unbelievably tired. You did not just simply walk through the jungle. You fought it every inch of the way. It was relentless— it never gave up. And slowly we realized that it would still be here long after we were gone — mostly unchanged by our passing. Every jungle vine had a purpose — to reach out and grab, trip, or stick on your pack. It was almost as if they were human. When we were not dodging vines, we were crawling under trees or through bamboo thickets. The jungle was like a Venus flytrap — it grabbed you and held on for its dear life. You, and you alone, were responsible for trying to crawl out and away from its insatiable maw. After the attack on the log bird, the jungle took on an even more ominous tone. We knew Charlie was around. He was not only here, but he was close. Every sound, every movement, every rustle of vine or leaf could be Charlie. We walked with our hearts in our throats— eyes and ears alert for anything. Yet it was impossible to move quietly.

Sgt. Gambill had approached me the day before log. Good news! He informed me that a rear job as Company clerk was going to be available and he had been talking to the CO (Commanding Officer of Bravo Company). Gambill told me my chances looked good for landing the job. Inwardly, I was thrilled. ANYTHING to get out of the field! Things were looking up — or so I mistakenly thought.

Three days later, we experienced what was probably Army Standard Operating Procedure (SOP). It was the last day in May, and we had received word the night before that we were going to pull LZ duty, which we looked forward to doing. Upon arising the next morning, however, we learned that instead, we would get resupply and remain in the field another eight days. We got log and then waited to CA to a new area. The choppers arrived and CA'ed us to another jungle LZ. As soon as we landed we were told that we would have to march 300 meters through the jungle to another clearing, where we would be picked up and CA'ed to Barbara. It all seemed so foolish. All the money wasted to CA us to an LZ, prep that LZ with artillery, only to have us leave again. We saddled up and had not advanced five meters into the jungle when all of a sudden everyone started running out. Several grunts were almost trampled as the guys in front of them rushed back to the clearing. I was in the rear, and scared shitless. We all thought someone had spotted a bunch of NVA. Alas, several men had stumbled into hundreds of swarming bees that fiercely attacked and stung them around their heads, necks and arms. We threw smoke bombs at the bees and tried to bypass them, but their defense was pure, unadulterated hell and it was impossible to move through them. Evidently, the artillery prep had KO'ed a bee's nest. They were determined to vent their wrath on us and they did. All of us were stung. One got me over the eye, which immediately puffed up and partially affected my vision. We tried to breach their defenses several more times but were turned back by the ferocity of their attack. Finally, one grunt passed out from the stings, and the CO decided to head back for the wood line, not 300 meters from where we had first entered the jungle. We waited two and a half hours before we CA'ed to Barbara. It had been a long, boring day filled with frustration and pain. It was not, however, to be my last encounter with bees.

JUNE

Bees, Rats, Lizards, and Sleeplessness

Older men declare war. But it is youth that must fight and die. And it is youth who must inherit the tribulation, the sorrow, and the triumphs that are the aftermath of war.

Herbert Hoover (1874–1964)
(Speech at the Republican National Convention,
Chicago, on June 27, 1944)

Barbara was to be our home for only one night, and then we were off again to the ubiquitous jungle. This time, our LZ, we were told, was "hot"—i.e., our landing was to be opposed. I was scared. On a hot LZ, the choppers usually did not set down, but hovered from four to eight feet off the ground, so you had to jump out. I still had not mastered the fine art of exiting choppers while they hovered. I jumped, landed, staggered, and fell. Off came my pack and helmet. Because I was so scared the LZ might be hot, I did not give a damn about my stuff. Abandoning everything except my M-16, I ran like hell for the wood line because I had been instructed to reach it no matter what. When the area had been secured, and found to be cold, I returned for my equipment. We then marched 300 meters through the jungle, set up in ambush, and, late in the afternoon, after no action, were CA'ed back to Barbara.

On Barbara the next day, a grunt wearing black pajamas showed up. He had been a POW and had escaped from captivity. He brought word that a nearby VC/POW camp was holding five other GIs as prisoners. In less than fifteen minutes, we were CA'ed into the jungle.

38

We had been cautioned to exercise the utmost quiet in moving through the jungle. Miraculously, we glided, quiet as church mice, through the vine-entangling morass. As we were traveling in the wood line right next to a clearing, word passed back to take a break. Just as we paused, disaster struck. A grunt inadvertently hit a bee's nest. This time we did not stand a chance. Grunts took off in all directions as if involved in a Chinese fire drill — some broke into the clearing exposing themselves (and our position) while others fled into the depths of the jungle. Chaos reigned supreme as men screamed in agony. I was forward of all this, but could hear the commotion. We popped smoke like crazy in a futile attempt to drive off the bees. Our actions, however, only intensified their relentless attack. One grunt, stung numerous times, started screaming and screaming. He screamed for over ten minutes before lapsing into unconsciousness. Hardly a soul escaped being stung. It was much worse than our prior episode with bees. Many grunts had 15–25 stings on their necks, faces and arms. One grunt went into convulsions. We had no other choice but to call in the medevacs.

The medevac ships certainly got a workout in Nam. We were constantly using them. When the jungle was not encircling you, or the insects weren't chewing on your ass, there was always something else. Four days before this attack, we had called for a medevac because a grunt had been stung by a scorpion. Two days later, two more grunts received scorpion stings. The morning of the bee attack, heat exhaustion felled a grunt. So, not only did we have to fight Charlie, but also Mother Nature was not kind to us. I was never quite sure which of those two forces got the better of us.

Having blown our position, we had a slim chance of locating the POW camp. We did discover a rather large, well-used bunker complex but not much else, other than *beaucoup* (a French word meaning many) trotters.

After the bee attack, I was moved up in my squad. I had been walking rear security but my squad sergeant, a guy named Bruce Buck, assigned me to the point team. While this was a move up, I hated it. Each platoon in the Company alternated as the point team — the first grunts (when Blackfoot was point) that Charlie would knock off if we stumbled upon him. I was not reassured.

On June 4 Bravo Company had its first contact since I had been assigned to it. We set up that evening along a trotter. Aztec and Cheyenne were on one side of the trotter (which, in this particular case, was a well-used road) and Blackfoot was about 100 meters away on another trotter near a clearing. The following diagram shows our ambush positions:

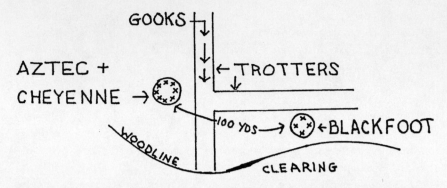

This diagram shows two trotters (enemy paths) intersecting at right angles just inside a wood line. Aztec and Cheyenne Platoons were set up in ambush at the intersection of the two paths alongside the more heavily used trotter. Blackfoot Platoon was set up in ambush about 100 yards away alongside the smaller trotter. The gooks, or NVA soldiers, came down (as indicated by the arrows) the more heavily used trotter and surprised Aztec and Cheyenne, killing one GI.

The enemy came down the well-used trotter and evidently heard Aztec and Cheyenne. They opened up on, and surprised, the grunts. Sporadic M-16 and M-60 machine gun fire continued for fifteen minutes or so, and was coupled with the resounding explosions of claymores and grenades, while Blackfoot remained silent in hopes of surprising and killing an enemy soldier. The enemy killed one grunt and suffered no casualties. Artillery, firing from a nearby LZ, was called in (almost on top of us) so we really had to lay low as pieces of shrapnel were flying everywhere.

More surprises awaited me when we were CA'ed back to Barbara the next morning.

Being appointed to the point team was bad enough, but my squad sergeant also decided that I was going to be the person who would carry the point team's M-79 grenade launcher, instead of my M-16. On top of the weight I was already carrying, I would also have to haul a minimum of fifty grenade rounds, which weighed half a pound each! The Duper was a good weapon (an exploding round had about a fifteen-meter casualty radius), but I was not thrilled at having to carry all that extra weight. I now knew I was going to be in the field a long time. Each day, my hope of escaping from the jungle faded a little more. Now that I was carrying the Duper, I realized I was indeed stuck. Having to carry all that extra weight really concerned me.

On June 5, my first night back at Barbara, I pulled LP. We were the early warning system in case of attack and got to carry a radio. I loved radios. For some reason, they have always fascinated me. The Army radios that we used in Nam weighed about twenty-five pounds and were nick-named "Prick 25" because their Army designation was PRC-25. That night turned out to be one of the worst I had experienced so far in Nam. We grunts went out on LP after dark so Charlie could not detect our movement. That evening, we set up on what we thought was level ground. The drizzling rain soon turned into a downpour, and we discovered the flat area we set up in was, in reality, a depression. Within minutes we were lying in two inches of water, so we moved to higher ground. I was miserable, but somehow managed, wet as I was, to sleep until 0300 hours when I was awakened to pull my time at guard. At 0325 hours, Charlie struck the LZ with rockets and mortars. I woke up the other guys, but, being experienced old-timers, they yawned nonchalantly and went back to sleep. Three mortar rounds landed within 100 meters of our position, but no closer. No one was hurt on the LZ, and the rest of the night was peaceful.

That Charlie was ever present, ever watchful, was brought home to us by an incident that occurred during the night of June 4, the day before we arrived on Barbara. Just outside the berm was the LZ's log pad, which measured about 150 by 150 meters. Someone forgot and left fifteen 175-mm artillery rounds on the pad that night. LZ Barbara was the only firebase I ever saw that had these big artillery pieces which, I was told, could fire up to twenty miles. So, these rounds really packed a wallop when they landed. The next morning not one round was left.

After four weeks without a bath, I finally managed to shower on Barbara this time. I felt so good after taking it. After all, it was only my second bath since arriving in Nam. Of course, I could not tell whether or not I was washing the dirt off or cleaning a sunburn! The next day, we got a laundry drop, and I received not only clean clothes, but also clean socks. This was my first sock change in a month so I felt like a king. When you are used to bathing often, or changing clothes regularly, it is difficult to describe how you are affected by being dirty all the time, and wearing the same old smelly clothes reeking of sweat and dirt. There was so much dirt and dust in Nam that we finally adapted to being as dirty as a pig and smelling like one. We may not have liked it, but we got used to it. Meanwhile, Charlie could probably smell us a mile away upwind!

On Barbara, I was introduced to pot. I had never heard of grass, or ever used it, until I arrived in Vietnam. I had been so sheltered while growing up that I had no idea what marijuana was. The use of grass in the combat zone was the rule rather than the exception. I once estimated that perhaps at least 95 percent of the grunts in my Company, including the officers, smoked grass. With three exceptions, everyone in my platoon smoked it, and I can understand why. The grass I smoked in Vietnam was the best grass I ever had in my life. Nothing I ever smoked back in the States the first few years after I returned could compare to it. It was super stuff, exceptionally potent, and I know why guys came back to the States and continued smoking it. We grunts, however, did have our own rules governing the use of grass. One was allowed to smoke it any time on the firebases, but when we got to the boonies, it was strictly off-limits. No one was allowed to smoke it in the field. This was an unwritten law and woe to the man who tried it in the jungle. If a guy smoked in the field, two things usually happened to him — he was turned in, or worse, his fellow grunts beat him up by using their rifle butts on his head. The philosophy behind this was that out in the field you had to be on top of things, but on the LZ no one gave a damn. Also, in the jungle, the sweet, pungent smell would easily blow our position. Even our Company lieutenant smoked grass. It was easy to tell when someone was smoking pot. It had a sweet, smelly odor like raw mown hay that could be detected a mile away. Over there, we were all under so much strain that we had to do something to relieve ourselves, and since alcohol was not generally available, this was the next best pacifier.

One evening on Barbara, I climbed to the top of our bunker and found Patrick, our machine gunner, calmly smoking a "J." I sat down. He handed me a lid and said, "Have a toke." The first few tokes did absolutely nothing for me. Then, all of a sudden, I began to feel high. It was the greatest feeling in the world. I felt as if all my troubles were infinitesimally small. I had no worries. I sat there on the roof of my bunker and got peacefully blown away. It was the best feeling I had ever had. Afterwards, I got the giggles. Everything anyone said was as funny as hell to me. It was indeed an enjoyable (and unforgettable) night. That night, I got my best night's sleep since I had arrived in Nam.

The next day, on Barbara, I was a witness to a sight that really disgusted me. I had been assigned to garbage detail. We drove around the firebase and picked up all the garbage, which consisted of, among other things, used C-ration cans and slops. We then took it out to the dump, which was located about 100 meters outside the LZ gate. Just down the road was a village and 30–40 children from the village were awaiting our arrival. We kicked the garbage off the truck onto the nearest pile. Before the filth had a chance to hit the ground, the kids were grabbing for it. We had to physically push them off the truck before they swarmed over it to get at the refuse. I just could not believe people would stoop so low in all that filth to get a piece of used food, etc. Such a sight was disgusting, shocking and sad. For the first time in my life, I saw poverty and it became something tangible to me. It was ever present in Nam, and it manifested itself all over the place. I could see that a lot of the kids were wearing used, ripped and torn GI fatigues, which they had probably found in the dump.

This entire incident caused me to reflect upon my outlook towards hunger and poverty, since I was saddened by what I had witnessed. We all like to sit back and push the image of starvation from our thoughts and minds. If one has never encountered it, it does not exist. It is not real to you. But here, right before my eyes, was living proof of hunger. What these children had to endure for a piece or scrap of food turned my stomach. My eyes could hardly believe the truth of the situation. That people could demean themselves so much was just incomprehensible to me, and I found it hard to countenance such acts. But what could I do? Those children fought like animals for a few stale, rotten pieces of food. I thanked God I lived in a society where there was more than enough food to go around, for everyone. Americans, by and large, have no conception of how well off we really are in life. Starvation and hunger just are not in our ken. They are abstract concepts, something to file away and not worry about during our daily life. Yet, here we were, the greatest nation on earth, spending millions of dollars to save South Vietnam, and these children were not being helped one bit. They were still groveling in the trash heaps of Nam, looking for rotten bones to suck or gnaw. God only knows how many worms, maggots, or bacterial diseases they picked up.

When we were not fighting bees and all kinds of other insects in the jungle, we were fighting off rats on the LZ. To survive in Nam, to adapt mentally to the pressures, you had to like rats. Otherwise, you would freak out. We have all battled the elements, but to fight insects and animals, well ... that is different.

The rats thrived at night. Nighttime was their chance to shine. At night they dominated the ground around and the space inside the bunkers. Their high-pitched squeaks were distinctive calls to all rodents to come and eat, and we heard these squeaks all night long as they feasted joyously on whatever they unearthed. The one thing that we could not control on the LZs was the rodent population. There was just too much food, left-over C's, crumbs, and marijuana for the rats to eat. As soon as darkness descended, the rodent population expanded its base of operations. The rats were not timid — in fact, they were incredibly bold and aggressive. Give them a mile and they would take ten. The bigger the LZ, the more food we had, the more rats there were. I soon found that, regardless of where I slept, they managed to be there.

If you have never been exposed to rats, you do not imagine that they can climb. I constantly found them crawling over me even when I slept on the top bunk inside our bunker. They loved to use your chest, or back, as a racetrack while you slept. One night, one of our platoon sergeants awoke to find a rat gnawing on his shirt. His comment on the whole matter was, "The rat gave me the shirt back because it was too small for him!" Another grunt woke up one night with a rat running all over his chest. At first, I found it hard to give credence to these tales. One night, however, I awoke to find a rat sitting on my chest, gnawing at one of my shirt buttons.

There was no rest for the weary in Nam. One would have thought that on the LZs we would have achieved some respite from being ever watchful. It was just not to be. On the firebases, the rats told us when we could sleep. In Nam, I learned that the rats usually would not appear if we left a light burning in our bunker. I hated to sleep in a bunker that was lit up at night. In fact, I find it extremely difficult to sleep with any type of light on, no matter how tired I am. So, on top of everything else that hemmed us in, we had to adapt to sleeping with light. We lit candles and burned them all night. Their light usually warded off the four-legged demons that infested our bunkers. To my knowledge, no one was ever bitten by the furry monsters. Evidently, they were adjusted to man and decided that he was just not worth the effort.

One night, I went peacefully to sleep in our darkened bunker. The rats that inhabited our bunker were squeaking fiercely and running all over the place. Something, probably our beer or grass, had excited them. One rat decided that my chest would make an excellent racetrack, so he proceeded to run up and down my body. After brushing him off several times, I gave up, lit a candle and slept peacefully thereafter. Those rats, they hated the light, but in the dark they went hog wild!

I was thankful that, up until that time, I had not had to kill anyone. At times, I prayed that, if I shot someone, he would not know what hit him. Now that I was firing the Duper, I knew that a grenade would, or could, prolong the agony of death a lot more. Not a pleasant thought to say the least. I did not, however, care or give a damn. I was in Nam to do a job — a messy, dirty job that I prayed I could do to the best of my ability. The thought of taking human life did not affect me deeply then because I was inexorably enmeshed in a situation that dictated that we kill or be killed. Today I know that human life, *all* human life, is valuable and should be preserved. To kill is wrong. It is a pity that governments force us to kill. Human life is sacred. It should not be taken. Unfortunately, governments dictate otherwise. It was funny, or odd, but being in Nam, we grew to realize one inescapable, inevitable fact. Your life was the most precious thing you have. *Nothing* else mattered. Nothing — not how rich or poor you were — made any difference. All that meant nothing in Nam. We soon realized that whatever we thought was important in life — status, marriage, money, a job, a car — was so minutely inconsequential. All that was important was life — our life.

It was the 6th of June. On this day, twenty-five years earlier, the Allied forces launched the invasion of Europe to bring peace to the world. Now there was no peace. There would be no peace for years to come in Nam. I wondered how many more young men would have to pay the supreme penalty before people in our government would wake up and realize that we were indeed fighting a fruitless war. When would we come home? I wished someone with brains would stop this senseless war. We would never win in Nam — only temporarily contain.

That night on Barbara, my lieutenant, Edwin J. Hill, came by the bunker while I pulled guard duty. A lifer, who had been in the Army nine years, he was a forthright, sincere, articulate man who tried his best to accomplish the goals set before him. Unfortunately, because he had risen from the enlisted ranks to become an officer, he was probably slated to never achieve high rank. I respected this man because he was sincere and cared about the men whose lives were entrusted to his command. The other grunts and I considered him a good leader, but his peers, the college-educated brass, would never let him achieve his full potential or admit him to their privileged ranks. A man could follow Lt. Hill. It is a pity that the powers that be in the Army would not allow this to happen.

While on guard duty that evening, I had a most enjoyable time as we sat and conversed about Europe for two hours. He had been stationed in West Germany for three years as an enlisted man, and I had toured Europe during the summer of 1964 after my senior year in high school. We reminisced about places we had been in Europe and also discussed operas. As it turned out the first opera that we both had seen was Verdi's *Aïda*. We had a wonderfully fulfilling time discussing the different places we had seen and visited in West Germany, from the Rhine to the German castle of Neuschwanstein — the fairy-like castle of the Bavarian King Louis II, a.k.a. Mad King Ludwig, that served as a model for Disneyland's castle. He had visited other castles that Ludwig had constructed — especially Herrenchiemsee, which was situated on an island in a lake, and had a hall of mirrors. We chatted through the night. His wife came from Billings, Montana; so I told him I had visited the Custer battlefield — whereupon we talked about the tactics of the battle of the Little Big Horn. Lt. Hill had been in the Army since the age of seventeen and had been an officer three years. He was an intelligent individual who could communicate extraordinarily well with his men. He probably had more cultural experience than most people. All in all, it was a most interesting evening.

As we talked, Charlie dropped a few rockets and mortars on the LZ.

We kept talking and paid little attention to the incoming rounds. For the first time in Nam, it was so nice and relaxing for me to talk to an intelligent individual and share the same impressions about places we had both visited. Lt. Hill deserved much better than what the Army ended up giving him. If anyone deserved to be a leader and attain rank, it was Lt. Hill. I will never forgive the Army, and one lieutenant colonel in particular, for the ill treatment that was later perpetrated on this noble, hardworking, zealous, and service-dedicated individual.

One of the perks to carrying a Duper was that I was also issued a Colt .45. Any individual who carried a Duper was issued a .45. Perhaps it was a status symbol, I just do not know. .45s were a pain in the ass to clean because they rusted so quickly, and most of the time, they never got cleaned because they rusted so fast. It was nice to have one on your hip, but I never found mine to be of any particular use. It was just more weight to carry. Had I ever been involved in hand to hand combat, however, then the pistol might have been useful, because when the Duper was fired, its round had to travel about fifteen feet before it was armed and would explode. In close combat situations, the Duper was useless, so the .45 had to serve as our protection.

It is hard to imagine, or even contemplate, how any one individual will react to seeing someone actually die. Nam was an excellent classroom in this respect. It did not care for you or your feelings. War never does. Death was always present — always hovering — waiting to be asked to join the party. Forget the rockets, forget the mortars, forget the sappers, forget the AKs, death was always at hand. It waited on you and your friends. Next to having your balls shot off, death ranked as the biggie to avoid. The name of the game was survival. We did not go to Nam to fight a war or win one. Our year in Nam was known by some of us as Tour 365. All we had to do was somehow manage to survive for 365 days, and avoid a death sentence in the process.

Up until June 7, death had always been removed from my ken, in one way or another. First, it was someone else in the next bunker. Next, it was someone in the jungle and finally, it was someone in the next platoon. Death had not moved in on me yet. It had managed to strike someone else who was removed from me — someone I did not know personally — someone who had not touched my life. I had never witnessed someone's death.

It is difficult to describe seeing someone die. We all want to hide that from ourselves and from everyone else. Death is so … quick … so final. It was like being a Jew in the gas camps. They were lined up against a wall, knowing that someone was going to be "chosen" to go on a detail. It was a detail to the ovens. Death stalked each of us in Vietnam. There was no reprieve from its clutches. Like a soaring eagle looking for prey, it chooses and strikes. The result is so final — so permanent. There can be no turning back.

To experience death for the first time is unreal. Here is someone alive — living and breathing. Then, seconds later, their body is offered up on the altar of death. I wonder what the jewelry-laden Mayan virgins thought as they were shoved over the cliff edges to fall into the sinkhole waters below. Knowing you are about to die, knowing there is absolutely nothing you can do or say to prevent it, must be one of the most terrible horrors of the world that some individuals are forced to face. It is difficult for anyone to imagine — not being there.

I saw a man killed right before my eyes. It was a tragedy and the most needless waste of human life I had yet seen. Sitting on top of our bunker at Barbara the morning of June 7, I watched a small light observation heli-copter (LOH), a Hughes OH-6A Cayuse, which we called either a "Loach" or "bird dog," crash-land outside the berm. The VC, or NVA, had shot the hell out of it. The tail assembly was completely gone. That it even made it to Barbara was a miracle. The pilots must have had a lot of guts and savvy. As the chopper landed, its skids collapsed. The rotors were barely spinning. Fearful of an explosion, the two pilots leaped out of the chopper. They had not been wounded. As they jumped out of the cockpit, the rotor blades collapsed. One blade caught one man in the back of the head and another blade caught the other aviator on his side.

"Medic! Medic!" we screamed. Within five minutes, the two men were on stretchers in another chopper bound for Tay Ninh. The pilot who was hit in the head was dead before his body was even placed on a stretcher. His death made me realize the futility of this war. This experience tore me up on the inside. Had those men only taken the time to duck, they would have been alive and well. As it was — one was dead and the other mortally injured. All that training and time over in Nam, and to die for that. It was all so senseless ... so ridiculous. I kept asking myself — why do young men have to die in Nam? There was no reason, yet death plays no favorites.

My appeals for Kool-Aid were paying off. Not only were my parents sending it, but also their friends, my friends, and several of my girlfriends. By this time, on Barbara, I had over forty packets of Kool-Aid, which was more than enough to last me and my buddies. I knew I would never use all forty packages, so I gave all but ten packets to the guys in my squad. Because I always had so much Kool-Aid on hand, I would soon acquire the nickname of "The Kool-Aid Kid" among some members of my squad.

My father, John S. Wise, had observed in one of his letters, which I received on Barbara, that the communists were our real enemy. In Nam, the enemy was elusive and ethereal. The bullets were real. In Nam, we did not really know who was the enemy. He struck quickly and then disappeared, melting into the jungle. Our enemy was the local peasant, the VC, or the NVA. They probably were not communists, but their leaders were. They were just as scared of us as we were of them and, like us, fighting for a cause or idea. We soldiers were the sheep. The VC did as he was told. We did too! In Nam, our orders were firm — if it moves, kill it. Don't worry about killing an innocent bystander, shoot first. Forget guilt or innocence. If it moves, kill it. Even the South Viets were enemies. My father wrote that if we did not win in Nam, we would lose everywhere else. I wrote the following back to him:

> We won't win in Nam. We never will. Nixon has admitted a military victory is impossible — and it is. We can only contain — here and everywhere else — but win here in Nam? Never!

I speculated at that time about fighting for liberty. I just did not know if we really were fighting for such a noble cause. When you could not trust anyone, you wonder whose liberty you are fighting for and protecting. The South Viets did not care — all they wanted was the Yankee dollar. We were just another meal ticket to them. What a waste — what a sacrifice it all was.

Because there was little to do while we were in the jungle, I always had plenty of spare time, so I was always writing letters. The big, deep pockets on my fatigue pants came in handy. I carried my writing paper in a plastic bag and, every time we took a break in the jungle, I whipped it out and started writing. Usually, by 1600 hours, we were set up and dug in along a trotter somewhere, so I had two or three hours of daylight in which to write. I was forever begging my parents and friends to send scotch tape. Dampness permeated everything, making it impossible to seal our envelopes, and I needed tape for that. What tape I received only lasted a week or two before the dampness made a sticky goo out of it. So, among other things I was constantly receiving scotch tape in the mail, along with Kool-Aid.

My hopes for a rear job depended on Sgt. Gambill, our platoon sergeant. He was my one link to leaving the jungle and acquiring a rear job. Without him, I was lost — hopelessly bound to serve out an indeterminable sentence in the jungle. I was fervently looking forward to an R & R (rest and relaxation — a mini holiday) at Tay Ninh, which had been promised us for weeks. In Tay Ninh, Sgt. Gambill would perhaps free me from my bondage. I prayed each day for our R & R to come, and the chance to get a job in the rear, away from the jungle. Sgt. Gambill was a kind, thoughtful man from North Carolina. Although black, he was a father figure to us, and we all came to love this wonderful, gentle soul. He did not deserve to die in Vietnam. He should have died at home of old age. But death played no favorites in Nam. It struck quickly and took whomever was in the way.

On June 7, while on Barbara, Sgt. Gambill died in a tragic, senseless accident — one of many that occurred throughout our convoluted involvement in Vietnam. That it had to happen to the most respected, most loved individual in our Company made things all the more bitter tasting and tragic. It was a disgusting and excruciating tragedy to witness.

Sgt. Gambill was out on the earthen berm surrounding Barbara with two new cherries who were on my point team. One grunt, Frank, an African American, had been with us only six days—two of which were spent in the jungle and the rest on Barbara. In the brief time he had been with us, Frank impressed us as an extremely scared person who jumped at the slightest sound. Everything seemed to spook him. In all my time in Nam, I never met anyone else who was literally scared of his own shadow. We immediately nicknamed him "Fraidy Kat." The other grunt, Cory, who was white, had also been with us several days. I was standing in our bunker with my back to the gun ports and could not see what happened. All three of them were working on the berm with claymores and C-4 (dynamite). Suddenly, a gigantic explosion ripped through the air. We all thought it was incoming (rockets or mortars fired by Charlie). So loud, so near was the explosion that for a moment I thought our bunker had taken a direct hit. After picking myself off the floor (where I had automatically fallen), I looked out while I brushed off the particles of dirt that had been shaken loose from the roof and fallen on my neck. I could see a red glare from the berm and someone was screaming "Medic! Meeediccc!" We rushed out to help, and I could not believe my eyes. What confronted us was a grisly and ghastly sight. Sgt. Gambill lay on our side of the berm with the side of his head open — blood and brains oozing out into an ever growing pool of blood. "Fraidy Kat" Frank lay on the other side. He had no legs from the knees down and one of his arms was gone below the elbow. Blood poured from the raw stumps. There was nothing left of the missing parts. They had vanished in the explosion. We called for a medevac ship.

After applying tourniquets to the stumps of Frank's limbs, the medics inserted an IV into his arm. We watched in stunned horror as Sgt. Gambill was tentatively pronounced dead. Then the medic started giving him CPR — but it was a fruitless effort. He was dead. Gone. So were my hopes of escaping from the jungle. Frank was a grim sight. He died on the way to the hospital. Cory had survived being blown off the berm, but he could not hear anything — the explosion had deafened him.

No one knew what had happened. Evidently an entire box of C-4 had been detonated and a depth cord, which not only connected several claymores but also burned at the rate of 20,000 feet/second, blew the claymores. Unfortunately, "Fraidy Kat" Frank was holding a claymore when the instantaneous explosion occurred. He would have lived, but it was obvious from his injuries that he was installing the claymore backwards. That day, Sgt. Buck, our squad sergeant, had caught him setting up another one backwards and had corrected him. Well, either he was stupid, or too scared, or he could not read. He did not learn and he faced the front towards himself. A claymore has 600 steel mini-balls backed by two pounds of C-4. Need I say more? Had Frank placed the mine (which says FRONT — TOWARD ENEMY on the front) he would have received the back blast and probably lived. Some people, like Frank, were nervous and uptight when they arrived. We all were. But Frank's fear did not go away. It killed him.

When the medevac left to fly Sgt. Gambill to Chu Chi for brain surgery, we returned to our bunker where we broke down and wept openly — tears flowed from every man's eyes. No one said anything. We just cried. We all loved Sgt. Gambill. He always treated us as if we were his own children. That made his death all the more hard to accept. He had once told me that, although married, he had no children. Well, he had children. All of us in Blackfoot were his children. We mourned his passing.

I guess about this time, I began to realize there was definitely something wrong with this war. It lacked a common thread — a goal — a happy ending, if such an outcome could ever be achieved. I now knew men would die, not for some altruistic goal, but uselessly, and in vain. I could not contemplate dying for such an undefined goal when the final objective was so ethereal. People, not ideas or goals, killed each other, but reaching or attaining a goal was a fanciful vision of sugarplums in some far-off general's mind. There was no glory in dying on a dirty mound of earth, in some godforsaken outpost, which no one would remember or care about in ten years. I would meet death, come face to face with him, many times in the next few months, and he would win more often than not. It was not totally a question of survival. Mistakes were to be avoided assiduously. If repeated — well, we knew the penalty for carelessness. It would be difficult, mentally, not to err a second time. The pressure would always be there. We had to strive to attain some nebulous perfection. We would be pushed, driven, to do better and better. We had to be on a constant winning streak so that our lives would not be forfeited. In the months ahead, I would search into the inner reaches of my soul, and learn a lot about the mettle I had, which would enable me to conquer the impossible odds I might unwillingly have to face.

What brought this tragedy even closer to home was that "Fraidy Kat" Frank, Trent (another grunt on our squad), and I had just drawn lots to see who would go on LP that night, and who got KP the next day. Frank had been assigned to our bunker while Bravo Company stayed on the LZ. Frank drew the LP straw (I got KP) and had just left the bunker when Sgt. Gambill saw him and asked him to come help. The explosion was so powerful that people who were within seventy-five meters of the berm were blown to the ground, and a few had been hit by the mini-balls from the claymores. That thought, coupled with the knowledge that I might have drawn the LP straw and left the bunker to be grabbed by Sgt. Gambill, sent chills down my spine. I was in shock the whole night, thanking my lucky stars that I had been spared.

This senseless tragedy had its own side effects. The next day, while on patrol, I was still incredibly jumpy. The horror of war and the agony of tragedy are the two things we constantly lived with in Nam. I was sick to my stomach — and scared. I was so scared that, when something moved in the bushes, I had my M-16 on full automatic ready to fire — before I saw that the sudden movement had been caused by a bird. The patrol was a long one — over five hours. We had to follow the entire wood line surrounding Barbara, which was two klicks (a klick was a kilometer, or 1000 meters) away from the LZ. We had seven checkpoints to make — but only made three. There was absolutely no way we were going to get close to the wood line where Charlie could easily pick us off. We were all too uptight over Gambill's death, so we patrolled in a smaller circle than we were supposed to because we did not feel like staying out until late evening. When we got close to a checkpoint we would radio in that we were there even though we were nowhere close to it. There was no way anyone on the LZ could check on us anyway, so it was easy to lie to the guys on the firebase. The only good thing about that day was, instead of being on KP, I took Frank's place on LP.

When I returned to the LZ, a huge package from my Aunt Katrina was awaiting me. Aunt Katrina wasn't my real aunt. She and her husband, Uncle Preston, were close personal friends of my parents and I had grown up calling them Aunt Katrina and Uncle Preston. The contents of Aunt Katrina's package were almost staggering. She had sent Kool-Aid, candy, four cans of apricots, cocoa, lemonade, Vienna sausages, V8 juice, canned tomatoes, shampoo, chewing gum, Coppertone, deodorant, a can opener, plastic bags and a much-needed mirror. Thank goodness I was on the LZ when I received this package of goodies, because I could eat most of the food before we CA'ed out. In the jungle, there was just absolutely no way I could have carried all the stuff, and I would have been forced to abandon most of it. We could not use the Coppertone, shampoo, and deodorant in the jungle because there was always the strong possibility that Charlie could smell it, and thus we would give away our position.

Because we were so late returning from patrol, there was no lunch left for us. That was OK — I feasted on the Vienna sausage, V8 juice, and some apricots. I also took stock of my Kool-Aid. That day I had fifty packets of Kool-Aid. I gave twenty packets to my buddies, plus some of the candy I had received. I knew I would never use or eat it all. Plus, a lot of the guys were not as fortunate as I — they did not have a lot of family or friends to send them things.

Being in Nam was an incredibly lonely experience for most of the men I knew. Oh sure, everyone had a girl back in the World, but few received letters from them. Still others had wives, who, I am sure, were probably not faithful for a whole year. So Vietnam ate at our insides emotionally. I knew many guys who received "Dear John" letters. To this day, I have no idea how they ever survived mentally. I was so damn lucky. I had lots of friends. People wrote to me constantly, and I was forever keeping the door open by replying to them right away. I had several girlfriends and developed a regular correspondence especially with one, Mary Garth Flood, who was from my old neighborhood. Few of my correspondents quit writing to me. I am sure that, if I had just one girl, or a wife, I would have gone nuts had I received a "Dear John" letter. Had I been married, the knowledge that my wife was living footloose and fancy-free for a year would have had a profound effect upon my thinking and reactions. I, especially, did not envy the married guys. What torture, what hell, they must have gone through wondering if their wives were slipping out and screwing around on them. They probably were, because, according to statistics compiled in the late 1970s by the Disabled American Veterans, a significant number (in excess of 30 percent) of all married Vietnam veterans were divorced within a year of returning from the war zone.*

Life in Nam was one big revolving complication. Inadvertently, I stepped on and smashed my glasses while on Barbara. All I had left were my prescription sunglasses, which were useless at night. I especially needed to see in the early morning and late afternoon — Charlie's favorite times

---

*I have been unable to locate the source of this information, which came from a publication issued by the Disabled American Veterans in the 1970s, so I have generalized my facts rather than using an actual percentile figure.

of movement. I was as good as wounded — a blind bat, with little or no useful eyesight at all. The nearest spare pair of plain glasses were in my duffel bag, which was locked up in Quan Loi. Lt. Hill nonchalantly told me that it once took him two months to get his clear glasses. By that time, I would be dead, or I would be shooting at anything that moved.

On our last night at Barbara, my bunker mates and I decided to have a feast. There was no way I was going to be able to carry everything my Aunt Katrina had sent. So Bruce, Trent, MacClary and Patrick opened our C-rations and got some bread and cheese. I opened my two cans of tomatoes, and we fixed heated cheese and tomato sandwiches. They were delicious, and sitting together in the bunker, with candles flickering, my friends and I grew a little closer.

Our interlude at Barbara ended, and we CA'ed via a CH-47 cargo helicopter, known as a Chinook, to LZ White, which was about thirty klicks from Barbara. LZ White was in a godforsaken area. Barbara was the Hilton of firebases, but White was the open-all-night-one-bed-for-$5.00-for-one-hour-only LZ. Surrounding White were the ubiquitous bamboo thickets that would cause us much grief. Whereas the area surrounding Barbara had little bamboo, White was engulfed in it. Bamboo is hell to move through. You literally and physically had to crawl on your hands and knees through the stuff. We were CA'ed off White by birds to a nearby area and started to move the two klicks we had to cover to arrive at our nightly ambush site. By evening, most of us were dead tired after having worked so hard to crawl so far.

That night, we set up next to a clearing adjoining the most well-defined trotter I had yet seen in Nam. Well trodden, it was obviously heavily used by the enemy. Unfortunately, we blew our position. While entrenching ourselves and readying for an ambush, a grunt cut himself with a machete as he hacked at the bamboo. The medics could not stop the bleeding, so we had to call for a medevac. Our grunt was lifted out, and we settled down for what could have been a long night. After all, Charlie now had our number and could have launched a sneak attack on our position at any time. For some reason, it seemed as if everyone and his brother had a cough that night. I was on LP and we could hear them coughing seventy-five meters away. If Charlie had had his shit together that night, he could have definitely laid a number on our asses. Either that, or he was not going to come diddy-bopping (walking carelessly) merrily down the trail and give us an opportunity to blow him away.

The next day, after moving about a klick, we discovered a four-foot by four-foot storage area. It seemed unused and abandoned. Another grunt and I opened it. It only had a depth of about a foot. Nothing. So we had to dig, and dig, and dig to make sure nothing had been buried in it. At a depth of five feet, Lt. Hill told us to stop. Hell, if we'd dug any deeper we might have broken through to China! What a wasted effort. But Uncle Sam had to have his pound of flesh. At the time, I resented having to dig up so much. Later, I realized our Company commander had probably seized on this as an excuse for a much-needed rest stop. Well, it may have been a rest stop for the Company, but I sure as hell did not get any rest. We all needed rest in the jungle. Any excuse would do. Our field officers really were considerate of us in the long run. By the five-foot level, I was totally exhausted; and I was still carting that damn Duper and all the M-79 ammo around.

That night on LP, I really unwound. I was exhausted from having to fight bamboo and dig up a non-existent cache. My backpack was killing me. The extra weight of the Duper rounds (twenty pounds) was certainly no help at all. I was finding it hard to sit up. My body was racked with pain, which I could only get rid of when I laid down or stood up straight. I was fast reaching the point of telling my squad sergeant that I wanted my M-16 back. The Duper was for the birds. The pain was depressing. With Sgt. Gambill gone, my fate to remain in the jungle seemed to be sealed. There appeared to be no avenue available for me to leave the field and get a rear job. I had met guys who had been in the field 350+ days. Was it to be my fate also? I did not know, but the thought really depressed and frustrated me to the point of believing that my life was a fruitless endeavor. I started to think that my life was just not worth living anymore. Sgt. Gambill had been my only hope for getting out of the field. Now that hope had vanished in an accidental explosion and with it, all chances of my getting out of the boonies. Life seemed so unfair.

The next day, I went over to talk to Lt. Hill about my glasses and he told me that I would have to wait until we got to an LZ. Once there, he would try to get me on a bird to Quan Loi, so I could pick up my spare pair and order two more pairs. As we talked, I noticed that he had been studying physical geography. Having majored in geography at TCU, I talked to him for fifteen minutes or so about my favorite college subject. I began to have great respect for Lt. Hill. He was a self-educated man, and I had never really met a self-educated person before Nam. He was definitely better informed and more intelligent than some of my college classmates. My overall impression of Lt. Hill was that he was a go-getter, the type of person who would always seek self-improvement.

The plastic bags that my Aunt Katrina had enclosed in the care package I had received on Barbara came in handy one evening. While on LP the night everyone was coughing, some son of a bitch stole three quarts of water from my ruck. We used to tie the four corners of our ponchos to nearby trees and use them as hooches. The next evening I used the bags to catch rainwater as it ran off the side of the hooch. I was able to fill my five-quart canteen in ten minutes. I collected two quarts of water in my steel pot and helmet liner, so was able to quickly replace the stolen water. It was fortunate that I did so, because bad news awaited us.

It was June 11. We were supposed to get log (resupply) the next day. We had only brought enough C-rations for three days and now we were out of food. News filtered down that an enemy battalion was supposed to be in the area. An NVA battalion numbered about 180 men compared to a U.S. Army battalion consisting of 500–600 men. We were set up in ambush and the powers that be felt we had a good chance of ambushing them. Our starving bellies were sacrificed so that we might have a chance at nabbing Charlie. Most of us had eaten all of our food. That afternoon, grunts rummaged through their rucks and the backpacks of anyone else who was foolish enough to leave his alone for long. Usually, I only ate two meals a day. This time I only packed a three-day supply. So, I barely had enough for myself. I had two meats and two fruits left that I guarded closely because, when we got low on C's, guys would not hesitate to steal anything. I ate that morning and had hot chocolate for lunch. We were all thankful that it had poured rain the night before, so everyone got water resupply. Otherwise, we would really have been in bad shape. Now, we were faced with going one and a half days without food. Just as our spirits were at their lowest point, good news reached us—we would receive log the next day. Fortunately Charlie did not do us the courtesy of showing up so we could ambush him. We got to eat and live another day.

On June 12 we learned that there would be a 25,000 U.S. troop pull-out from Nam. Although this good news excited us, most of us knew there was no way we would be in it. The only infantry people eligible would be short-timers—those who had only two to three months left to serve in country. If the brass did take a division like the Cav out, I knew I would not be going back to the World. They would simply transfer me to another division and transfer in short-timers from other divisions. I had too little time in country to be leaving so soon.

When we CA'ed back to White on the 13th, Lt. Hill was as good as his word. He informed me he had arranged for me to return to Quan Loi to pick up my glasses. My trip to Quan Loi turned out to be a quick round-trip. I was going to try and stay as long as I could, but while I was gone, Blackfoot had two men wounded by chicoms (enemy hand grenades) in an NVA ambush while on patrol outside of White. So, I rushed back to be with my platoon. Prior to leaving for Quan Loi, I had a premonition that something was going to happen while I was gone, and indeed it did. Again, I had been lucky. I had missed out on dodging some of Charlie's bullets. I did not know whether it was luck or fate that walked with me. During my brief stay in Quan Loi, I ran into a guy who had been my squad sergeant in AIT (advanced infantry training) at Fort Polk. We chatted awhile about people we knew and then bid each other good-bye. I learned he was in another division of the Cav. Although the Army is so big, one really does find that it is a small world. You were forever running into guys who had served with you at a previous duty station.

Being away from my platoon and the jungle was nice, but an emptiness followed me the whole time I was gone. When I stepped off the chopper which had flown me from White to Barbara (I had to catch another to Quan Loi from Barbara) a feeling of loss and emptiness hit me. I actually missed being away from the guys and felt as if a part of me was gone, making me rather sad at being separated from them. In the boonies, you developed a strong bond of camaraderie with your fellow men. While I hated the jungle and wanted out of it desperately, I missed my friends. Now I was away from them and Blackfoot had been ambushed. Victor B. "Vic" Tenorio, a cherry from Guam, who had been with Blackfoot less than a week and was on my point team, had been recommended to receive a Bronze Star for his actions during the ambush. I was almost jealous and just a little envious. He had been with us a week, had been in a firefight, and here I was not having seen any real action at all! I wished, in a way, that I had been in on the action, but then, if I had, I might have been killed.

An unwritten rule of the jungle stated that one always thought of his buddies when he got to the rear. So, before I left Quan Loi, I went to the PX and brought four six-packs of beer and three cartons of cigarettes for the guys in my squad. I knew they would appreciate both items. When I reached Barbara on my way back, someone told me that Sgt. Gambill had died the day of the explosion. The brass had not confirmed this for a whole week, although we knew he was gone when he was flown to Chu Chi.

Back on White, I contemplated my time left in Nam, which I worked out to be 319 days, or 7,656 hours, or 459,360 minutes or 27,561,600 seconds! I always was one for figures, but sometimes the tedium of Nam drove us batty. At that time, I also learned I had been recommended for promotion to Spec. 4. I was pleased — at least my superiors thought I was doing a good job. Little did I know that I would not receive my promotion until August 23.

My first night back on White turned out to be rather long. I had no sleep because intelligence had informed us that the enemy would attempt to overrun the LZ that night, so everyone was placed on a 100 percent alert, which meant that no one was allowed to sleep. During the night we had a "mad minute," which was the first time I had ever participated in one. During a mad minute everyone on the LZ opens up with whatever weapon he is using and fires into the wood line outside the perimeter, as fast as he can load and reload. Mad minutes were lots of fun. They were almost like playing games. Guys with M-16s would try to see how many clips of ammo they could go through. Duper men, like myself, tried to fire as many grenade rounds as possible. Usually, we Duper men were able to get off 15–20 rounds, although once I saw a guy fire off 27 rounds. Sometimes there were two or three mad minutes a night, and we usually had illumination during them, so we could see where to shoot. The main purpose of this exercise was to scare the shit out of Charlie, and if he were readying for an attack, this mad minute might discourage him. In the future, during other mad minutes, I had a lot of fun shooting at the rats running around in front of our bunker.

After one and a half months in country, I had acquired not one but two nicknames. The guys in my squad called me either "The Professor," because I had been to college, read so much, and wrote so prolifically to people; or they called me "Tay Ninh," which was the capital of the South Vietnamese province by the same name where we operated. The "Kool-Aid Kid" moniker had faded away by this time. Grunts were funny about names in Nam. You spoke to a man by using either his first or last name, or rank, or by calling him by his nickname. Generally, nicknames appeared to be more popular. Not only did we want to project an image of ourselves as we wanted others to view us, but also as to what we hoped, perhaps, to achieve in life. It was rare that we knew, or even cared, what a person's real or full name was. It just did not matter that much. Some men earned their nicknames by their achievements (like "Doc" for medic), while others acquired them naturally by their appearance or actions—hence "The Professor."

By now, I was getting to know the guys in my squad. At age 24, I was the oldest man in both my squad and our platoon, plus, in addition to our captain, I was the only other college graduate in Bravo Company. Patrick was a big, hefty, tall (about 6' 6"), curly-haired guy from California, whom I liked and respected and who, along with a guy named Frank Graham, was our machine gunner. Frank, from Clairton, Pennsylvania, was stocky, blond, good looking, serious and had been in country two weeks longer than I. He did his job well. Ben Bolt, from Dallas, Georgia, had a southern drawl and a great sense of humor. Jim "Hillbilly" Kelly was a real loveable guy from Greenville, South Carolina. He was a riot and a half most of the time — a happy-go-lucky guy who kept our spirits up when we were down.

He had been put in for promotion to sergeant the same day he was busted to PFC (private first class). Joe Musgrove, Spec. 4, was a quiet, soft-spoken country farm boy from Warrior, Alabama, who never complained. He was a true buddy and good friend. Randall "Chief" Carter, from Gallup, New Mexico, was a rather portly Navaho Indian, who was rather outspoken about the fact that he wanted to be a hero and win lots of medals. On several occasions Chief told us that his role model was the great Indian Olympian Jim Thorpe (1886–1953). To ensure that he never ran out of ammo, or water, Chief always carried 20–30 M-16 clips and double the amount of water we normally humped. Bill Rohner, Spec. 4, a stocky, curly red-haired individual from Matamoras, Pennsylvania, was our point man and damn good at it. He had been in country eight months and knew his stuff. Then there was MacClary, Sergeant (E-5), a tall, curly blond, also from Pennsylvania, who was fun loving, happy-go-lucky, and a darn good man to have on your side, although he had a tendency to go to sleep on guard duty. You still could not help but like him. Trent, from Pennsylvania, was blond haired, quiet, did his job, and hung around with Rohner and Mac-Clary. Jackson F. Winter, an African American from Saint Pauls, North Carolina, knew his stuff and was an extremely good man to have on rear security. His specialty was digging foxholes and he could dig one faster than you could blink an eye. He loved digging, and once dug a two-foot by six-foot by four-foot-deep hole in twenty minutes with no help! He and I were close buddies. Another African American, Collier, from Dallas, Texas, was our bad apple. He was a shammer — a person who never pulled his weight in Nam. No one liked shammers. Collier never would pull his share, was lazy, shiftless and got out of anything he could. Vic Tenorio, from Guam, was a short, dark-complexioned individual who looked like a Vietnamese. It was this one facet of his looks that probably saved his life a few weeks later. Lastly, there was Bruce Buck, our squad sergeant from Iowa — an NCO school graduate. He was a nice guy, big-bodied football type — quiet, knew his stuff and was most conscientious. All in all, it was a good squad, made up of solid individuals who were not going to let anyone walk over them — a damn fine bunch of men.

One day at White, I was on Observation Post (OP) with Vic. During the day men who were on OP walked out some 100–200 yards from an LZ's perimeter and set up in position to watch for enemy movement. Our objective was to prevent Charlie from sneaking up on the LZ during daylight hours and setting up mortar or rocket positions. So, Vic and I were lolling around under a bamboo clump when suddenly we heard a noise in the thigh-deep grass, not five feet away. We knew it could not be an enemy soldier, but were not exactly sure what it was. We slowly stood up, flicked our rifles off safety, and advanced toward the noise. Suddenly there was a swishing of grass and the biggest damn lizard rushed pass us. It had a fin about two feet tall on its back. We about shit in our pants! Those lizards scared the piss right out of us. We heaved a big sigh of relief that it was only an animal and not a Charlie. Besides the iguanas, Vietnam also had its own unique "fuck-you" lizard. I had heard about the "fuck-you" lizard when I arrived in Nam, but just did not believe they really existed. When I heard my first one, I was dumbfounded. The lizard would begin its plaintive cry, like a cuckoo clock striking the hour, "Fuck you! Fuck you! Fuck you! Fuck you!" Each call was a little less in volume until it faded off and ceased. I used to count how many times they would shriek "Fuck you!" Seven to nine times was about average. They were everywhere and we were seldom far from the call of one.

LZ White was beginning to get to us. We were on 100 percent alert every night until 0300 hours and only managed to get two or three hours of sleep because we had to rise at 0600 hours. At times, I hated LZ duty because I got so little sleep, and as much as I hated it, I prayed to return to the jungle. After seven days of LZ duty, we were itching to get back to the jungle. On the LZ we were sitting ducks—Charlie knew where we were, had our position plotted and was ready to dump all over us. At least in the boonies, we got four to six hours of sleep a night—and we were safer there.

While on White, we were assigned a new squad sergeant, David L. Elia, from Hilo, Hawaii, who had been called up by the Army Reserve. Although we still had Sgt. Buck, Elia had more time in grade (a.k.a. TIG—the length of time one has held a specific rank in the military), so he was in charge. He proved to be a damn good man, and a capable leader. Not only did he know his stuff but he also *always* kept us informed of everything.

One night on White, the Redlegs (artillerymen) had tree practice. They lowered their guns so that the 105s would be firing right over the bunkers. When this occurred you had to get off the top of your bunker or you could easily get blown away. For three nights in a row, they had tree practice. We blew away so many trees in the wood line that Charlie must have thought we were all stark raving mad.

Yet, intelligence informed us that the NVA were massing for an attack. They were either going to hit LZ Ike or us, on LZ White. On our daily patrols, we found lots of signs that the enemy was in the area. Then, on June 19, they struck at Ike. Could our tree practice have discouraged them? The gunfire from Ike reached our ears that night. Snoopy was called in and worked out all night over Ike. Snoopy, also known as "Puff the Magic

Dragon," was a Douglas C-47 cargo plane that had been adapted to a gun-ship role in Vietnam. It was outfitted with three General Electric 7.62-mm mini-guns which, in a one-second burst, could cover every square inch of an area the size of a football field. Snoopy also carried ARA and illu-mination flares. It could stay in the air a long time, giving air support to grunts on an LZ. To see the tracer bullets blazing from that plane so high in the sky was a beautiful sight. It also gave us a lot of confidence that, if we were in trouble, the Army could give us good, strong backup support.

The enemy attack on Ike failed but we were told that seven grunts had been killed while over 100 dead enemy bodies were recovered. We were also informed that their attack on Ike was the biggest offensive the NVA had ever launched against an LZ in III Corps, but this was probably typ-ical Army propaganda to keep us on our toes. Later, on LZ Becky, I was to be a part of one of the most massive attacks the NVA would ever launch against an LZ. On White, we really thought the enemy was aiming to hit us. Two days before the attack on Ike, we had spotted two Charlies out-side our perimeter. Gunfire scared them off. The day before the attack, we discovered that a whole section of trip flares, which had been set up along the wood line, had been tampered with — Charlie had put all the safety pins back in them!

At 0600 hours on the 20th, after the attack on Ike, I was sitting on top of my bunker, which faced the log pad. A chopper was coming in when explosions started going off near the wood line located 200–300 meters in front of my bunker. At first, I thought they were Duper rounds, but after the third explosion I realized it was incoming enemy mortar fire. One of my bunker mates woke up and nonchalantly said, "Hey, that's incoming." "Yep, sure is," I replied. No sooner had these words passed than I could hear the thump of the mortar round as it left the tube. We quickly shot an azimuth and gave it to artillery. But, by the time they returned the fire, the incoming had ceased. Charlie had probably didi maued. Besides, Char-lie was a terrible shot when he tried to aim mortar rounds accurately. Only twice, during the whole time I was in Nam, did Charlie hit his target with mortar rounds. The training that enemy mortar men received must have been atrocious— or rudimentary. Thank goodness it was so bad — other-wise, there would have been a lot more grunts killed in Nam.

By the 21st of June, our Company had been on White nine days. I was averaging 2–2½ hours of sleep a night. It was the longest we had ever pulled LZ duty. Only once had I been able to grab some shut-eye in the daytime. Somehow, I managed to plod onward — praying to get back to the jungle where I knew I would have no trouble getting some sleep. The Army was definitely getting its pound of flesh and blood out of us. Even though I was getting little sleep, I did not feel extremely tired. I guess we all passed a point of no return. Exhaustion took a back seat to our will to live. Survival kept us alive — kept us plodding onward. I was also suffering from an earache, which was the result of firing three LAWs (light antitank weapons) during a mad minute, several nights earlier. A LAW was a small, portable, lightweight (about 2–3 pounds) one-man shoulder-fired single-shot 66-mm rocket, which we carried in the jungle. Evidently the concussion of the rocket fire had been too much for my left ear. I was taking pain pills (Darvon) and anti-infection pills, but the Darvon made me feel as if I was flying in the clouds. So, besides being dead tired, I was doped up. Despite this bad experience, I still wanted to fire the rockets. They were a blast. That day was just another long, hot, dusty day for us. We spent the whole morning filling sandbags. Then we returned to our bunker, tore it down, and rebuilt it bigger and better. Personally, I think it was a make-work detail. We had learned several days previous that the Army was going to abandon White in about ten days. If that was so, then I did not see why we had to enlarge and strengthen our bunker. The brass were beginning to spin their wheels— they had to keep us busy — otherwise, discontent would surface.

Discontent was close to rearing its ugly head anyway. After no sleep all night, filling sandbags all morning, we were told we had to go out on patrol. All of us, including me, were pissed. Here we were, working our asses off, staying up all night and then having to go out on patrol. How any fool of an officer expected us to be alert and ready was beyond me. That was the iniquity of Nam. We, the common work horses, were driven into the ground day after day, and then expected to be mentally and physically alert. It was just too much. I will never understand why more men did not succumb to exhaustion. Perhaps it was because we all were so young and in such good physical shape that it did not matter if, mentally, we were zombies. Perhaps we were all past caring. As we prepared for the patrol, we decided that we were going to take several long breaks and cut a lot of corners by taking shortcuts and bypassing checkpoints. Sure, these actions, in particular missing checkpoints, might have hurt us, but we were past caring. We were robots by this time. The nine days on White were beginning to get on our nerves. Since I was on Darvon for my ear, I was flying most of the time. So I was really high when I left for patrol. Charlie could have walked over to me, said, "Hi, how are you?" and shook my hand, and I would not have known the difference, or cared.

We had no sooner entered the wood line than we came across *beaucoup* footprints. Gooks! Then we found three or four new and well-used trotters seventy-five meters further on as we moved cautiously through the

bamboo thickets. We radioed in to the LZ and told them we were changing the direction of our patrol — we had decided to go head-hunting. It was
amazing how fast our fatigue vanished. This sure beat the dullness of
White! After all that moaning, groaning, griping, and bitching about going
on patrol, we wanted some action. A few minutes later, we entered a savannah-like area. The elephant grass reached to our hips. We had advanced
about 200 meters when we discovered two mortar pits. One showed recent
use — perhaps from the missed barrage of the other morning. As we called
in the location of the mortar pits, we heard Vietnamese on our own radio!
Charlie had probably captured some of our radios and was using them.
We were all keyed up. We made every effort to move as quietly and cautiously as possible. I was about the fourth in line in the patrol's point team.
Moving slowly, we were spread out about ten yards apart. The first three
men moved forward abreast so that, if seen from above, our patrol looked
like a "T." Suddenly, they hit the ground. Seeing them go down, I hit the
ground. We had almost walked into an enemy company! Fortunately, our
guys had heard foreign voices and been forewarned. Had they not been
instantly alert, I am sure some of us might have been blown away, especially me, since I was floating along on my Darvon high. We lay there, then
quietly, by using hand signals, regrouped into a perimeter. The enemy still
had no idea of our nearby presence. As we sweated profusely in the hot
afternoon sun, our FO (forward observer) called in artillery and mortar
fire. It took him three mortar rounds to adjust so the enemy had plenty
of time to didi mau. Then the mortars rained down right on target, not
seventy-five meters in front of us. We hugged the ground as shrapnel fragments whistled by overhead.

       After the barrage we were supposed to go in and check for bodies. There
was, however, no way in hell we were going to do that. Had there been any
NVA around, they would have had time to figure out they had been spotted and would have set up an ambush for us. So, we called in and said all
we found was a blood trail — then we hauled ass back to the LZ. Our battalion colonel, known as Stone Mountain in radio lingo, who just happened
to be on White, took off in his chopper and flew around after the mortar
barrage. Later we were told that he spotted about twenty-five of the enemy
hauling ass. He called in the Cobra gunships. As we were heading back to
White, we saw more movement. Gooks! Then the news reached us via
radio that *beaucoup* enemy soldiers had been seen east of the firebase. It
looked as if Charlie was definitely up to something, and we were the bait.
Proceeding cautiously, we finally arrived back on White in the late evening. Some kind soul had ordered the chow line to stay open for us and
the food tasted really good, after our long, hard, harrowing afternoon.

My father had written me that Vietnam was a cancer eating at the soul of America. I could not have agreed more with him and replied:

> I'm reminded of some words a great gentleman spoke in Richmond in a church, "Peace, Peace, Gentlemen may cry for peace, but there is no peace. The next gale that sweeps down from the north will bring to our ears the resounding clash of arms ... etc." It is to be thus for America— continual war. Will we ever get the peace that made Patrick Henry say, "I know not for you, but as for me, give me liberty or give me death?" Will America get peace (liberty) or will she continue to butt into other affairs and seek death? Only time will tell. Wars, like Vietnam, are cancers to the U.S. They cannot bring us (in the U.S.) complete liberty, for cancer eats away at society and ruins it thus, we find the death Patrick Henry so aptly spoke of.

As I read those words some thirty-four years later, which I had written to my father on June 21, 1969, I still agree with them. Vietnam was a cancer to our society. It almost devoured us. America paid a heavy price and still has not learned to stay out of other countries' affairs. America can only hope to survive if it does not send her sons off to die in useless foreign wars—and Vietnam was a lost cause for 58,193 GIs. It was more than a lost cause. It was the end to their lives. How many people were affected by those deaths? How many lost someone dear? And now, it is déjà vu all over again—the same mistakes are happening with America's involvement in Iraq. Our country should not be allowed to sell its young men and women down the river of lost causes. We Vietnam vets have a sacred duty to prevent the reoccurrence of such a travesty.

My predictions on the troop withdrawal were proving true. By June 21, we had heard that the 9th Infantry had been chosen to pull out of Vietnam. Men who had been in Nam a short while were being transferred out of the 9th to other divisions like the Cav. Short-timers were being transferred into the 9th, so they would be leaving Nam soon. The troops going home were, in actuality, a conglomeration of short-timers. The knowledge of this policy made many a grunt bitter—especially ones who had been in country at least six months. Nixon, however, had promised peace in Nam. Peace to us was getting out of Nam, and it appeared he was keeping his part of the bargain. Morale was high over the troop withdrawal. We did not, however, appreciate the backstabbing the Army was perpetrating on us. Our last night on White was a total loss to me. All those days of little or no sleep finally caught up with me. I collapsed about midnight. I went into my bunker and woke up the next morning, six hours later, in my own sleeping hooch next to the bunker. I have absolutely no recollection of walking from the bunker to the hooch, but somehow I did.

Finally, the Army consented to let us return to the jungle. We were CA'ed off White to a nearby river, which was the largest flowing stream I had yet seen in Nam. Upon landing, we walked through some high elephant grass. It was so tall and thick that we could have passed within five paces of an enemy company and not spotted them. Pushing our way through the tall grass, we came to a large clearing that had lots of trotters branching out from it. We set up in a large bamboo thicket next to this clearing. We knew we had a good chance at contact because the enemy infested river areas and located their hospitals there. The clearing in front of us was about 100 meters wide and rose in elevation to our right. We were just sitting there smoking and shooting the breeze when my sergeant whispered, "Gook!" We hit the ground just about the time three grunts opened up on him with their M-16s. Then Patrick, our machine gunner, started laying down fire. A second enemy soldier was walking about 75 meters behind the first one. With the eruption of the first fusillade of bullets, the first NVA went down and the second didi maued. Firing through the bamboo canopy that covered our position, I got off two or three Duper rounds that landed near the position of the second enemy soldier. We were extremely cautious. We knew the first NVA was out there, but whether he was dead or alive was another matter because the knee-deep elephant grass concealed him. Three of our guys advanced toward the enemy soldier and threw frags. Then they rushed the downed man. Out of all the bullets fired at him (at least 100 rounds) and the tossed frags he was only hit once — in the lung. After calling a medevac, our medics immediately went to work on him.

So, now I had seen my first real live Charlie. Like us grunts, he wore green fatigues. In his rucksack was a can of U.S. Army issue C-rations—spaghetti and meatballs. He had obviously found it at some log site where a grunt had chucked it away or he had obtained it from villagers who were forever scavenging around local firebases or abandoned LZs. Our POW's AK-47 was new and had just been cleaned. He only had one banana clip of ammo that contained thirty rounds. He also had a flashlight that was most unusual due to its parts and construction. The batteries of his flashlight were parts of a Prick 25 battery. Whenever a Prick 25 battery ran low, we were supposed to break it into at least two parts and either throw them away or bury them. I did this, but lots of other grunts did not. Our POW had probably found a discarded Prick 25 battery and had ingeniously made his own flashlight. This gave me a much deeper appreciation as to how clever and ingenious the VC/NVA were. This one example clearly showed their desire and determination to beat us at our own game. To insulate his batteries, the fallen Charlie had covered them with tinfoil wrapping from an accessory pack, known as a 101, which came with every C-ration box.

The accessory pack contained cigarettes, cigars, sugar, soap, toilet paper, razors, shaving cream, matches, stationery, envelopes, M & Ms, chewing gum, Lifesavers, and chocolate plus other types of candy. Clearly, the enemy were good scavengers. When we got log, we never used all the C's we received. Those we did not use, we were supposed to open and throw in a common pile to be burned. Well, most of the time we did not open our cans, we just chucked them away. We also emptied the articles from the cellophane-like covering of the 101s and would usually forget to throw the wrappers on the pile to be burned. The last thing we usually did upon leaving a log site was to burn the pile of trash and C-rations. Sometimes, we were in a hurry and did not bother to light the pile. If Charlie was near by, he would wait until we left and then go scavenge all the good stuff we had left. We were constantly finding C-ration cans in the enemy bunkers. So, indirectly, we were supplying the Charlie with food that probably gave him a little extra energy to fight us. The belts that the NVA wore usually had a buckle with a star on it symbolizing the star found on the North Vietnamese flag. Our POW had had one such belt, but by the time we loaded him on the chopper, it was gone. Grunts prized such trophies and this was a perfect time to get one.

Our whole attitude towards the POW was one of casual indifference. Basically, we could not have cared less about him. This was a callous attitude on our part; however, we just did not have time to be sympathetic to his plight, no matter how seriously he was wounded. This was the enemy. He was lucky. Had we killed him, we would have left the body to rot in the grass, just like a dog's body that has been hit by a car and is left to fester alongside the roadway. This man was a soldier just like us. His only mistake had been to walk into our ambush and take a bullet. Considering how the enemy treated our POWs, this guy got off easy.

Lt. Hill took the AK-47. Since I had never seen one, he not only showed it to me, but broke it down (disassembled it) for me. All enemy automatic weapons, such as the AK-47, had to be turned in to Bravo Company's supply sergeant back in the rear. Grunts, however, could keep semi-automatic weapons like the Soviet-made 7.62-mm SKS rifle, if we were lucky enough to find one. The next day, when the AK-47 went on the log chopper, it was minus its bayonet. Those we were allowed to keep.

As we were eating breakfast on the next morning of June 24, gunfire broke out. We made the ground become a part of us, we were so flat! Three enemy soldiers had tried to sneak up on us and had been spotted by an ever-alert sentry. I do not think we hit any of them, but while we waited, the pungent smell of grass wafted over our position. The damn enemy had the audacity to sit out there, on the upper side of the clearing, and smoke pot! A lot of guys had their tongues hanging out tasting an imaginary toke. After treating us to a savory, olfactory repast, Charlie left and we moved out.

We had advanced about 100 meters into the jungle when we stumbled upon the largest bunker complex I had yet encountered in Nam. It contained about thirty extremely well-built and heavily entrenched bunkers. The enemy had been in the bunkers that morning because we found some open food — tins with mackerel in them — so we carefully checked out each bunker. One grunt found a Christmas card to some GI, from someone back in the World. Charlie must have picked it up after a careless soldier had dropped it in the jungle. We also found some carved wooden chicoms. The enemy, always low on ammo, had used these wooden grenade mockups for practice. I picked one up and kept it. It would be mailed home as a war souvenir, if I ever got to Tay Ninh.

As we moved further into the jungle, we had jet fire support that day and the next. Evidently, our battalion colonel, known as Stone Mountain, figured we would need this backup support. It was comforting to know we had it, but we were wary of what awaited us ahead. Would we corner Charlie, or were we merely chasing a will-o'-the-wisp? Later, we were told that we, along with six other companies, were involved in a sweep designed to net Charlie. Those first two days in the jungle were a blessing in disguise. Out in the boonies, we were able to sleep, and I got a lot of sleep those first two nights. The second night out, we cheated a little bit on guard duty and got some extra sleep. We combined guard duty with the guys in the hole next to us so that each of us only had to pull one hour of guard duty. It was so damn good to sleep again. I got about eight and a half hours of sleep that night, and I needed it.

The next day, we moved into an area that had been hit by B-52 strikes. Evidently we were there to assess the bombing damage. In a letter home, dated that day, June 24, I wrote:

> Here's how the report will probably read. Said air strikes were most effective — there were 379 trees killed, 5,293 ants blown to hell, and 6,378 vines killed. No sign of gooks!

My sense of humor was obviously beginning to return after a long time of sitting around on White. We saw no sign of the enemy or any bunkers. It was a day of stops and starts. We would advance a little way and stop. A patrol would then be sent out to do a cloverleaf. I was on two cloverleaf patrols and found it to be a pain in the neck. A cloverleaf patrol is exactly what it sounds like. We would stop in our line of march and patrol out in a circle on one side. Then we would march a little farther, and send a patrol out on the other side. It took a lot of time and increased our chances of detection, which was not something we wanted to happen.

One of the more pleasant aspects of Nam was seeing the different kinds of butterflies that inhabited this part of the world. I had always been attracted to butterflies and, at one time, collected them. I was intrigued by all of Nam's varied species with their bright colors. The butterflies in Nam evidenced little fear of man and, in fact, they almost appeared to be tame. One day, one lit on my glasses and simply would not get off. I brushed it off several times, but he was a determined cuss, so I relented and let him stay. Sometimes, I found myself wishing I could tramp through Nam with a butterfly net instead of an M-16!

I saw my first rice paddy that day. We had moved across an open space and then up to the top of a small hill. The hill did not rise more than twenty feet in elevation over the plain, but it was the first physical terrain of any note that I had encountered thus far. We spent the night on top of the hill, then wandered down to the paddy the next morning to be CA'ed back to LZ White. I sat on a dike while waiting for the choppers. We made such tempting targets that the enemy could have picked us off so easily. We were out of water, so some guys scooped up the rice paddy water and brewed some hot chocolate. Someone must have forgotten to put a water purification tablet in the water. That night, after being CA'ed to LZ White, quite a few guys had the trots. I was lucky — I had boiled my water about five minutes before drinking it.

The inevitable happened while I was on White. My prolific letter writing was paying off, in lots of return mail. I was unprepared, however, for the nineteen letters that awaited me at White! I had always prided myself on answering every letter I received in Nam. Now, a formidable task faced me. How I ever found time to answer them all is a mystery, but they all received a reply.

Back on White, I discovered a new way to eat my C's. In every accessory pack which we received with our C's, there was usually a tin of cheese or jam. I had been eating my jam with the C-ration bread. One day, after I had finished off my bread, I had some excess jam. What to do? I just could not toss it away. I was eating some boned chicken that I had heated, so I mixed the blueberry jam with the chicken. It was delicious and made my meal so much more enjoyable.

Some people may wonder how we cooked hot meals. It was really quite simple. We would take an empty C-ration can, usually the one that contained bread, which was about 1½ inches tall by 2½ inches wide, and entirely remove either the top or bottom lid with our can openers, which

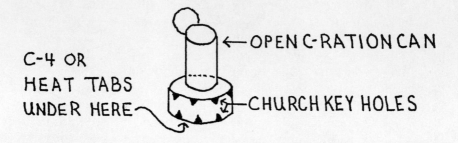

C-4 OR
HEAT TABS
UNDER HERE

←OPEN C-RATION CAN

CHURCH KEY HOLES

This diagram shows how we made a crude stove for heating our C-ration meals. First, we took a small round C-ration can, usually the one that contained bread, which was about 1½ inches high by 2½ inches wide, and entirely removed either the top or bottom lid with a P-38 can opener. Second, using a church key–type can opener, we put triangular holes in the can's side bands around both the remaining lid and the now open lid area. Third, we dropped our C-4, or a heat tab, on the ground, lit it, and placed the open end of the can over the now burning heat source. Fourth, we set an already opened can of food on top of the remaining lid and heated our food.

were known as P-38s. Then, using a second can opener, known as a church key, we would put triangular holes in the can's side band around both the remaining lid of the can and the now open lid area. We then dropped our C-4 (or a heat tab, if we were lucky enough to have any) on the ground, lit it, and placed the open end of the can over our now burning heat source. Next, we set an already opened can of food on top of the remaining lid. Thus, we had a crude, but effective, stove. See the above diagram for further detail.

The physical work needed to survive in Nam is something that cannot accurately be described in words. Our willpower, I am sure, played a rather large part in our ability to adapt to the rigors of jungle and LZ life. It was not easy. You might get down, but you knew you had to keep on, or death awaited you. We rolled up the sleeves of our fatigue shirts to walk through the jungle. In some cases, we wore our green T-shirts as we humped. Our arms needed the air — and we found, with no sleeves, that we sweat less. Unfortunately, from the elbow down, our arms took the brunt of what Nam had to offer — sun, flies, ants, and innumerable cuts and scratches. My hands and arms always had cuts on them. Because I was young and in good health, my body was able to fight off infection. Grunts were always getting small infections, which they shrugged off. The dirt and the grime did get to us, though, because I never knew any man who did not get boils. A boil was extremely painful and the treatment not much better. The brass could not afford to let grunts go into the LZ to have minor infections, such as boils, treated by the LZ medics. Out in the jungle, you were needed. You were part of a team. We were constantly getting blisters on our hands, which popped and became raw sores. This was one result of having to dig a 2' by 6–8' long by 2½'–4½' deep foxhole every night when we set up in ambush. The pain from the broken blisters was excruciating at times, yet we endured it. We had to—there was no relief. The medics did not use iodine for the numerous cuts and scratches that we managed to acquire. Instead, they used hydrogen peroxide, which stung like hell when applied. Many times, I yearned for my own bottle of iodine or mercurochrome; however, that would have stung too, when applied to the raw flesh of my hands. I was lucky—I had no signs of jungle rot that appeared on one's feet from sweat and trudging through the innumerable streams we crossed. I had foot powder and used it often. Plus, I tried to wring the water out of my socks at least two or three times a day. This desire to stay healthy, and my determination to keep my feet dry, paid off. I saw several men with terrible jungle rot who had to leave the field when they got to a point where they could hardly walk.

On June 27 I received a letter, dated June 18, from Major General Alfred G. "Tubby" Tuckerman (Ret.), who was a close personal friend of my parents. At one time, Tubby had been in command of the same 8th Cav to which I now found myself assigned. What a coincidence! Parts of his letter, which was deeply touching, read as follows:

> ... I was pleased to learn that you have been assigned to the 8th Cavalry, which is the Regiment I commanded when the First Team landed in Yokohama on 2 September, 1945. Prior to that I had been briefly in command of the 2nd Brigade, which included both the 7th and the 8th Cavalry.
>
> ... I was with your great Division from January, 1942, until mustered out in March, 1946. Thinking that you might wish to wear them, I am enclosing two 1st Cav. patches I wore all the way through World War II, on my left shoulder while with 1st Cav. and on my right shoulder while with I Corps, and again after the war as Commanding General of the 77th Infantry Division, USAR. I send them to you, as the son of one of my closest friends, and pray that these patches will protect you as they did me.
>
> Most sincerely,
>
> Alfred G. Tuckerman
> Major General, AUS (Ret.)

I was deeply touched and honored that Tubby, as my parents called him, would send me some of his 1st Cav patches, which he had won in

World War II. I did not sew them onto my uniform because the bright yellow coloring might have given me away; instead, I tucked them away in my rucksack for good luck. I still have those lucky patches that now reside in my Vietnam scrapbook. Perhaps they did indeed bring me good luck.

That same day (the 27th) I thought a lot about killing. Being in Nam could have been a killer's dream come true. At one time or another in our lives, we all dream of committing murder or killing someone and getting away with it. Well, Nam was the perfect killer's paradise. It was an environment that lent itself to murder. A person could really get rid of all his pent-up emotions and take them out on Charlie, or, if he was lucky, on some superior officer he did not like. In Nam, we truly felt "above the law." There we could actually commit murder and get away with it. We were hired killers for our government, and were legally free to kill any Oriental person we saw in the jungle. Plus, in a firefight, if you did not like your sergeant, lieutenant, or captain well, you could swing your M-16 a few degrees to one side or the other, and nail him. I know this actually happened to one of our platoon sergeants, a man who was hated by everyone in Blackfoot. What a terrible thing to know that you could actually kill someone — and get away scott free. For, out there in Nam, there was no law except the law of the gun. It was like the Old West. Sure, eventually law came to the West, but in the early days, the law of the gun prevailed. It was the same here. He who shoots the quickest, survives and rules. A gun was power. The thought of being able to kill indiscriminately gave one a great sense of exhilaration and power. It was almost sexual. I could not believe that I would ever think such thoughts, yet I did. Power is an extremely dangerous weapon — even more so when you have unlimited power to do what you want. How could any nation give such power to its young men, and then expect them to return to an orderly society as normal human beings again? It just cannot be done. It is no small wonder that many Vietnam vets could not handle their reintroduction to civilization. We lived like animals — kill or be killed — and yet were expected to reenter society as tame, ordinary people. I am sure many adjusted, but many more will carry the scars of uninhibited freedom to kill as long as they live. Personally, I am not as afraid of death as most people who have not seen it face to face, as I did. Given the right set of circumstances, I know that, today, I would not hesitate to kill someone. It is the knowledge of this sublimated thought that scares the hell out of me. I have assiduously avoided all situations, since Nam, which might even place me in such a position. Nothing — animal or man — likes to be cornered. In Nam, we learned that the way out of that corner was to kill.

While traveling through the area that had been subjected to B-52 attacks, I could not help but observe that, despite the tremendous explosions that had taken place here, there were still ants. No matter how hard we tried to kill Charlie, we still could not put a dent in the insect population! In the bombed-out area, we discovered the largest bunker complex I was ever to see while in Nam. We first estimated that it probably covered seven to eight acres. Slit trenches ran back and forth between bunkers that were also connected by well-built tunnels. Our Company split up and each platoon set up in ambush — hoping Charlie would oblige us by walking down one of the numerous trotters in the area. Unfortunately, he didn't. I was beginning to get an itchy trigger finger. I had been in country two months and had seen no action. I was dying for action. As we explored this bunker complex, it turned out to be much bigger than our original estimate of seven or eight acres. For three days, we traveled slowly through it, and never left it. It was probably a klick long by a klick wide. Without exception, there was a one-man fighting position every 25–30 meters, which had overhead cover, making it similar to a small bunker. Some of the bunkers had three sets of logs covering them, thus making them extremely well fortified and well nigh invincible to ground assault. I would have hated to try and move Charlie out of these well-built bunkers.

One day, while still in this complex, we discovered a supply area of sorts and unearthed thirty homemade ingots of aluminum, or some steel-like metal. We found 70–80 half-inch by twenty-foot-long steel rods that were used for reinforcing concrete bunkers. We even found a cement mortar mixer that had obviously suffered from a case of the B-52s. Some U.S. Army water cans— the type that were used to bring water to us during log, also turned up. Last but not least, we discovered our first booby trap, which we disarmed. It was a 60-mm U.S. mortar round that had been wired to explode if someone stepped on the trip wire.

Walking in the bunker complex was easy because we used Charlie's trotters. No vines or bamboo to fight off. What a relief! Of course, walking down a trotter was not conducive to one's health and well-being, if Charlie was around. In that case, he had a tendency to take shots at your ass and make things mighty uncomfortable. In this case, Charlie had probably didi maued the area, so we did not worry about him showing up.

I finally got out of the point team towards the end of June and got in with the gun team and rear security. So, I was walking last in the line of march, making sure Charlie did not sneak up on our asses! It was a job I grew to love.

JULY

LZ Becky's Birth

A war, even the most victorious, is a national misfortune.

Helmuth von Moltke (1800–1891)
(Letter, 1880)

July 1st came in with a bang. The Army abolished serial numbers and substituted our social security numbers in their place, plus it (or Congress) gave us a 12½ percent pay increase. Considering our pay, it was not much, but at least it was a raise.

Washing in Nam was almost a lost art. Baths were a rarity and almost non-existent. Most guys were content not to bathe at all. On our last log in June, I took a half bath—from the waist up. Every log day, we each received 101 packs, which were extremely valuable because they always contained items that we wanted, needed or would trade for something else. That log day we had lots of extra water, so I got some 101 soap and, using the excess water, lathered up from the waist. Chief then poured water over me to wash off the soap. I cannot begin to describe how good this "semi" bath felt. It was my first (and only) bath that I took while I was out in the jungle, and it felt wonderful to be clean for just a little while. I could not believe my hands were actually clean. I smelled so much better that I was sure that Charlie could have detected me a mile away.

I would need to feel clean because, on July 2, we were faced with a rather grim and ghoulish task. We had been wandering down a trotter, which we had been on for three days, when we discovered a grave. Orders came down to unearth it—after all, it might have been an arms cache. Unfortunately, it was no more than a grave. Thank goodness, it was an old grave and not "ripe," because there was no stench of rotting, decomposed flesh. We covered it back up rather hastily and moved onward. So, now the stain of desecrating a grave was upon our souls. It was a mark I cared not to bear, but nothing was sacred or holy in war — even if it was an undeclared war at that!

On the morning of July 3, Blackfoot platoon killed its first enemy soldiers. I had just awakened and was making breakfast when our claymores went off. Then all hell broke loose as gunfire erupted all over the area. Three NVA had walked down the trotter where we were set up and stumbled into our ambush. Two of them did not get away. We reconned the entire area by fire and then a security team went out to check the bodies. We could hear one of the enemy soldiers moaning loudly. Our security team took care of that. Frank Graham, our machine gunner, who was on the security team, told us later, "One was moaning, so I raked him with my gun and he stopped moaning!" One of the enemy soldiers had an AK-47, but the other one had a *brand* new M-16, with lots of M-16 ammo. It appeared that the M-16 had hardly been used. A member of the security team removed a belt from one of the bodies and gave it to me. I kept it and later sent it home as a trophy.

The next day, we "sort of" received log. I say "sort of" because the choppers could not land since we were in thick jungle and had no desire to hack out a thirty-yard-wide clearing with our machetes. So, they hovered about fifty feet in the air and threw out our C's. All the canned crackers were ruined, although the food tins survived. Then they threw our Cokes out. That was just about the icing on the cake. Oh, were we mad! Most of the Cokes burst — literally exploding upon impact. Everyone was pissed as hell. We all gave the finger to the log bird and its crew and screamed a few obscenities.

It was on that day, July 4, 1969, I entered the world of combat veterans. On that day, I was under fire for the first time in the jungle, and participated in a kill.

As we were saddling up and getting ready to move out, the NVA opened up on our platoon. After all, they knew our position due to our July 3 ambush, which had cost them two men. I started firing my Duper. Somehow, miraculously, not one of our guys had been hit. We pulled back and called in artillery and jets, which bombed the hell out of the area in front of our platoon. After the strikes, Cheyenne was sent out on patrol. They set up an ambush and soon trapped two NVA in two different bunkers. The encircled enemy soldiers soon realized that continuing to fight was hopeless, so they started yelling "*Chieu Hoi,*" which means, "I surrender." They refused, however, to leave their bunkers, and they had managed to wound one of our men. By wounding the grunt, they sealed their fate. All afternoon Cheyenne closed in on the bunkers, pulling the noose just a little tighter every few minutes, as they inched forward. Not only could we hear the NVA frantically screaming "*Chieu Hoi! Chieu Hoi!*" but they also yelled "*Lai day,*" which means "come here." "*Lai day! Lai day!*" we yelled back. Still, they refused to surrender or leave their bunkers. Considering what we found later, when we reached them, I doubt they could have crawled out.

To take a bunker, especially a well-constructed one, is a difficult task as they are virtually impregnable to small arms fire. Well, Ranger — the radio code name for our CO, Captain John D. Mooneyham — decided to send in my squad to help Cheyenne. So, off we went with Ranger following us. Linking up with Cheyenne, we found the wounded grunt and several of our guys carried him out. But, I was to be in on the kill!

We surrounded one bunker and threw everything we had at it — Duper rounds, M-16s, machine gun rounds, frags, and an M-72 LAW. It was definitely a case of overkill. Two guys rushed in for the kill only to find the bunker empty!

Then, as if on cue, from two different places came the plaintive shouts of "*Chieu Hoi! Chieu Hoi! Lai day! Lai day!*" Upon locating them, we tried to talk them out — but none of us spoke Vietnamese. All we could do was to yell back — "*Chieu Hoi! Lai day*! No shoot! Come out!"

They would not come out. I think they were too severely wounded to leave their bunkers.

Cheyenne stormed one bunker and found a live enemy soldier. He moved. They raked him. My Blackfoot squad closed in on the next enemy soldier. We threw frags. I hated frags — especially in heavy vine-infested jungle. This experience really confirmed my suspicions. Jungle vines would not part for frags; instead they caught and bounced them back towards us. For every two frags we threw, at least one would hit a vine and tumble to the ground, forcing us to duck each time to avoid shrapnel fragments. After our frag attack, the VC still yelled, "*Chieu Hoi! Chieu Hoi!*"

He still refused to come out.

Ranger got really pissed off. He yelled to us, "Frag the son of a bitch!" So, we fragged the bunker again.

Bill Rohner had inched close enough to spot the NVA's rifle, and then the enemy himself. The man moved and three of our guys raked him. He was still alive as we closed in and stormed the bunker. Somehow he had miraculously survived!

Our sergeant gave him the *coup de grace*.

I decided I wanted to see a dead enemy soldier since I had never seen one. He was extremely perforated. Part of his hand had been shot in two, and he had been trying to sew it back together. We found a few morphine capsules on him and a couple of morphine needles embedded in his flesh, so he was probably out of it. Amazingly, after he had received so many wounds, there was not a lot of blood — not even enough to fill a couple of shot glasses. This was a sad sight I would not soon forget.

Here was once a man. How he must have suffered in his last hours! But, we had no choice. We had to kill them. Even though each one was mortally wounded, they might have had a chicom and tried to take one or two of us with them. Then again, they had wounded a grunt. When an infantryman was hit, or killed, any nearby enemy soldier sealed his fate. Grunts gave no quarter.

One thing really bothered me after this episode. The NVA soldier, who had been in the process of sewing his hand back together, must have been terror stricken when he realized that we were not going to let him live. Those must have been the toughest three hours of his life, lying there in the bunker knowing he would soon be dead.

Knowing that you are going to die within a short period of time must be one of the most frightening feelings that anyone can experience. I certainly felt that way several times in Nam. That thought of impending death, coupled with the knowledge that there is absolutely no hope for escape, that you are going to die no matter what, must not only have its own special kind of horror but also must, indeed, be a hell on earth.

When I read about the Iranian firing squads in 1979, part of me went out to those poor souls who had no chance to defend themselves before they were unceremoniously dragged out, put up against the wall and shot. It is almost impossible for anyone to imagine what it's like; but knowing, by seeing and participating in the eventual extinction of a human being, gives me great empathy for all people who must face their God by sudden, violent means. God have pity upon their souls.

I learned a lot about myself in Nam. Not only had I been involved in my first kill, but also I had been shot at for the first time, and I had stormed an entrenched enemy in a bunker. Yet, despite all this, the thought of fear never crossed my mind. I know and realize that I should have been afraid — but I was not. I could not understand why. Perhaps I was becoming numbed by what was happening around me. During our final assault on the two bunkers, I realized that I was extremely bored by the whole process. There was no fun in killing. It really was not as heroic or glorious as portrayed in World War II movies, or John Wayne thrillers. Killing is something most people just do not enjoy doing. I was not afraid to kill, but it just did not turn me on. Nam was more like a game of hide and seek. As long as we were both able to miss stumbling upon each other, we stayed alive. And staying alive was the name of the game. Killing was an incidental part of the game. It all came down to surviving for 365 days. Play the game right and you survived. Fuck up and Charlie took your number. It was just that simple, and all so damn insane — killing until you were killed. Nothing we did as infantrymen would ever really make any sense. I was not able to participate actively in the kill because I had a Duper — and you just did not fire those things at close range with a bunch of grunts standing around. It was not good for your health — if you wanted to live.

After our kill, the brass decided to CA us out of the area. Since there was no landing place for choppers, we blew a bunch of trees with C-4 to make enough room for two choppers to land. While some of us prepared an LZ for the choppers, the rest scattered CS (tear gas) crystals in nearby bunkers. Tear gas was no fun and the CS crystals were like mothballs except worse. We were forced to wear our gas masks as we spread the CS crystals. One whiff was all one needed to make him cry. The crystals were supposed to last at least six months — after that I wondered if we were supposed to come back and put more out.

Survival in Nam did not just depend upon staying alive physically — we had to stay alive mentally. For, without that mental will to live, to survive — there was little hope of making it. Not only were we pitted against Charlie, the ants, bees, rats and jungle, but also we were in a continual struggle to stay alive mentally. We were forced to think. If one gave up thinking, he became a robot; and if Charlie did not knock him off, the jungle got him. It was difficult not to become depressed or discouraged in Nam. At one time or another we all got depressed. But, if someone labored too long on thoughts of death, he usually made a mistake (like "Fraidy Kat" on Barbara) and died. Perhaps it was good that we were on the go a lot; it gave us something to do, and doing something, whether it was filling sandbags or humping three klicks through vine-infested jungle, made us forget some of the things that were depressing us. The conditions under which we labored were mentally and physically strenuous. It is hard to describe to an outsider what it was like. Every breath we took might be our last. If one slept he might not wake up. In fact, we lived in constant fear every second, every minute, every hour, every day that Charlie was going to blow us away just around the next bend in the trotter, or with his next mortar barrage on the LZ. To know that you might be killed, and to realize that death could happen at almost any second, was indeed extremely unnerving. The mental strain we all were under was, at times, unbearable. It is difficult for anyone to realize what it is like, never knowing when you are going to buy it, or cash in your chips. The ever-constant pressure was there — like a monkey on your back just waiting for you to err. It was relentless. Every move, every thought was centered on the one immutable idea—can I make it? Will I survive?

I am sure we all became discouraged and downcast at times. I never really saw anyone, however, who would admit to being depressed. Somehow, we managed to hide it. To bring it out into the open might open Pandora's box. We all depended upon each other. To voice or communicate our fears might be construed as failing your fellow squad members. We did not, under any circumstances, want to let our buddies down, because we needed and depended upon them. Even though we might feel depressed, we knew that all of us were vital to each other's survival. We could not afford to break the chain and endanger the group. We depended on our own little groups, which nurtured, supported, and reinforced not only our belief in ourselves but also our knowledge that the others would keep us alive. It was our sole protection. It offered survival—or a path to survival. To depress others in the group (and we all formed our own little cliques) was taboo. It threatened stability and security. Thus, for the most part, we all held our fears within ourselves so they could eat away at our insides. Yet fear gnawed at all of us a little at a time. So, our insides eaten away, we returned home as hollow shells of our former selves.

When you learn to survive, you learn to let nothing stand in your way. Survival is, or must be, a primal instinct. Without it, all is lost. When placed in such a primitive environment, as the Vietnam jungle, you survive or die. I did not make it *through* Nam, I *survived* Nam. Some of us survived better than others. I wonder how many of us needed, received, or did not receive, psychiatric help after Nam?

After all, the average age of the Vietnam combat veteran—the grunt—was 22, compared to 26 for both the World War II and Civil War veteran.* For the most part, American soldiers were young boys, not men, who had not reached their potential yet, or matured enough to cope with the terrible stresses thrust upon them by a nation hell-bent on emerging victorious from an unwinnable war. Is it no small wonder then that these men were bound eventually to come apart at the seams mentally upon their dishonored return to the World? I guess I was fortunate in one respect. I had been to college, and that extra four years of education along with the maturity that goes with it enabled me to cope a little better with the situation.

For a society to place a man in a live-or-die situation is easy. But is society willing to accept the consequences of his re-entry? Is it prepared

---

*Dunnigan & Nofi, 3. The average age at death for the ultimate "grunt"—the 18,465 "Eleven Bravos" who died in the war—was 22.55.

to handle the consequences of its actions? History points out that somehow, society has survived doing this. But when will the final straw break the proverbial camel's back? When is society going to test the waters just once too often? It came deadly close in Vietnam. The residue of this fiasco is going to affect most profoundly the outcome of our decisions for years to come. There is much bitterness and anger, dissatisfaction and discord, over what our nation did to us. It will pay an extremely heavy price for what it forced upon its young men. This may not manifest itself for years to come, but the effects will eventually be seen.

You cannot give someone a rifle and tell him to kill over there, but not here in the real world. You cannot condone marijuana in one place and forbid it in another. You cannot spray Agent Orange in one place and deny those affected by it their right to medical help. What did we survive? How did we survive? By sheer guts and will to live, and the knowledge that, to accomplish that objective, it had to be a no-holds-barred fight. You do not simply kill an enemy — you beat him into the ground. People who get in your way are to be stepped on — squashed. Nothing matters but the objective. Indeed, Vietnam taught us all a lesson, and the knowledge we gained cannot help but be carried over into the society in which we now live. Woe be unto those who will stand in our way in the future — for they shall be pushed aside, smashed like the ants we stepped on in Vietnam.

I battled with myself every day I stayed in the jungle. I was incredibly discouraged numerous times. By July, after one and a half months in the jungle, I had almost given up hope of ever leaving it. The thought of spending ten and a half more months in the jungle was oppressive and weighed heavily upon my mind. Every day I stayed increased my chances of dying. In fact, because I was an infantryman, there was nearly a 50 percent chance I would be killed or injured in Vietnam.* Those of us who did manage to end up in combat in Vietnam saw a lot more of it than our fathers or uncles did in World War II. In Vietnam the average infantryman saw about 240 days of combat in a single year.†

I despised and hated the jungle. I cursed the country that would do this to its young men. I hated the nation that had enslaved us and forced us to participate in this tragic farce. The physical torture of putting on my sixty-pound rucksack was indescribable. I hated every vine and bamboo shoot that caused me to trip. I was always tripping, stumbling, or falling with the crushing weight of my pack there on top of me, to remind me that Jesus, too, carried a heavy cross up the hill of Calvary. My shoulders

---

*Ibid, 20.
†Ibid, 16–17.

stayed raw from where the straps bit into my sunburned flesh. Towels served as pads and abated the pain somewhat, but the pack straps had rubbed raw places on my back and chest. Pain shot through me more often than not. The pain was hell. I just couldn't understand how I, a college graduate, could ever have found myself in such a position. I wasn't dumb. I just couldn't rationalize why I was doing such a lowlife job with other men who were (I thought at the time) not as intelligent or as educated as I.

Not only that, but I also found it exceedingly difficult to take orders from younger men. I did not respect, or trust, their ability to use good judgment. This was a prejudice on my part, which I never fully resolved. I just lived with and accepted it somewhat grudgingly. By July, I had abandoned all hope of ever escaping from the jungle's clutches, which seemed to loom ubiquitously and ominously over me and strangle every last ray of hope I might have had of being freed from its clutches.

My dream of a rear job had vanished with the explosion that took Sgt. Gambill's life. He had been my last link with civilization. I was now a wounded animal in pain, awaiting slaughter. Badly wanting to be out of the field, I wept inwardly — and, at night, when others couldn't see, I cried openly, but silently. I was pissed off too. I hated carrying the Duper because, being a small man — I only weighed 110 pounds when I left Nam — the extra weight of the fifty Duper rounds (each weighed half a pound) was a bit too much. So, I conveniently lost thirty rounds, which lightened my load considerably. After all, what could they do? Send me to Nam? I told my platoon sergeant that I wanted to give the Duper up, but he demurred on my request.

Actually, I couldn't blame anyone except myself. I did not have to join the Army — I could have joined the Navy or Air Force, except then I would have served a four-year term of enlistment instead of a two-year term. At least I had been smart enough not to join the Marines! So, in the final analysis, I could blame no one else except myself for the predicament in which I had become entangled. We all have choices in life. Because I was young and believed in my invincibility, I was willing to bet that I could survive unscathed. I could have gotten out of the field had I been willing to sign up for one or two more years of service. So, I knew what the roll of dice could mean. I just was not willing to serve my country one goddamn fucking more minute than absolutely necessary. If that meant living like shit then I would risk it. So, I did have avenues of escape — which I knew about — but I just did not believe in serving in the Army one more minute over two years. I had chosen my own stew and now I was in it. I was not about to sign up for more of the same bullshit to get out of the field. I would sit it out and pray a whole hell of a lot.

Sometimes, I wanted to get out of the field so badly that I prayed that I would get wounded — just badly enough to get out of the jungle and stay out, as I am sure others did too. Had I known then about the price of the emotional wounds I would bear later on in life, I might not have prayed for any kind of physical wound. At times I even seriously contemplated taking a risk to get wounded, which would enable me to get out of the field. I never thought about wounding myself. That thought was abhorrent to me. Let it be by Charlie's hand and not my own! So depressed had I become, that I honestly thought I was going nuts. The days grew longer and longer. Mentally, Nam was working its power on me. I began to wonder if I could make it until tomorrow and then the next day and the next one after that. The strain was telling. Something had to happen soon, or else my fear, which was eating away at my insides, would conquer me. I could not afford to let that happen. I was not ready for the nuthouse yet, although I was praying I could go! I said it well in a letter home to my folks—"Truly, there can be no God who would want men to suffer thus."

I have previously mentioned the rodent population in Vietnam. Not only was it present in force on the LZs, but in the jungle field mice also made their presence known. As I slept during the night of July 3, a field mouse decided to explore my leg and back. I shooed the little critter off. The poor wee thing was probably freaked out since it was likely that it had never come into contact with a human being. Having no fear of man, the field mice probably took advantage of every opportunity offered them. Thank goodness, they did not bite; otherwise, a lot of grunts would have been getting rabies shots.

On the 4th of July, a Kit Carson was assigned to our Company. A Kit Carson was an ex–NVA soldier who had gone over to the SV side and had agreed to actively work with American infantry forces. He was touted as being extremely helpful and knowledgeable concerning all the little tricks the NVA could pull on us. In other words, he was a traitor whose ass would get shot off if the VC or NVA ever got him within their rifle sights. Somewhere along the way someone must have realized that we needed a Kit Carson, especially after we had failed to get the two enemy soldiers to *Chieu Hoi* after we trapped them in the bunkers.

After two months in the jungle, Bravo Company finally got a respite. On July 7 we humped three klicks to LZ White. It was a grueling and exhausting march, which made me feel dead tired. Once on White, we boarded a Chinook to Tay Ninh for a long-awaited three-day R & R! From the first day I had joined the Company, we had been promised an R & R in Tay Ninh, which was the capital of Tay Ninh Province and was located about forty-five miles northwest of Saigon. There was, however, always a catch to what the Army did. No sooner had we landed in Tay Ninh than we had to line up and receive a smallpox vaccination and a cholera shot. After two months of the jungle, those pinpricks hardly hurt. Having been inoculated, I immediately went to the PX where I purchased some much-needed stationery and Band-Aids. I definitely needed something for all the cuts and scratches the jungle seemed to hand out so freely. While I sat around writing to all my friends back in the World, espousing the grandeur of Tay Ninh, the rest of my buddies were getting drunk. Perhaps, had I known what lay ahead, I would have gotten plastered also.

Tay Ninh had one attraction that most grunts managed to use — a sauna bath. The sauna was more than a sauna — it was a front for a whorehouse and provided us with the opportunity to indulge in the pleasures of the flesh that the Vietnamese women had to offer. I was somewhat paranoid about fucking Vietnamese women since I had heard so many tales about the VD that we might contract. I guess I was scared my penis would rot off or something. I went to have a sauna and massage. That is all I wanted. When the masseuse removed my towel and touched me, I thought I would go bananas. Yet I did not get an erection, and when she indicated she would give me a blow job, I shook my head. So, despite the fact that I got a complete body massage and despite the fact I had not made love with a woman in close to a year, I survived. Had I known then what was about to happen to me and my buddies, in the not too distant future, I probably would have gone ahead and paid her $5.00 for a blow job and a fuck. Most of the men in our group had two or three saunas. I could not blame them. After all, why not? Our attitude was— Tomorrow we die, so fuck the future.

Much of our R & R time in Tay Ninh was spent drinking. Sadly, Chief drank far too much alcohol and stayed inebriated for most of our sojourn to the rear. He ended up getting into several fights, looked rather foolish, and thereby lost the respect of some of the guys in Blackfoot Platoon. This incident is a perfect example of the real tragedy of Vietnam in all its stark reality. The Army not only made copious amounts of alcohol available to its infantry troops when they were in the rear echelon areas, but also supplied them with limited amounts of beer while they were patrolling the nether regions of the jungle. Our unimpeded access to alcohol enabled us to banish our fears and frustrations, albeit for only a short while. It was a deceptive panacea akin to a traveling salesman in the Old West who offered up bottles of snake oil to cure every ill. Yet we drank to excess to blot out the horrors of this insanely unjust war that continued to chew us up and spit us out either dead, mangled or scarred indelibly for the rest of our lives. Alcohol was our temporary way to sip from the waters of Lethe in our fruitless quest to find oblivion. For those individuals with an inborn predilection for alcohol—like some Native Americans—the Army, inadvertently, made alcohol their drug of choice. Thus, somewhat unintentionally, the Army supplied its contingent of American Indians with Socrates' cup of hemlock. The debilitating effects of alcohol abuse by so many young men in Vietnam would have far-reaching and, for some, deeply tragic consequences when they returned home. It not only led many combat infantrymen down a tortuous path of self-destruction but also gave them and their loved ones a lifetime of heartache. Unfortunately, and most regrettably, alcohol would finally claim Chief's life in 1989.

While I rested in Tay Ninh and prepared myself for the rigors to come, I could not help but reflect in one of my letters home on something rather ironic. Basically, communists do not believe in the ownership of private property. Well, in the jungle, we were much like communists. Everything in the boonies became common property, so to speak. For instance, my machete was anyone's machete. Everyone used an entrenching tool at one time or another, especially since we were not permitted to take a shit in the jungle without digging a little hole and making sure the crap was deposited in it. So, entrenching tools were commonly used. We drank out of the same canteen cup. If you had something, like Kool-Aid, as I often did, you shared it. We shared our spoons and our food. In the jungle, what was mine was someone else's. Not to share only invited distrust and hard feelings, and, when you considered the fact that you might stand a good chance of getting shot in the back during a firefight for not sharing, you shared everything, except when it came to beer. That was the unwritten law. No one *ever* asked to share your beer.

One day in Tay Ninh, while I was busy writing, a shower of propaganda leaflets descended upon me. The U.S. printed *Chieu Hoi* leaflets, which were three-inch by five-inch pieces of paper, usually with the South Vietnamese flag on one side and a picture of an enemy who had surrendered on the other side, exhorting the VC or NVA to give up, surrender, or change sides. They were safe conduct passes. A surrendering NVA, or VC, could carry this and surrender without fear of being shot. Our PSY-OPS dropped these passes by the millions all over the jungles of Nam. I found them almost everywhere I went in Nam. So, we managed to trash up Nam's jungles with a lot of extraneous garbage, while back home environmentalists called for us to clean up our own country. At times I wondered if there was a square foot of jungle left in Nam that did not contain one of these leaflets.

In Tay Ninh, I had a chance to relax, shop at the PX, and mail home some war trophies that I had collected. I shipped home the NVA leather belt and the wooden chicom practice grenade that I had acquired. At the

PX, I saw two beautiful velvet prints depicting an old Vietnamese man smoking a pipe. I knew they portrayed pot smoking, but realized that few people back in the World would know what the old men were actually doing. So, I purchased the two velvet prints and sent them to my parents. I also bought a velvet painting of a tiger — a truly awe-inspiring print — as I could not resist the $23.00 price tag. I wanted to splurge and I did.

At this time, I also managed to finish *The Girl in the Plain Brown Wrapper* by John D. MacDonald, which my Aunt Katrina had sent to me. I had never read a "detective" story prior to this and had read it out of obligation, since Aunt Katrina and Uncle Preston had sent it to me. Little did I realize then that John D. MacDonald would, until his 1986 death, be one of my top ten favorite writers. I really came to enjoy his writing; however, in 1969, I just was not ready for him. On July 8 I wrote my parents:

> I can tell you, I definitely don't like John D. MacDonald. Too much sex and too too complicated. It took him 10, yes 10, pages to unravel the ramifications and complexities of the multi-complex and deeply involved web of intricacy he had woven. In other words, it was so goddamn complicated that you couldn't tell heads from tails. I almost gave up on it. I am not sending it home. They have a TV lounge — writing room here at the R & R center where I've been most of the time. One shelf contains a hundred or more paperbacks. I'm leaving it here for someone else to read.

How I could ever have thought so ill of MacDonald is beyond me. At that time, I was so naive that I actually believed if a book had sex in it, it was dirty. Thank goodness, I saw the error of my ways and started reading MacDonald in later years. Oh, what I would have missed! Sometimes I wonder if that paperback is still in Tay Ninh, or whether the communist regime, having perhaps found it, has judged it to be too decadent and consigned it to fire — or has Nam's dry rot turned it to dust along some dusty, dirty jungle path?

On our last night in Tay Ninh, we were treated to a floor show by a Korean band, which consisted of three girl singers, who put on a fantastic show. The band played while the girls sang popular American songs of yesteryear, which reminded me of my high school days. The girls danced, sang, and changed costumes several times. Unfortunately for us, the costumes were not risqué. I guess if they had been, a few women might have been raped. We raped them in our minds anyway. The girls not only sang American tunes but also sang and danced several native Korean numbers for us. I was glad to get a little culture for once and really appreciated what they were doing; but I doubt the rest of the herd fully understood or cared what they were seeing. All they wanted to see were tits and ass.

7/9/69: Day 1 of building LZ Becky. We arrive on site.

Tay Ninh had a MARS (Military Affiliate Radio Station) that allowed one to call overseas. I desperately wanted to call home and let my parents know I was alive and well. I went to the station and waited a couple of hours to no avail, because the generator had broken down so they were unable to transmit. I had been counting on calling home and was upset at not being able to do so.

I was present at the birth of LZ Becky, and either fate, or coincidence, placed me on her, the night of her death, some four weeks later. Becky was constructed approximately ten klicks south of the Cambodian border, and was about four and a half klicks south of the abandoned (except for the NVA) Vietnamese settlement of Bo Tuc. The NVA artillery stationed in Cambodia was to have no trouble zeroing in on it.

On July 9 Bravo and another company were flown from Tay Ninh to ground zero — a small clearing in the jungle — to begin construction of LZ Becky. I was dumbfounded by the size of the field where we would construct the LZ. The wood line was no more than 250 feet from all sides of the low earthen berm that we would construct to surround Becky. What fool decided to place Becky here should have been taken out and shot. It

7/9/69: Day 1 of building LZ Becky. CH-17 Chinook helicopter delivers a 105-mm howitzer artillery piece.

was a perfect setup for Charlie. I had heard of putting your head in the lion's maw, but this was ridiculous! We were going to be bait, or mincemeat, for Charlie, who would have *absolutely* no trouble sneaking up on the LZ and fixing the position of every artillery piece, every mortar pit, every bunker and the Tactical Operations Center (a.k.a. TOC, the LZ's headquarters and communications center). Becky would become a slaughterhouse where many young American boys would die needlessly. There was no excuse for the Army building such a death trap. Desperate to get Charlie into massing for an attack so the Army could whip him in one decisive blow, the brass overcalculated and allowed many young men to be uselessly slaughtered in this modern-day Thermopylae.

Building an LZ from scratch is an interesting process. If one has never seen the equivalent of a small village constructed in a day, then it is almost impossible to describe the process of instantaneous overnight construction. The forces, equipment, and matériel mustered by the Army to build such an installation were staggering. Chinooks CA'ed us to the clearing that was to become Becky; along with our arrival, bulldozers, which swayed in

7/9/69: Day 1 of building LZ Becky. Our sleeping hooch with earthen berm behind it.

slings, were airlifted in by Sikorshy CH-54 "Skycranes" (huge helicopters which looked like gigantic mosquitoes). Other Chinooks disgorged trucks and backhoes. Tons of lumber, especially four-inch by four-inch wooden beams, were brought in for the bunkers. An entire eight-piece 105-mm artillery battery was flown in along with Redlegs to man it. Hundreds of engineers and infantrymen swarmed like ants over the area and worked at a feverish pace to complete this ill-fated LZ. Boxes of ammo, C's, concertina wire, and supplies, along with half sections of steel culverts (to build our sleeping hooches) were flown in and dumped.

That first day we sat around a lot, guarding the perimeter. In the late afternoon we constructed our sleeping hooches out of the half sections of steel culverts, which had been delivered late in the day. Putting the steel together was easy, but filling the innumerable plastic green sandbags to cover our hooches was not as easy.

By the end of the first day, 90 percent of the earthen berm, which was to surround Becky, had been thrown up by the bulldozer crews. The rich,

LZ Becky from air. Note: Defoliated area in upper right from use of Agent Orange.

black earth moved easily, and smelled good to our nostrils, despite the fact that future rainfall would soon turn it into quagmire. All sleeping quarters were completed that first day and the TOC, where the radar was housed, was partially finished. The first night it rained and flooded us out of our hooch. Two other grunts and I moved to higher ground and constructed a poncho hooch. The black mud sucked at our boots as we moved about in the rain trying to make a temporary shelter for ourselves.

We surrounded every LZ with concertina wire. In Becky's case, they decided to put down three rings. On the second day, one and a half rings of wire had been laid out. The bulldozer crews completed the earthen berm, then thickened and increased its height. That day, I had ammo detail. We picked up the ammo from the landing pad, sorted it out, and delivered it to the ammo dump inside the LZ. On the third day, we constructed the bunkers. First, we placed a heavy wire mesh shield, supported by steel pipes, in front of the bunker. This was, ostensibly, to protect the bunker against having a sapper throw satchel charges through the firing ports, should he be lucky enough to crawl that close undetected. Charlie would soon show us that he could indeed creep that close. Next came the bunkers. Building them was easy, but we found it tiring and difficult to fill the hundreds of sandbags required for each bunker. A bunker was a wooden structure, approximately ten-feet by ten-feet by eight-feet high, with gun ports in the front and a rear entrance. The roof was partially protected by three layers of sandbags. Having constructed the bunkers, we cleaned and loaded hundreds of M-16 magazines. Since this was an easy task, we took our time completing it so that we did not have to continue filling the ubiquitous sandbags.

On that third day, July 11, a little excitement occurred. The Army had some small choppers known as LOHs. Usually, LOHs flew together in teams (about 500–600 meters apart) looking for Charlie. Their main purpose was to fly at treetop level and draw Charlie's fire, so the Cobra that followed them high above could put some smoke on Charlie's ass. Two badly shot-up LOHs landed at Becky that day, with numerous bullet holes that had perforated every side of each chopper. One of the pilots had been wounded in the ass and had to be removed by stretcher. At the same time, a Cobra also landed nearby and I had my first close look at one of these fire-breathing machines.

Charlie was definitely in the area. We were building an LZ right in the middle of a hornet's nest. That day a Chinook bringing in more supplies took heavy ground fire from an NVA .51-mm–caliber machine gun, which was the enemy's heaviest piece of field equipment. It could shoot anything out of the sky. The day before, a flying crane took on fire, but landed safely at Becky without too much damage.

Also, on our third day at Becky, B-52s dropped bombs within a klick of the LZ. A Cav company near the LZ stumbled upon eleven NVAs that day and killed them all without one friendly casualty. I had a sneaking suspicion that we would be patrolling in this area a lot in the near future and, with luck, would make contact. It was not something pleasant that one could look forward to, especially when, on that same day, Charlie shot down a chopper near Becky. He was not going to fool around; and, like hornets who find their nest disturbed, he was letting us know that he would not tolerate our intrusion, which would be hotly contested. We were cocky — after all, we were the U.S. Army. No one could kick us around. Little did we know, or realize, how badly Charlie would kick the shit out of us in the near future.

By July 11, Charlie was scoping us out. Two enemy soldiers were spotted outside the barbed wire, near the wood line, and didi maued before we could invite them in for a lead supper. It was an unnerving time for all of us. Here we were, less than three miles from Cambodia, waiting for Charlie to pounce. We knew that, because we were so close to Cambodia, he could, with virtual impunity, fire rockets, mortars and artillery at any time and hit us. The U.S., at that time, had had the guts to bomb Charlie in Cambodia, but that did not stop him from doing the same to us. I prayed we would soon return to the boonies, where I would be a little safer. Here on Becky, we were sitting ducks! While there, news reached us about the two guys from Blackfoot who had been wounded in ambush outside of White, when I had gone to Quan Loi to pick up my glasses. One was back in the World with a broken jaw. We were told that the other man had died not from his wounds, but from a heart attack. He had developed high blood pressure, evidently brought on by the excitement of being wounded, and had been given medication to lower it. We were told he had taken an overdose and had died from a heart attack. This was sobering news. Perhaps the overdose had not been a mistake. His wounds had been superficial, and he would have been able to return to the field soon. Nam, or the fear of it, made men do incredibly strange things.

On July 12, we received word that NVA soldiers had been seen throughout the day, in great numbers, all around Becky. We were told to expect an attack that night, which led me to write the following to my high school girlfriend, Linda Beasley, who lived in my hometown in Virginia. Little did I know how prophetic I was to be:

> We can expect to get attacked tonight. I say bullshit!!! The gooks won't attack this place for at least a month. First, they'll case the area and map the entire LZ, so they'll know where everything is. They won't attack until they know exactly where every bunker is, where every machine gun position is, where all the artillery pieces are, and where the ammo dump is! Once they've thoroughly mapped the place out and know exactly where everything is, then they'll attack!

Had I known then on July 12, 1969, how unfailingly accurate my words were to be, I probably would have tried anything to get out of the jungle. All that I was to offhandedly predict in that letter home to my girlfriend, Linda, came true with tragic clarity.

On July 14, we finally got off the LZ for awhile. We ran a patrol and, as luck would have it, encountered some NVA soldiers. We had four checkpoints to make and were heading back to the LZ after the last one. It was late, and we did not want to miss chow, when we spotted the enemy soldiers. Curses! As they were between us and the LZ, we decided to backtrack. My readers may wonder why we did not engage the enemy. First of all, it was late and we were tired and hungry. Secondly, we had no intention of getting stuck out in the jungle at night. In this case, we were in an open grassy area, where Charlie could have at our small ten-man patrol all night and then set up a nice, juicy ambush to spring upon us in the morning.

So, we backtracked 500 meters, skirted around the enemy, and made it back to the LZ. We were late for chow. No one had called the mess and told them to save some chow for us. Boy, were we pissed. After grumbling that we just might take a few cooks out and shoot them, someone managed to hastily scrape up some food for us!

On July 15, we were still on Becky. I received another friendly and informative letter from General Tuckerman (Ret.) who had previously written to me. I had replied to his first letter and had asked him about a rumor I had heard about the Cav, which purported to say that the Cav had disgraced itself in Korea and therefore could never return to the U.S. His reply straightened out the entire matter, and gave me a brief history lesson concerning the Cav, which I found most informative:

> Thank you for your prompt reply to my letter of 18 June.
>
> Yes, I did see some of your letters which your Mother showed me, ... and I fully understand your inability to rationalize the necessity for our having gotten ourselves into such a messy situation in Southeast Asia. It stems back to a commitment we got ourselves into at the Geneva Conference in 1954 to oversee "free elections" in Vietnam supposedly in 1956. Since then subsequent administrations, and in particular LBJ's, have mishandled the situation, as history will show, leaving a mess for the present administration....
>
> This brings me to the false rumor you have heard about the 1st Cav Division having disgraced itself in Korea and lost their colors. The truth of the matter is as follows:
>
> 1. The 1st Cav Div did an outstandingly fine job in Korea and enhanced the great reputation they had gained in WWII.
> 2. It is true that one of the units, which I believe was the 8th Cav, was overrun one night south of the Yalu River by a Chinese Cavalry unit on Mongolian ponies causing very heavy casualties among our troops. They rallied and beat off this attack with devastating casualties among the Chinese. The next morning the 8th Cav reorganized themselves into a strong fighting force and were able to do their part in the ordered general withdrawal of all troops to the 38th parallel. Had General MacArthur been permitted to utilize the Air Force to destroy the enemy's potential north of the Yalu and the munitions plants in Mongolia, this disaster to the 8th would never have happened and we would have won the war, instead of an armistice, and would have controlled all of Korea instead of one-half of it.
>
> The above facts will make you even prouder to be a part of the First Team. Kindest personal regards.
>
> Sincerely,
> Alfred G. Tuckerman
> Major General, AUS (Ret.)

The above facts stand for themselves. I was proud to be a member of the First Team and to have served in it. I am also most thankful that it was an AM (Air Mobile) Division. That fact made it easy for us to move quickly and strike unexpectedly. The air support supplied by its gunships was a comforting fact, and I was glad to know, on more than one occasion, that we had gunships at our beck and call. Our wounded were medevaced quickly and therefore had a greater chance of survival than those in other less fortunate units, which did not have air support. If I had it to do all over again, I would fervently pray to be a member of the 1st Cav. It was a hell of an outfit, with a lot of fine individuals.

On July 15 word filtered down to us that Becky, which we had helped build during the last seven days, was destined to have a life expectancy of only three weeks! We were stunned. This was almost unbelievable. We were told the main purpose in building this firebase was to entice Charlie to muster his forces and attack it. The brass evidently wanted the NVA to gather all its troops and attack the LZ so we could have one big wipeout. Well, there was going to be a wipeout all right, but we knew we were the ones who were going to have our asses kicked, not Charlie. I was sickened that so much money and labor could be put into the building of an LZ, only to have its life expectancy be three weeks. It lasted a little longer, but not much. In letters home, I decried this useless waste of taxpayers' money. I estimated that it probably cost the Army close to $100,000.00 (in 1969 yet, when money was not that inflated!) just for the first day, to bring in all the equipment, manpower, and matériel. I was a taxpayer, and I was paying for this incredible waste. I was paying for something which, after three weeks, would not have any use. I could scream, and I wrote home about it. The thousands of dollars spent to put up the berm, lay out the concertina wire, build the bunkers, and all the labor gone into filling sandbags was wasted. All of our labor of the last seven days was to be for naught. It was extremely difficult to believe that this was all going to take place.

In a letter home to my parents, I lamented:

> How can the American people stand for such useless waste of money? Everyone wants to know why this war is so expensive. Well, I know. It just makes me sick to see all the money wasted, just so we can get the goddamn gooks to concentrate and attack us! All this labor and effort just to wipe out a few hundred gooks. Why, I'll never know!

I know now. It was spent so Charlie could stomp our asses into the ground and kick us out of his backyard.

July 15 was a good day for me. We had several cherries assigned to us and one of them got to carry my Duper. No more weight! My rucksack would only weigh 50–60 pounds instead of 65–70. I was so relieved to get my faithful M-16 back. Somehow I managed to persuade one of the cherries to take it, and my sergeant OK'ed it. No way was I ever going to take that son-of-a-bitchin' weight back! I was so happy at being relieved of that onerous burden.

July 15 was also payday — my third in Nam and the first time I actually drew pay — $35.00. I was low and had to pay for my Coke rations for the next month. Every month we each paid $5.00 for Cokes. Then, every log day, plus every day on any LZ that we happened to be on at the time, we would get two Cokes — most of the time on LZs we received two Cokes and one beer. We usually received enough so that the cost averaged out to less than 20¢ a drink, which was not too bad in the late 1960s. At times, on the LZs, we were fortunate enough to have ice shipped out to us from the base camp, so we were able to ice down our beer and Cokes. Cold beer tasted so good! One day on Becky, some guys in the squad gave me two beers because they did not want them. I still had my beer and a Coke ration to drink. It was an extremely mellow day.

Tuesday, July 15 was a notable day in other ways for us in the 2nd of the 8th. On that day, we had a semi-holiday because the 8th got a new battalion commander — Lieutenant-Colonel Felix T. Lewis, a man in his late thirties who had been in the army for almost twenty years and had already served one previous tour in Nam in 1966. He was to become one of the most despised and hated men we ever encountered. I have nothing good to say about LTC Lewis. Because of his apparent willingness to sacrifice men at any cost and his uncaring attitude for the health and well-being of the troops under his command, he was directly responsible for the deaths of several hundred men. Of that I am sure because I was almost one of the dead. He was a go-getter who believed in body counts, and evidently his plan was to let *absolutely nothing whatsoever* stand in his way to achieve high body counts. He did not appear to give a damn how many grunts were killed or wounded, just so he could report more NVA dead to the Cav's headquarters. It seemed to us that the man was overzealous, and in his determination to beat the indomitable NVA, he really lost. I would not want to shoulder the burden of knowing that I was directly responsible for the deaths of several hundred of my own men — all to achieve some nebulous body count. It appeared to us that he was a fanatical Army lifer — the type of man the Army, and we in the 8th Cav most especially, did not need. Thank goodness he was finally relieved of his command.

To celebrate his arrival and taking over command, we got steaks cooked over a charcoal fire for lunch. That night we were served loads of fried chicken. Boy, did we ever feast! Those two meals were probably the best two meals I had had since joining the Army. For some unexplainable reason, at least to me, the food we ate in Nam always seemed so much better than what we received in the States. I loved the Army chow in Nam, but hated stateside food. The two meals on Becky that day were exceptional — and the cooks made it up to us for previous slights and errors.

After the fried chicken dinner, we relaxed and watched some grunts play football. At our end of the LZ we had a large open area, where the guys could play tackle football. Three nights earlier someone had produced a football from out of nowhere. How a football ever managed to get to Nam, much less out there in the boonies, was indeed a miracle. The game was a lot of fun and really relieved our tension. I wondered what Charlie, if he was watching, would think of us playing football in the middle of the jungle!

Unfortunately, LTC Lewis soon let us know what kind of a gung-ho lifer he really was. Word came down that infantry companies would be in the boonies for thirty days and then pull ten-day tours of LZ duty. Plus, according to Lewis, since we had been spoiled by the last battalion commander, we would have to toughen up. Log would be every four to five days, instead of every three. That meant more C's — more weight — to hump. What weight I had lost by not having to carry Duper rounds, I would gain back in C's and extra water rations, which really added to the weight of our rucks. I would now have to carry ten quarts of water, instead of my usual seven. It was a never-ending cycle.

On July 17, we escaped from the dirt, grime, mud, dust, and boredom of Becky. We watched a B-52 strike from our positions on the LZ, and then were CA'ed to the area that had just been bombed by them. We soon uncovered a rice cache. It was the first one I had ever seen. There were 110 burlap bags of rice, each weighing approximately 200–500 pounds. As we were in no position to have it airlifted out, we were forced to destroy it. It took two, sometimes three, of us to drag each bag about twenty-five meters to the nearest bomb crater, cut it open, and spill its contents into the crater. A slick dropped diesel oil and CS crystals for us to use in burning and contaminating the rice and the residue that did not burn. I was amazed, and infuriated, to learn that the rice had originated in Cuba as there was a stamped seal on each of the burlap bags proclaiming in English, "Product of Cuba." It was bad enough knowing that the Soviets and the Chinese were aiding and abetting the NVA; but to learn that a two-bit banana republic, ninety miles off the U.S. coast, was also involved in helping the enemy, was a bit too much.

That morning, three LOHs had been shot down by communist .51-mm heavy machine gun positions. Our Company was also acting as a quick reaction force to try and locate those gun positions. Charlie was around in force. That we knew. The NVA was firing at every chopper coming near Becky with alarming frequency and, as more and more choppers flew into Becky, we could hear them taking enemy fire. It was an ominous sign. We had invaded and occupied the hornet's nest, and it was not about to let our intrusion go by uncontested.

On our first night out from Becky, the brass felt Charlie was around in significant numbers to warrant all the protection they could possibly give us. Incoming artillery rounds from Becky bracketed our position. Cobras flying directly overhead blasted away with their ARA and mini-guns. We had not even had contact! It was spooky. One would have thought that the enemy was massing right outside our perimeter. Every night while we were out in the boonies, after we would set up, the local firebase (LZ) zeroed in our night log position with its artillery. This was done in case we were attacked at night and needed artillery fast. This particular night, they really made the bracketing tight. The FO would direct the artillery until they got a fix on our position. That night our FO was bringing the 105-mm artillery rounds within 75 meters of our night log. Shrapnel was flying everywhere, so we were forced to keep our heads low.

By this time, I was getting rather aggravated with our new squad sergeant. Elia and I did not see eye to eye. Since he was in the National Guard and was only going to be in Nam six months, his command experience was somewhat limited. It seemed to me and Joe Musgrove that he picked us for every work detail that popped up. We thought that he did not evenly distribute work details so, naturally, we felt we were being treated unfairly. We decided that if he continued picking on us, we would ask Lt. Hill to rectify the situation. I believed that I was being treated unfairly because I was the only one in my squad who had been assigned to drag the incredibly heavy 250-pound bags of rice to the crater to be destroyed. I thought I was doing my job to the best of my ability. In fact, at times, I felt that I was doing more than my fair share. But it appeared to me that Elia had a case for me, so I decided to see Lt. Hill, if he did not ease up. Fortunately, Elia soon eased up on both of us and the perceived tempest in a teapot was over and quickly forgotten. He was learning the ropes of combat command and it just took some of us longer to adjust to his style of leadership.

It is hard for anyone who bathes regularly to conceive of the dirt and filth that we were forced to endure in Nam. We lived under the most unclean and insanitary conditions, with little chance of washing our faces or hands, much less taking a bath. Sweat, coupled with dust and dirt, rolled off our faces, chests, and backs constantly, making us feel as if we had a film of dirt all over our bodies. My entire face had terrible acne, and the dirt and dust also caused boils that were the most painful sores one could have. Boils formed on any part of your body and generated a dull, constant, throbbing pain. I used Wash and Dry towelettes (which had been sent to me) to clean my face, but ten minutes later the sweat and dust had returned to form a film over it. It was a never-ending battle — one that we all invariably lost. I knew that when I returned to the World, I was going to have to make some adjustments. Sleeping without boots and clothes on would be strange and using a bed would be uncomfortable for a while. The knowledge that I would be able to bathe and wash my hands when I pleased was definitely something to look forward to once I returned to the World. I had not sat in a chair since arriving in Nam. That would be nice. To be able to use a napkin, instead of my jacket sleeve, would be a pleasure. Of course, being able to use a bathroom — and a toilet! — would really be super. Plus, wearing underwear again would be a big improvement! If only people back in the States realized how fortunate they really were to have all the luxuries we have by living in such a free nation. Being in Nam made me realize that the little things in life that we all take for granted — i.e., soap, napkins, good food — really meant a lot. Plus, we were so damn fortunate to grow up in a country that had these items available to everyone at such little cost. If, and when, I made it back to the World alive, I knew that I would appreciate each little thing so much more.

C-rations, while filling and nutritional, just did not cut it as far as taste was concerned. Now that log was every four to five days, instead of three, we had to carry more C's. Each C-ration carton contained twelve meals. Usually, during log, we would get one carton per man. In the past, knowing we would get log every three days, we went through our carton and picked out the meals and cans of food that we liked. The rest (approximately six meals) would get thrown away because they were far from delectable. Now, with log every four to five days, we had to hump more C's and eat stuff that we did not like. My favorite C-rats were turkey loaf, boned turkey, boned chicken, beef in spiced sauce, and beans and franks. I could not stand the ham slices, beefsteak with juices (ugh!), ham and lima beans (gag!), pork slices with juices, and meatballs with potatoes (yuck!). Now, I was going to have to carry and eat some of these meals that were enough to make a grown man regurgitate. I was most thankful I had friends back in the World who sent care packages. Without their care packages of Vienna sausage, fruit, raisins, etc., I doubt I would have made it. In every twelve-meal carton, there were only four cans of fruit. Because I loved fruit rations, I used to scrounge or trade on log days and get enough fruit for my two meals a day. The juices (in the fruit cans) were a treat in themselves, but one had to guard his fruit because some grunts would steal what they could if given the opportunity. People always spoke in terms of how bad C's were. All in all, I think they were damn good, and they certainly had enough nutritional value to sustain us in times of much stress and physical labor.

By July 22, the siege of Becky had begun. Intelligence reported that Charlie was collecting in large groups around it (as if we did not already know this fact!). A few days before, Becky received its first incoming rocket, which landed right on the TOC, which was located in the middle of the LZ. This was obviously no fluke — Charlie had our hides rightly nailed to the wall and was getting ready to cure us of our impetuosity for building the LZ on his turf. Two grunts on top of the TOC were blown off by the rocket and were uninjured. The rocket then penetrated two layers of steel, three layers of sandbags, and a six-inch layer of wooden beams, and killed the radio man inside. So tight was the NVA ring around Becky, that we learned the usual day-to-day patrols could not even get out to reconnoiter. Echo recon platoon went out with thirty men one day and was ambushed. All but two were wounded. None killed. The NVA fired on our patrols before they reached the wood line. Grunts were so shook up at this turn of events that nighttime LP positions were hard to accomplish. We even heard the brass was asking for LP volunteers. This turn of events was not out of the ordinary for this particular time, place and situation. A grunt could be ordered to go, but, if he refused, what could they do — send him to Nam? So what if he had to face a court-martial? Because it took too much time and paperwork — plus the fact that it was a good way for a man to get out of the field for a while — the Army rarely used this form of punishment. So, while the brass and Non-Coms (NCOs) could have resorted to threats, they did not. There was always a thin line, and the Non-Coms and officers knew that they had to tread lightly. After all, it would have been so easy to put a bullet in the back of someone's head. The higher-ups knew this. So, volunteers were asked for, and usually found. There was always someone who was willing to risk being killed if he was given a chance at killing Charlie.

We were told that our intelligence had intercepted an enemy radio message which said, "We can take Becky any time we want." How true it was. Meanwhile, choppers coming into Becky took continuous heavy fire. One chopper pilot reported seeing so many enemy .51-mm machine gun and mortar positions that he could not count them. The noose was drawing tighter and tighter every minute. Like the condemned criminal, we all wondered when the hangman would spring the trapdoor and prayed none of us would be around for the final drop. On July 22, 1969, I wrote home:

Becky could be easily taken. The wood line is too close to the perimeter and there are only two barb wire rings [they had apparently decided not to add a third ring as mentioned earlier] about the firebase. I only hope Bravo Company isn't the company on the LZ when the gooks decide to overrun it.

My hope was in vain. We were. We had ringside seats for an incredible massacre.

That week, I received my first medal for being in Nam, the CIB (Combat Infantryman's Badge), which signified that I had been under hostile fire. So now, I was part of the team — officially. It was an impressive metal badge that depicted a Kentucky long rifle, surrounded by laurel leaves. I wore mine proudly.

My friend, John Sivick, was still in Bravo with me, but served in another squad. He too, like me, was unscathed so far. Three new cherries had joined Blackfoot. Rocky, although he hailed from northern New Jersey, really had the nasal accent of a New Yorker. He was cocky and seemed to take everything for granted — that this was all a game. But he would soon lose his devil-may-care attitude. Daniel L. "Dan" Webster, from Cedar City, Utah, was tall, serious minded and appeared to have his shit together. Virgil Renfro, from Richmond, Kentucky, was a tall, dark, curly-haired young man from the coal fields who would become one of the best dynamite men we ever had. He and C-4 took to each other naturally and for a short time, he became our demolitions expert.

July 24 turned out to be a long, long, LONG torturous day of pure, unadulterated hell for us. We saddled up and started humping at 0730 hours, and pushed through thick jungle all day until 1730 hours. That one day made me realize that some of the things that I was carrying just had to go. I had been spoiling myself on three meals a day for a while. No more. It was going to be two meals per day from then on! I went through "house-cleaning" my rucksack and threw out food and lots of other stuff that I could not carry. It still did not feel lighter, so I decided some of my water had to go. I cut back from ten to seven quarts. Times would be lean to say the least, but, at 110 pounds, I just did not have the stamina, or physical strength, to carry all that weight.

That same day, we discovered a 15 to 20-ton cache of rice, which was probably enough to feed an entire NVA battalion (or about 200 men) for five months. As usual, we destroyed it.

After such a long tramp the day before, we were allowed to rest on the 25th, and lay around in ambush. I got a lot of reading done. I started and finished Ayn Rand's *The Fountainhead* that Mrs. Liz Cox, a friend of my parents, had sent to me. People were always sending me books because they knew I loved to read so much. In fact, I read over fifty books during my tour of duty in Nam. Thomas Costain, Daphne du Maurier, Helen MacInnes and Frank G. Slaughter were among my favorites. While there, I read such books as *Rebecca, Profiles in Courage, Red Sky at Morning, The Silver Chalice, Sayonara, Airport,* and *Bleak House.* Upon finishing *The Fountainhead* that day, I started Kenneth Roberts' *Lydia Bailey.* So, when I was not writing to someone, I was constantly devouring books. I had to read, or write; otherwise, I would have gone nuts from the tedium of Nam. A lot of the time, there was nothing for us to do but sit around and wait for something to happen. I felt obligated to do something constructive with my time, which my nervous energy just would not permit me to waste. So, while most grunts sat around with their backs against a tree trunk, staring off into space, I made use of every second by either reading or writing. I was one of the few who used his spare time in this manner. As a result, one of the nicknames that I acquired among my squad members was "The Professor."

Time — that is all we had in Nam. Time was something to kill. In a firefight, a minute was an hour, an hour became a day. Most of the time, we sat around in the heat, sweating, doing nothing. But a day under fire was an eternity — much longer at that moment than the year we were forced to spend in Nam. We had to survive time. Many grunts drew calendars on their camouflaged green helmet liners, which they numbered from 365 backwards. Every day they X'ed off one more revolution of the earth from the timeless insanity that was Nam. We were all bound to Nam by the chains of time. Under fire you aged many times faster than the guys who sat back in the rear in Tay Ninh or on the nearby LZ. When we pulled LZ duty, we were much more somber and reflective than the men who manned the firebase. They did not get hit as much as we did. Under fire for a week in the bush, we aged a year and left them so far behind. Our fight for survival was really a never-ending battle with time. It held us there in its implacable grip and allowed us to depart only when our 365 days were over, or a bullet found us. Vietnam became a prison sentence of time. It appeared we would be there FOR-FUCKING-EVER! So each day was many years.

One day, while I was involved in writing, I had to fight off a butterfly that insisted on using my writing pad as a landing zone. It was an exquisitely beautiful insect with bright yellow and blue wings, with white dots on its blue-tipped wings. I pitied this beautiful piece of God's art, which apparently had no fear of man. It was so colorful in such a godforsaken environment.

Of the many days in Nam that are memorable to me, one stands out clearly. July 26, 1969, was a date in destiny for me personally. What occurred on that day — what might have happened — will follow and haunt me the rest of the days of my life.

Parents often wondered how their sons died in Vietnam. Many grunts died as a result of "friendly fire" — their own artillery or mortars blew them away. Sometimes their buddies, through no fault of their own, would err and blow them away. On July 26, I almost blew away some of the members of my platoon. During log that day, we were surprised at being served our first-ever hot meal in the boonies. We could hardly believe our good fortune, but were told that new battalion policy dictated that we receive one hot meal a week in the field, which really perked up our spirits. Along with that log, I also received another care package from my Aunt Katrina, who sent me three mirrors. As I already had a mirror, I distributed the extras to my buddies.

After log and the hot meal, we moved down a well-trodden trotter, through savannah-like terrain, with elephant grass five or six feet high on either side. Every so often, this grassy area was interspersed with huge, thick clumps of bamboo. We walked about fifteen yards apart, so that if there was an ambush, fewer grunts would be injured, because we were not bunched up. Chief and I were walking rear security. We were tense and extremely jumpy. First of all, we were moving back up a trotter we had already traveled down. Secondly, about thirty NVA soldiers had been sighted by the log choppers where we had set up our ambush three nights previous, on this same trotter.

We knew the enemy was close — perhaps even closer because they had obviously heard or seen us receive log. Moving on trotters was just not easy. While they facilitated movement (because we did not have to break bush) we knew the enemy just loved to ambush grunts on their home ground. Visibility along this trotter was difficult due to the height of the elephant grass and the fact that the trotter wound back and forth between the large bamboo clumps. Therefore, it was impossible to see where the trotter led. We had to rely solely on the guy in front of us to pass the word back about any communication from the front of the column. What made this patrol even more difficult was the fact that Chief and I usually walked backwards when we were on rear security so as to prevent a rear attack.

The bamboo clumps on either side of the trotter were extremely thick. One could easily pass within ten feet of some enemy soldiers and never know they were there until it was too late. Plus, usually when we set up in ambush alongside a trotter, we did so under bamboo clumps because they had an open space underneath the foliage that enabled us to move around easily. Chief and I had heard what we thought was movement to our rear, and we had reported it. Our platoon stopped and set up a hasty ambush for about a half hour but nothing happened, so we started moving cautiously down the trotter again.

Now imagine the situation. Chief and I were convinced that perhaps the NVA were both ahead of and behind us. We knew that the choppers had spotted thirty NVA at our former ambush site, and we were headed back in that direction. It was a tense and touchy situation and our nerves were not the best. Every day news had reached us about the incredible numbers of enemy soldiers who were seen in the area surrounding Becky. We could hear our choppers being fired on relentlessly. To say we were keyed up would be an understatement. The elephant grass was tall. There was absolutely no way I could see in which direction the trotter led, especially since I was walking backwards and looking over my shoulder every so often to see where the man in front of me was walking. The grunts up front were out of sight except for a man about fifteen yards ahead of me. We were extremely wary about the possibility of an ambush.

Someone goofed. Someone really fucked up. Someone forgot to pass the word back to Chief and me that Blackfoot had left the trotter, had circled back, and was entering the rear of a bamboo clump immediately to our left, not ten feet away! I thought our platoon was still moving down the trotter, but it had, in fact, turned off the path and circled around to set up in ambush. Suddenly, I heard the distinctive crack of a branch breaking in the bamboo clump not ten feet away.

I immediately reacted by flipping my M-16 off safety, onto semi (semi-automatic), which allowed me to fire one shot at a time, and opened up on the bamboo clump. I guess I had emptied three-fourths of my eighteen-round clip into the bamboo before I heard a familiar voice coming from inside the clump. Then the horror of what I had done reached me — I had opened up on my own men! Needless to say, I went to pieces, got hysterical, and wept openly. Miraculously, no one had been killed or wounded. I had missed Sgt. Elia's head by six inches. Another guy told me a bullet hit his rucksack frame.

So, a near tragedy was averted. One may ask — well, who was to blame? Somewhere up ahead, someone had failed to pass the word back that Blackfoot had left the trotter and was executing a cloverleaf formation along the line of march. It is my belief that one of the cherries was responsible for this oversight, which could have cost the lives of several grunts. That night was one of the longest nights of my life. It rained, and I did not get one wink of sleep because I could only think about what might have happened. I was also scared to death that someone would blow me away for fucking up so badly. Absolution, however, was not long in coming.

The next morning, Lt. Hill assembled the platoon and exonerated me by telling them that I could in no way be held at fault. "The fault lay with the individual who had failed to pass the word back," he said. In fact, he commended me on my quick reaction, and affirmed that I actually had no other choice but to open up and fire. I was relieved to be exonerated; however, had I killed or wounded someone, I doubt my life would have been worth a plugged nickel.

This near tragedy was even more significant in light of the fact that during log the previous day, we had heard about an amusing incident (with near disastrous overtones) that had taken place on Becky a few days earlier. At that time, Alpha (A) Company was pulling LZ duty on Becky. Late each afternoon they were not only sending out two platoons on night ambush but were also sending two LPs about 100 meters into the woods. Both LPs radioed in that there was a lot of enemy movement around them, so they were both told to return to the LZ. One LP had started back in when they saw enemy soldiers behind them, beside them, and in front of them. The four grunts hid in a bomb crater near the wood line and radioed in, "Hey, we're surrounded by gooks out here in this bomb crater!"

Meanwhile, the other LP was radioing in, "Hey, we've got four gooks surrounded in a bomb crater out here!" You can imagine the chuckles everyone had when they learned the truth of the matter. To say the least, this was a funny and amusing incident, yet, like what happened to me when I opened up on my own men, it was fraught with danger. They could have easily started shooting at each other.

We operated in an area of Nam known as a free-fire zone, where our orders were specific. If it moved, shoot first and ask questions later. There was no middle ground. If you hesitated, you could be dead. We were cloaked by a mantle of heavy responsibility. The weight of that burden was, at times, onerous. These instructions were an awesome responsibility. To be able to handle something of this magnitude proved to be extremely terrifying at times. It was so easy to shoot first. How one handled the consequences of such actions depended on his mental stability. Some guys shrugged it off, while others, such as myself, felt the crushing weight bear down upon their shoulders.

Our last ten days in the field had been absolutely miserable weatherwise. Rain poured sporadically every day, giving us only a few hours' respite. The rain made us hear things—things we would rather not hear—things we hoped we were not really hearing—like Charlie sneaking up on us. We had been sleeping, eating, and living wet. Our clothes had no chance to dry out. By midmorning, the rain would usually clear and then, in the afternoon, the heavens opened to drench us some more. Our clothes rotted off our backs and our pants ripped and tore like paper until the pant legs were in ribbons. We appeared to be a ragtag guerilla band and, in actuality, that is what we were.

During log on the 26th, I received a book from my Aunt Katrina entitled *The Choices We Face* by Lyndon Baines Johnson. Little did I realize at the time what part this book would play in my life.

On the 27th, the day after my fiasco in the jungle, we chopped down trees and used C-4 on those we could not drop, so that we could clear an area for choppers to land and CA us out of the boonies. The slicks took us to LZ Ike, which was about ten klicks south of Becky and was being abandoned. When an LZ was abandoned, grunts usually left lots of stuff that Charlie would find useful. So small groups of us were dropped into the jungle around the LZ, where we set up in ambush. If Charlie came to pick over the LZ, we might be able to kill a few NVA. On July 29, the LZ was finally abandoned, so we hunkered down to get a few kills. I decided to catch up on my reading, so I finished Kenneth Roberts' *Lydia Bailey* and started reading Thomas Costain's *The Silver Chalice*. Some of the guys in my platoon were so bored, they would read anything. I had a copy of Kenneth Roberts' *Northwest Passage* that I loaned to two guys. When one got tired of reading, the other one took it and read a while. I even got Hillbilly to start reading *Lydia Bailey*. I prayed that somehow I was bringing a bit of culture to the guys in my platoon — after all, I did have to live up to my nickname of "The Professor."

After two days of idleness, we humped in to deserted Ike, tore down a lot of things and shipped them out. I could not believe all the items that had been left behind. No wonder abandoned LZs were so attractive to the enemy. Scores of towels, fatigue shirts, pants, socks, fully loaded M-16 magazines, air mattresses, ponchos, T-shirts, poncho liners, paper magazines, boots, flak jackets, canteens, canteen cups, soap, and steel helmets lay in disarray, all over the LZ. Chief even found a radio that worked. We left everything there. I could not help but ruefully wonder how much Charlie's eyes would light up when he found all this matériel. We burned a lot of the bunkers that afternoon. I felt like a pyromaniac. We would pile timber up, throw gas on it, and light it. I had a ball burning everything I could get my hands on, and then, as the LZ burned, we were airlifted to our old nemesis, LZ Becky.

AUGUST

LZ Becky's Death

It will be a war between an elephant and a tiger.... If ever the tiger pauses, the elephant will impale him on his mighty tusks. But the tiger will not stand still.... He will leap upon the back of the elephant, tearing huge chunks from his side, and then he will leap back into the dark jungle ... and slowly the elephant will die of exhaustion and bleed to death. Such will be the war in Indochina.

Ho Chi Minh, September 1946

We stayed on LZ Becky one night — July 30, before Blackfoot Platoon was CA'ed out the next day to the boonies — ostensibly to locate a rice cache that a LOH had spotted. What followed for the next two days was pure, unmitigated hell. The heat was absolutely excruciating. The sun was unmerciful; Chief and I nearly fell out the first day. We were only supposed to hump 300 meters, but we ended up walking a klick. Then, our battalion commander, LTC Felix Lewis, radioed and told us that we were one and a half klicks from where we should have been. Demanding to know why we were out of position, he really got pissed off at our platoon leader, Lt. Edwin J. Hill. Well, if that jerk Lewis had ever marched in a jungle (which I am sure he had never done), he would know why we were probably lost. Retracing our steps, we were caught in a torrential downpour. A raging stream, which was too high to cross, forced us to set up and we slept wet and cold that night. Personally, I was a little pissed off at the rain. My wet clothes had had a chance to dry during the sweltering day. I hung my fatigue shirt over my rucksack to dry and wore my T-shirt. When the rains descended, my clothes were soaked, so I had to adapt to sleeping wet again.

103

The second day, August 1, was no better than the first. On that day, I experienced my first stream crossing in Vietnam. The current was swift and the water came up to my armpits. As the current tugged at me, I almost floated away and then, in the deepest part, I got stuck. With a fully loaded pack, which weighed 50–60 pounds, it was hard to get out as the mud-laden bottom sucked at my boots; but, finally, I reached the opposite bank of the fifty-foot-wide stream. We got lost twice and traveled about two klicks. Lewis had Cobras, LOHs, and slicks out looking for us. Personally, I believe we were CA'ed to the wrong jungle LZ and that is why we were so screwed up. We were supposed to link up with another element from Alpha Company. The Cobra that finally spotted us also located the other element — fifty yards away from where we had set up along the stream the previous night! We had been in the right place all along, but it seemed to us that the LTC had his head up his ass and was tooling us around and making our lieutenant look bad. This was not the last time something like this happened. At that point in time, we were 1500 meters from where we should have been. When we had first landed, we had been within 300 meters of our rendezvous point. All of us were upset and mad.

Besides having to put up with sleeping in wet clothes and walking around in circles during this unbelievable heat, I also had to contend with a boil on my face. At LZ Becky, the medics had put something on it to bring it to a head. While we were set up by the stream, our medic, William "Bill" P. Raley, a redheaded guy from Gadsden, Alabama, with whom I was good friends, decided to get the core out, as it had not come to a proper head and thus put me in considerable pain.

To remove the core of a boil, the boil has to be lanced (cut open). Usually it is opened by making two equal incisions crossing at right angles to each other, over the head of the boil. The medic can then see the yellowish core, which looks like an octopus with tentacles. Using tweezers, he clamps down on the core and rips it out. Usually, it had to be removed in parts. This was field medicine at its basic level. After most of the core had been removed, he would then cleanse the boil, put ointment on it, and then bandage it. Ripping out a core is not easy. It was painful and few of us survived such an ordeal without having tears come to our eyes. Once the core had been removed, I felt a lot better. The whole side of my face was swathed in a bandage. Sometimes, if one was lucky, the core could be brought to a head and then squeezed out. That particular removal process, however, was also excruciatingly painful.

About this time, we received some uplifting news. The 1st Air Cavalry Division Headquarters had been moved to the town of Phuoc Vinh (PV for short) located in the south central portion of Binh Phuoc Province.

Bravo Company had been chosen to pull perimeter guard, which basically meant we would secure, or guard, the area surrounding the village of Phuoc Vinh. We learned we were "supposed" to go there in about ten days. So, with any kind of luck, we would be out of the boonies by August 12–13. Well, we would be out of the boonies then, but not at PV! Phuoc Vinh, we were informed, was a safe and secure area. There had been only one contact in the last six months because, theoretically, it was an unimportant military target in a heavily populated area, with zero gooks, so we would have time to relax. Little did we know, or realize, however, that most of us would never live to see PV. We were told we might stay in Phuoc Vinh for three to six weeks. It was too good to be true. LTC Lewis had confirmed to Captain Mooneyham, Bravo Company's commanding officer, that we would be going. Once there, I would not have to hump any heavy ruck while on perimeter guard! If only we had known what awaited us in ten days, we all would have prayed to be out of the field a hell of a lot sooner.

By that time, most of Bravo Company had developed an overwhelming feeling of hostility towards LTC Lewis. To us, it appeared that he had an insatiable appetite for kills. No matter how many NVA we killed, it seemed that he always wanted more. According to our officers and platoon sergeants—who were more in the know than we common infantrymen—LTC Lewis wanted us to be more aggressive in the boonies. Confirmed kills seemed to become an obsession to him. He pushed and drove us unrelentingly. He continued to place us into more and more dangerous situations, like CA'ing only Blackfoot Platoon (consisting of about twenty-five men, at that time) out in the jungle to locate some godforsaken rice cache. I have no doubt that, had it been definitely 100 percent confirmed, he would have CA'ed us right into a mass meeting of an NVA battalion. We all believed that he was definitely flaky. Whether he was trying to impress his superiors to gain rank, or was merely a glory seeker, I will never know. What I do know is, had he gotten within the M-16 sights of a lot of grunts, he would not have lived very long. Because of him, we moved longer and harder each day than we had previously. That was hell, because when we were tired, we had a tendency to say to fuck it, and ignore the jungle around us. When pushed, or driven, to the brink of our inner mental and physical strength, we had a tendency to become automatons. We marched from Point A to Point B with little care, or concern, for what lay in between. Every move became automatic. Get up. Move. Stop. Rest. Get up. Move. Stop. Rest. We were zombies—men driven until their last reserve tank was on empty. Sometimes, I felt as if I wasn't really in my body—that I was outside of it, watching a robot move inexorably toward either a breaking point, or death and destruction. LTC Lewis's orders were driving us up a wall. We never liked exposing ourselves more than necessary, and now the glory-seeking battalion commander was forcing us to move at the same times Charlie was likely to move, which was extremely dangerous. As a result, late afternoon showers now drenched us before we could set up for the evening. Being wet and sleeping wet were not conducive to good morale.

To us it appeared that LTC Lewis could afford to be reckless with our lives and throw them away. The odds of his being killed were a lot less than ours, so, in the end, we grunts would pay with our lives for his tactical errors.* It is no small wonder that he drove us so relentlessly and sacrificed us so willingly. It was all so depressingly stupid and nonsensical. But then, our being in Vietnam was pretty absurd!

Besides being lost all one day, we did manage to have some excitement on August 1. We were traveling through an area that had been bombed in a B-52 strike. On the side of a crater, we found a partially covered cache, containing fifteen fifty-pound cans of fish. After we uncovered it, we were just lolling around when one of our men spotted six NVA walking, unconcealed, towards our position. The NVA point man was looking down at the ground. Our man put his M-16 on rake (full automatic), waited until the NVA were about twenty meters away, then opened up and emptied his entire clip. Caught by surprise, we all hit the ground because we had no idea what was happening. Alas, our man was a bad shot. He missed all of the gooks. We were not even able to find a blood trail! So, Charlie got away and we blew our position. Now, he would be waiting for us.

Meanwhile LTC Lewis was becoming a real pain in the ass. Word filtered down to us that he needed a scapegoat because we had been stumbling around and got lost in the jungle. Naturally, he seized upon the only individual whom he could nail for such an egregious and outrageous offense — Lt. Hill. We were informed that he claimed Hill was directly responsible for our being lost and causing him, the LTC, so much trouble (and inconvenience) in having to send birds out to search for us. Because he was a just and good man, Lt. Hill had endeared himself to the men of Blackfoot Platoon, who had complete respect, and the highest regard, for his leadership ability. When you follow a man for as long as we had, you become part of him, and he becomes part of you. You trust him and know he will not lead you astray. When your leader has an iniquitous injustice perpetrated upon him, you feel personally affronted. We all knew Lt. Hill was innocent, so our hatred for Lewis grew.

---

*Dunnigan & Nofi, 243. Only 126 LTCs were killed during the war, representing just 0.3 percent of all U.S. Army personnel deaths.

It really was difficult to get lost if you are landed at Point A and told to march on, for example, a 217 percent azimuth for 500 meters to Point B. All three of the point men in our squad, which had been breaking bush, had compasses. All three compasses could not have been wrong. Every azimuth we were given, we followed and checked. Yet, somehow, we had gotten inexplicably lost and, for this offense, we were told, LTC Lewis was going to try and hang Lt. Hill out to dry. There was only one plausible explanation for this foul-up. When we were originally CA'ed to the jungle LZ, the birds had set us down at the wrong LZ and that is why we were so far off.

But on log day, August 3, word came down that the Lewis was relieving Lt. Hill of command. Boy, were we ever gloomy. The first bird into our log site that day, which we had to blow so the slick could land, contained LTC Lewis and Capt. Mooneyham. They met with Lt. Hill outside of our hearing; so, we had no idea what was discussed, but somehow we all felt Capt. Mooneyham helped Lt. Hill. When Stone Mountain (Lewis's radio code name) and Ranger left, Lt. Hill was still with us! Our joy could not be described. We let him know, in no uncertain way, that we were on his side and would stand by him through thick and thin.

Not only did we get log that day, and keep Lt. Hill, but also we had a beautiful red and black German shepherd scout dog assigned to travel with us. These dogs were invaluable to our survival in Vietnam. They could smell out the enemy, food, and arms caches and, on more than one occasion, saved us. The saddest fact about these intelligent animals was that they were destined never to leave Vietnam. This was due to some regulation about diseases, which they might transmit if they were returned to the U.S. When the trainer's tour of duty ended, we were led to believe they were put to sleep as they were only loyal to one man.

LTC Lewis had left Lt. Hill with a final parting word, which endeared him to Blackfoot Platoon, and made us pray we could get him within our M-16 sights. His newest policy, according to Lt. Hill, was simple — if we saw gooks, we were "supposed" to make an on-line assault against their position. This highly dangerous maneuver required everyone in a squad, or a platoon, to stand up and walk abreast, towards the enemy's position, continuously firing until they reached and killed the enemy. LTC Lewis told Lt. Hill that he knew we would lose one or two men, but at least we would kill the enemy. Well, we could have told Lewis a few things. First off, he could take his new policy and stick it up his ass — sideways. If he really believed for one minute that we would make an on-line assault, he had to be out of his fucking mind. In our minds there was no doubt that his thinking was somewhat askew. It was obvious to us that he did not care how many American lives might be lost as a result of his misguided policies. We all concurred that there was no way in hell we were ever going to stand up during a firefight and make an on-line assault. We just did not believe in mass murder — of grunts! After all, we were sane. Why should we have risked our lives so some damn LTC could build his ego, and reputation, on confirmed kills to attain rank, glory, and more military medals? Sadly, this type of megalomania went on far too often in Vietnam, and a lot of good men died because some fucking asshole of a battalion commander wanted to gain rank and win combat decorations by using body counts to increase his personal stature within the chain of command.

The following imaginary conversation probably took place on more than one occasion in Vietnam:

"Hey, Lieutenant Colonel, heard you got ten kills yesterday."

"Yes, General, my men sure did. We lost twenty men, though."

"Oh, that's okay, Lieutenant Colonel. Kills! That's what we want. Kills! Go get 'em!"

Bullshit! By attempting to relieve Lt. Hill, LTC Lewis had no idea how close he came to getting shot down that day. Had Capt. Mooneyham not been on Stone Mountain's bird, we might have blown him away. Unfortunately, after Lt. Hill told us about Lewis's on-line assault policy, the LTC was long gone. I truly believe we might have shot him down. I know we all fervently prayed for Charlie to shoot him down, since we were unable to do so. Men like that deserved to die. On-line assaults were for John Wayne movies, but not for Vietnam. We all vowed that we would face a court-martial first, before we stood up and got zapped.

Log that day brought another surprise to us. For the first time, we got LRRP (long range reconnaissance patrol and pronounced "Lurp") meals, along with our C's. We had the following LRRP meals to choose from: pork with escalloped potatoes, chicken and rice, chili con carne, beef hash, beef stew, spaghetti and meat sauce, and one or two others. All we had to do was heat a cup of water and mix it with the meal. These meals were delicious and extremely filling. Each LRRP packet contained a cocoa package, coffee, cream, sugar, toilet paper and a chocolate bar. I did not like coffee then, so I threw it away, but I did drink the hot chocolate every morning. The Lurps sure beat humping C's, no doubt about it, especially since they weighed a whole lot less! They were so filling that one would have trouble eating more than two a day. We usually saved our Lurps by eating one a day and consuming C's the rest of the time. That way, we looked forward to eating something enjoyable.

By this time of year, the monsoon season was upon us. When it was not pouring during the day, it drizzled throughout the night. Life was miserable. In between the rain showers, our days were so hot that we would drink a lot of water. We had to quench our thirst because the sun's rays, filtering through the patchy jungle canopy, sucked the sweat right out of our bodies, and quickly dehydrated us. The overpowering heat was stifling. At times, we could hardly breathe. Within minutes of saddling up and moving out each day, our breaths inhaled the superheated air that quickly parched our throats. At night, we tied the four corners of our ponchos about two feet above ground, to nearby trees, or bushes, to cover us and collect the rainwater that dripped off the overhead trees. We usually left our steel pots out at night to catch water while we slept on the wet, soggy, cold ground. Sometimes, when it was not raining during the day and was hot as hell, we would scoop water out of the multitudinous bomb craters that dotted the jungle confines and pour it over ourselves. The bomb crater water, along with the water that dripped off of the trees onto our ponchos, most likely contained traces of Agent Orange. Had I known then about the pernicious side effects of Agent Orange, I might not have drunk the water that we collected in our ponchos or helmets. Agent Orange was a highly toxic herbicide that the military sprayed on the jungle for the purpose of defoliating the trees in the belief that it would be harder for Charlie to move around without being seen.

When I think about how dangerous and destructive Agent Orange is, it makes me wonder even more about my government. We were nothing more than guinea pigs, just like the troops sent into Hiroshima after the bomb, who were exposed to high levels of radiation. It was the same for us grunts. We were exposed to a highly toxic chemical — dioxin (a suspected carcinogen) which, Lord knows, has effects that may take 20–30 years or more to manifest themselves. Whenever people are exposed to highly toxic chemicals, like Agent Orange, there are bound to be some long-term health risks. Vietnam was Love Canal, only on a much larger, more grandiose scale. Our government covered up and is still covering up the disastrous long-term effects of dioxin. If Agent Orange could defoliate trees, imagine what it can do to the human body! Nothing will ever convince me, and many other veterans, that these chemicals had no effect upon our bodies or minds.

It is known that toxic chemicals, which are released into lakes and streams, have been traced and found to have moved up the food chain. Trees that received infinitesimal amounts of Agent Orange, which was washed off by the tropical rains, transmitted their poison to the ground into our poncho-like cisterns and the multitudinous bomb craters, from which we drank so often. There was no escape. Unwittingly, we drank Socrates' cup of hemlock. How else can one account for the uncontrolled spasms, the numbness in extremities and the high birth defect rates among American, Australian, and NVA/VC Vietnam combat vets? Is it merely a coincidence? I think not.

It is my firm belief that we Vietnam vets are part of a sad conspiracy that has been covered up and swept under the carpet by our own government. What our government did to us in Vietnam is inexcusable. What our big chemical corporations have done cannot be condoned. Surely, they knew from their own in-house experiments what the side effects might be. Yet, in their zealous greed to sell to our government, they swept aside the possible dangers to our own troops. We were expendable. If a bullet did not get us, a chemical was a more subtle way of maiming us. After all, the odds, which the big corporations well knew, were that the effects of dioxin would not show up until years after the Vietnam War. By that time, they would be home free and could claim "some other force" was the contributor to our genetic malfunctions, or the altered state of our minds and bodies. Thus, they would make a bundle selling to our government and escape liability for the effects of their deadly products. These corporations have committed a heinous crime and they, along with our government, should be held accountable for their Watergate-type coverup. The question is, will they ever be brought to trial? I doubt it, because they are too powerful, have too much money, and we downtrodden, chemically infected veterans do not stand a chance. With the meager $180,000,000 settlement of a class action suit in the late 1980s, this observation has sadly come true. A recent study in southern Vietnam showed dangerously high levels of dioxin still remain in the soil, some thirty years after it was dispersed.

Having the scout dog along with us paid off handsomely. We left the log site and broke bush most of the day, uncovering *beaucoup* trotters in the process. About 1500 hours, we paused to rest under a bamboo clump that also had an enemy bunker underneath it. So, we were not the only ones out there who hid under bamboo clumps—Charlie just reinforced his position a whole lot better. We found some papers scattered around the bunker which, although written in Vietnamese, showed, unmistakably, that they were homework papers consisting of spelling and math tests, with corrections!

As we rose, after examining our intriguing find, shots rang out. We hit the ground. The dog had smelled an NVA, and one of our men, seeing a gook, opened up. Charlie didied. We missed. We followed the trail he had taken and walked into our biggest discovery yet—an NVA base camp.

It was the most fascinating enemy encampment I had ever seen. Nothing I was to see later on could compare to the efficiency of construction. The whole camp appeared to be about 75 by 100 meters in area. The dining and meeting hall was about 25 feet wide by 75 feet long by 8 feet deep. Tables and chairs occupied the earthen floor. On one of the tables lay a deck of cards, with score pads and several hands next to it. We had obviously interrupted a card game! The entire hall was covered with corrugated tin and steel sheets. One part of the roof consisted of a large metal sheet with Schlitz Beer printed all over it. Obviously, it had come from a packing crate containing beer. It had probably been stolen, or discarded in Saigon, and had then been picked up and transported 40–50 miles on jungle trails to be used as part of this roof. Leading away from the dining area on one side was a tunnel filled with 10–12 bunks, and adjoining it on the other side was a huge kitchen, which was still under the metal roof. Pots, pans, and all kinds of silverware were stored there. Next to the kitchen was a food preparation table on which rested a pot of rice filled with enough food to feed twenty men. Adjoining the mess hall was a bicycle repair shop, with seven or eight bicycles lying around a central work area.

Our biggest discovery turned out to be a field hospital that was stocked with huge quantities of medical supplies. What was upsetting about this find was that we discovered many of the drugs and hypodermic needles came from the U.S. It made us mad as hell at the Quakers, who were sending these medical supplies to the enemy. It was one thing to fight the war; but to have your own people, your own kind, supporting the enemy was too much. Here we were, risking *our* lives, *our* blood, for some SOBs back in the States who were sending aid and comfort to the enemy. It was, indeed, a low blow.

The equipment that we uncovered was mind-boggling. We found a stainless steel medical kit, chicoms, an SKS (Soviet 7.62-mm carbine), NVA field telephone, and books filled with notes. We uncovered lots of U.S. Army entrenching tools — one, in particular, was a brand new lightweight one that had not yet been issued to American troops in the field! Knives, bayonets, seven or eight saws, an NVA claymore, a gallon thermos jug, chinaware, axes, lanterns, flashlights, a bottle of liquor, countless first aid kits, and steel surgical trays also turned up.

There was a thirty-foot-deep well with a bucket which, when reeled up full of water, could be emptied into a trough that was connected by pipe to another trough at the food preparation table. Running water — à la gook!

In one sleeping area, we found lots of hammocks strung up and nearby, on a shelf, a self-winding alarm clock just ticked away. Newly washed laundry hung from clotheslines, and I found a box that had the words "PEOPLE'S REPUBLIC OF CHINA" printed on it. Much to our delight, it contained bottles of insect repellant made in China. The repellant was incredibly effective, so we squirreled away as many bottles of it as we could possibly carry in our rucks.

The entire complex was perfectly camouflaged under a thick bamboo canopy, which made it virtually impossible to spot from the air. The metal roof did not even touch the lowest bamboo or tree branches.

The next day, we went out on patrol around the enemy base camp and found two huge rice caches and some large, fifteen-foot-square bunkers that were big enough to fit ten men comfortably. The outer walls were constructed of six-inch-thick logs. On top of them was a plastic cover to keep out, we speculated, seeping rainwater, with twelve inches of dirt on top of it.

The rice had to be moved to an open area where it could be airlifted out. That necessitated a 200-yard carry. We took the bikes, loaded each one with the 200–250 pound bags, and wheeled the rice down the trail to the PZ. From the PZ, we would ride the bikes back down the trail. At the site of one rice cache, we even uncovered a sewing machine. Indeed, the enemy had most of the comforts of home at his fingertips.

The complex was not without its animals. Chickens ran helter-skelter throughout the area. A pig, which had obviously been set free at our approach, played hide and seek with us for two days. He became a nuisance because he chewed the wires of the claymore mines that we had set out. Try as we might, we were unable to capture him. Sgt. Elia, our Hawaiian from Hilo, fashioned a spear with a hunting knife and stalked him. Elia's intent was to treat us to a Hawaiian-type luau. This pig appeared, however, to be as elusive as Charlie. We even made a primitive bow and arrows when Elia's spear failed to kill the porker. But it eluded our arrows with ease. In desperation, we even tried lassos, all to no avail. A stray black kitten wandered in and was a pitiful sight. It was maimed — perhaps by the gooks. Its tail had been chopped off and one front foot had been cut off. We fed it and tried to make it feel better. Sgt. Elia, who had failed in capturing and killing the pig, did manage to nab a chicken. So, that evening we had fresh chicken and rice for dinner. The rice was a bit hard, but palatable. The fresh chicken meat, however, was a feast fit for hungry grunts!

A new "atrocity" manifested itself while we were uncovering all these supplies. Our beloved LTC radioed Lt. Hill and informed him that all these supplies we had found were secondary. He reminded Hill that although Blackfoot Platoon had been originally airlifted out there to find a rice cache, killing gooks was our primary objective. He told Lt. Hill not to call or bother him unless we killed a gook. This made us furious. This SOB was, in effect, letting us know that our labor and efforts at finding and uncovering this supply depot were useless. Surely he must have realized that, if you took away Charlie's food, he would be hungry, and hungry people need food to continue fighting. Apparently, this simple fact eluded LTC Lewis. By denying Charlie the medical supplies that had been uncovered, the life of a wounded NVA would be harder. Deny the enemy food and medical aid, and he cannot fight half as well. Some people just did not seem to grasp these elementary facts. So, life under the "tyrant" continued.

About this time, I was beginning to notice a significant fact. My M-16 appeared to stay much cleaner in Vietnam than the ones I had used in the States. Back in the World, I had to clean my M-16 over and over again. In Vietnam, I only had to clean my weapon every three or four days. Usually, when I broke it down (disassembled it) for cleaning on the fourth day, it still had plenty of oil on the parts. We were told — whether it was true or not I never found out — that the M-16s in Vietnam had chrome in them, thus making them more rust resistant. Anyway, in Vietnam I took half as much time to clean my weapon as I had in the States. I had read and heard all the stories about how the M-16 was notorious for jamming. After Vietnam, I still find it hard to give credence to that rumor. I never knew or met anyone who had his weapon jam. Perhaps in other parts of Vietnam this was true, but not in our area. I had a fairly simple philosophy concerning my M-16. Every time I cleaned it, I rubbed cleaning oil on every part with great profusion. I would then, without wiping the parts off, reassemble my weapon and run it through its paces (without ammo) several times. Often a final few squirts of oil ended up in the bullet chamber. My M-16 never failed while I was in Vietnam. I had several different M-16s during my tour and always followed this simple, yet obviously effective procedure at keeping them clean. I have no complaints. It was an excellent rifle, and we were damn lucky to have such a lightweight weapon to lug around, instead of the heavy, long-barreled M-14.*

After shipping out all the rice that we had discovered, we burned everything we could get our hands on that was flammable, and left CS crystals in the bunkers and trenches surrounding the base camp. We were then CA'ed out to another jungle LZ. As we were being lifted out, we flew directly over the base camp. From an altitude of fifty feet above the canopy, I could not see the metal roof. The jungle matting protected it well.

At our new LZ we received log and then had to hump 1800 meters. With a fully loaded pack, I almost did not make it. Another boil had anchored itself to my neck. This one was huge and extremely painful. I was

---

*Without a doubt, one of the most compelling and descriptive accounts about the M-16, its development, and problems can be found in a book by Thomas D. Boettcher entitled *Vietnam — The Valor and the Sorrow: From the Home Front to the Front Lines in Words and Pictures*, (Boston: Little, Brown and Company, 1985) pp. 349–353.

unable to turn my head without experiencing pain. It was at least two inches in diameter and one half inch high. Doc Raley tried to get the core out, but all he got was pus and blood. The pain was so intense, I almost fainted. Doc put more medicine on it to draw the core out, but he did not want to lance it as it was on my neck. Cutting into my carotid artery would not have been conducive to my health! So, if the core could not be removed by the next day, I would have to make a quick trip to the battalion surgeon who would lance it.

While I suffered with my boil, others in the platoon suffered from another common ailment — the trots. Seven or eight guys had a bad case of the runs. Diarrhea was a serious ailment in Vietnam. One could become dehydrated rather quickly from it, and the hot, merciless sun drew the sweat from our bodies even faster. I was lucky — I didn't have it. The day before, desperate to quench their thirst, a lot of the guys drank creek water without boiling it or using iodine tablets to sterilize it. It was a foolish move on their part and now they were suffering. Lt. Hill could hardly walk. Every 200 meters we were forced to stop so he could evacuate his bowels. The poor guy was in a lot of pain but managed to recover as did the rest.

On August 9, Charlie probed the defenses of LZ Becky. It was his preliminary warmup for the real play that lay ahead. Sappers crawled through the two strands of concertina wire surrounding an LZ that needed, at a bare-bones minimum, three strands. The NVA blew one bunker sky-high. Four grunts wrapped in olive drab plastic bags went home to the World the next day. The NVA escaped.

Early on the morning of August 10, 1969, Blackfoot Platoon, Bravo Company, 2nd of the 8th, 1st Air Cav was airlifted inexorably towards its rendezvous with destiny. Little did we know, or realize, what awaited us. For some, it was to be their last helicopter ride alive — Becky awaited us with open arms, as did Circe with Odysseus.

After being deposited at LZ Becky, we were immediately sent into the jungle to search for blood trails that might have been left by the escaping NVA who had probed the LZ the previous night. As soon as we penetrated the jungle we found an NVA ammo belt and a blood trail. Stopping here for fifteen minutes, we hastily ate breakfast and awaited further instructions. We then progressed about 100 meters further into the jungle. Weary, uptight, and trigger conscious, we moved so stealthily that I doubt a footstep could be heard more than two feet away. Never in all our lives had we been so conscious of maintaining absolute silence. The inevitable gnats even sounded louder than our own breathing.

After moving 100 meters my squad conducted several cloverleaf patrols. During our second cloverleaf, we came extremely close to the wood line near the LZ. Suddenly, about fifty feet away, shots shattered the morning stillness. We hit the ground. Our point team had slipped up on two NVA and killed them while they lay on the ground observing the LZ from their vantage point. What astonished us was the fact that they had been set up in a position not twenty-five meters from where we had originally entered the wood line. They could not have missed seeing us leave the LZ and enter the jungle. These Charlies had definitely come prepared to lay some heavy shit on us. They had two large rockets the size of a 105 artillery shell, and a mortar tube with eighteen mortar rounds. Their mortar tube was set up in position for direct fire on Becky's TOC. They even had gas masks and a bangalore torpedo, which could be used to blow gaping holes in the concertina wire. LTC Lewis was overjoyed by our kill. He probably came all over himself when we radioed the news to him. Our platoon was now responsible for five kills in two months, compared to one NVA each for Bravo Company's other two platoons.

These two hapless souls had come to stay — permanently. The fact that they had so much firepower with them, however, portended impending peril.

On the night of August 11, 1969, I wrote the following to my parents:

> I think we'll have to stay on the LZ tonight, something I dread. The bunker where those four guys got killed is the one our squad built and the one which we use when we're on the LZ.

Indeed, it was to be a fateful night and a most unlucky bunker for the men of my squad. As if in a morality play, we moved towards an inevitable conclusion on LZ Becky, which became our own personal Armageddon. Becky was not a good cause. It was the tantalizing bait on the end of a small hook for a big fish, which would swallow and digest LZ Becky with ease. Despite what Army annals may say, or proclaim, we got our fucking asses whipped on Becky. Charlie had his shit together and he gave us an old-fashioned ass whooping. The NVA is not totally to blame for the American deaths that occurred during the early morning hours of August 12, 1969, on LZ Becky. Our division commanding officers must bear the weight of defeat upon their shoulders. It is especially theirs for permitting LTC Lewis to continue his misguided policies.

No one should be forced to experience what we had to undergo that horrible night. Our country, our Army, and the NVA forced us to pay attention. It was live or die. It was almost total and complete annihilation. It became our version of the 1876 battle of the Little Big Horn.

As long as I live, I will never forget the obliteration of LZ Becky. I will

never forgive the U.S. Army brass (and consequently the American government) for setting me, and many others, up to be the patsy in LZ Becky's
demise. I strongly believe that the deaths of the men on LZ Becky, during
the early morning hours of August 12, 1969, are directly attributable to the
actions and orders of one man, an incompetent individual, who should have
been relieved of command long before he ever set foot in Vietnam. Thank
goodness, in the future Major General E. B. Roberts, the 1st Cavalry Division's Commanding General (CG), would remove LTC Lewis from command, but, for us trapped on Becky, it was too late.

What was perpetrated upon us grunts on LZ Becky was criminal. It
was insane. We became the sacrificial lambs offered up to the altar of an
unknown God for a country that had no conception that there was a damn
good possibility we would lose this war — which, eventually, we did. One
cannot help but be bitter at his country, its leaders, and its philosophy, for
being set up to take a fall that cost so many men their lives. What our country, and our leaders, did to us on LZ Becky is inexcusable and unpardonable. Like a gaudy prostitute standing on a city corner, Becky awaited
Charlie so that he might avail himself of our favors and lose all his men.
Charlie partook of the favors, enjoyed them, and raped us. Those of us on
LZ Becky the night of August 11–12, 1969, truly met our God. If I were
asked, "What was the most significant day of your life?" I would be forced
to reply that it was the night I spent on LZ Becky, when the NVA decided
to annihilate us. What happened to me and the other grunts on LZ Becky
is almost beyond words. It was the longest night of my life and indelibly
altered my thought processes. It was a major turning point in my life. Up
to August 12, 1969, like a surfer, we had been riding the crest of a wave.
But all waves must break and cast up their contents. That night became
our Götterdämmerung.

There is an LZ Becky in everyone's life.

The jungle was our Charybdis, but Becky was our Scylla.

The night of August 11 started off as your usual night on an LZ. We
were tense. Charlie had tried a probe the previous night. He might try again.
We were keyed up tighter than a piano wire. You find yourself on the bull's-
eye. Sooner or later, someone's gonna score a direct hit. Our job was to
dodge the incoming bullet. But Charlie had us right where he wanted us—
by the balls. To entice the gooks, LTC Lewis had given orders that no illumination (flares) would be used at night on LZ Becky. Usually, on every
LZ, you sent up illumination at different times during the night. This was
done so that if Charlie was sneaking up on us, the flares might catch him
out in the open where we could spot him. The randomness of firing illumination also kept him off balance. LZ Becky had no illumination during its

brief three weeks of existence. Therefore, Charlie had a chance to really scope out the entire LZ and easily plot the position of bunkers, mortar pits, and artillery pieces.

We grunts hated the night. Night was Charlie's time. Charlie moved at night. Night brought death. We feared the night in Vietnam. Charlie struck at night. It was his secret weapon. After all, we were on his ground. He could easily control the action. Grunts died at night.

On the LZ, we never got that much sleep. On an LZ, like Becky, we had four or five men per bunker. From 2000 to 2400 hours we pulled 50 percent guard (two men awake), so one got two hours sleep at the most. From 2400 to 0330 hours we pulled 100 percent guard — everyone awake. Then from 0330 to 0630 hours, it was 50 percent again, so each of us only got about one and a half hours sleep. At the most, on the LZ, we got only three and a half hours sleep each night.

Rocky and I were pulling guard duty outside our bunker in a fighting position. It was 0330 hours — the early morning of August 12. We had just gone off 100 percent alert. The world caved in, and the ensuing fury, which Charlie unleashed, was terrifying in its intensity. How any of us managed to survive is remarkable. Dante's Inferno was tame compared to what was laid on us.

At 0330 hours a bright flash occurred in the wood line not seventy-five meters to my left. The long, yellow trail of a rocket whistled directly at my bunker and passed by overhead to explode in, or near, the mortar pit located directly behind us.

There were five men assigned to our bunker. When the first incoming explosion occurred, three men rushed from their sleeping hooches to the bunker. Rocky left me at the fighting position and joined the others. Rockets and mortars began, literally, to rain down on top of us. For some inexplicable reason, I decided not to go to the bunker. Instead, I ran over and crawled into my sleeping hooch, which was located about ten feet away from our fighting position. That decision probably saved my life.

Exploding enemy mortar rounds were pelting almost every square foot of the LZ. Shrapnel flew everywhere, and I could hear it splattering against my hooch. The concussion of incoming rounds landing as close as five feet from where I hid rang continuously in my ears. Not one single second went by without an explosion.

Incoming rockets exploded everywhere, digging out five-foot craters in the landscape. The bunker I was supposed to be in took a direct hit from a rocket that passed with ease through the wire mesh protective screen set up in front of it. The rocket entered one of the firing ports and exploded. I watched my bunker as it seemed to sway. Then, it slowly crumpled and

8/12/69: My destroyed bunker on LZ Becky.

collapsed. At the same time, the three 155-mm artillery howitzers, located directly behind my position about twenty-five meters from me, took direct hits and were knocked out of action.

Without letup, NVA mortars and rockets continued to rain down upon us. Explosions and fires were everywhere. The shouts and cries of the wounded and dying mingled with the screams of incoming rockets and mortars.

I peeped out of my hooch and witnessed one of the most god-awful sights I had ever seen in my entire life. Frank Graham, our squad's machine gunner, who was in our bunker when it took a direct hit from the incoming rocket, had stumbled out of what remained of our bunker. He was obviously in a daze. At the precise moment he exited, the mortar pit directly behind our bunker took a direct hit and all the ammunition in it exploded. The sky was illuminated by the explosion, and we were showered by thousands of shrapnel fragments, each carrying death in their journey from the mortar pit. I reeled back inside my hooch to escape this cataclysmic explosion and then looked out to see Frank. He was no longer standing, but lay on the ground facing me, a glassy look in his eyes, because half of his face had been blown away. I had never seen so much blood in my life. I couldn't take my eyes from it. I was oblivious to everything around me. All I could do was watch the blood pour from his head like water flowing from a garden hose when you water flowers. One eye remained open and stared in my direction. In all my life, I had never seen so much blood disgorge itself from a human being. Imperceptibly, the flow slowed and soon stopped when his heart either pumped itself dry or collapsed from the shock of death.

Seeking shelter, two wounded Redlegs crawled over from the 155s. By this time, everything over there had been blown away. One man was in a bad way. Above the continuing repercussions of the explosions, I yelled to him:

"Come on!"

"Come on over here!"

"You can make it!"

"Come on, crawl, CRAWL!!"

"It's only ten feet!"

"Come on, you can make it."

One of them started to crawl towards our destroyed bunker.

"No, don't go in the bunker — it's gone —come on over here to my hooch."

They both made it.

No other life was evident from the collapsed bunker. I had no idea if any of my buddies were still alive, and, after what happened to Frank, I was not going to leave my shelter to find out.

The second Redleg reached me. His leg was streaming blood, and he was in some pain. I turned into a medic. In a flash, my four hours of Army basic first aid training returned to me. I immediately started treating for shock by talking to him and telling him he was OK. The incoming explosions, coupled with the raging fires on the LZ, provided me with more than enough light with which to treat the wounded man's lower leg. I ripped his pants leg off and used it to stem the tide of blood. It took about ten minutes to calm him down. The other Redleg also talked to him and tried to reassure him.

The bombardment had not let up. It continued as Charlie pounded every square inch of what was LZ Becky. I had barely been under mortar fire before, but this took the cake. This was one hell of an attack!

For one solid hour, we suffered under a constant barrage of incoming that became such a steady stream that it appeared it might never end. Had Charlie followed it up with a ground attack by charging our position after his initial barrage, not one soul would have survived because we were all hiding. On three separate occasions Lt. Hill attempted to leave his bunker to rally his men, but every time exploding incoming rounds and their resultant shrapnel forced him back. Each time he was lightly hit by shrapnel. So heavy, so massive was this attack that no one could move about in the open without being hit. It was just too dangerous. An ant would not have survived that first hour in the open. Somehow Lt. Hill managed to leave his bunker during a lull and, limping over to each one of us, he rallied our demoralized spirits. His courage and bravery that night is beyond comparison and above reproach. Risking certain death or disfigurement, he went from man to man, making us leave protective shelter and go to our fighting positions on the earthen berm to repel any NVA who might be thinking of overrunning us. The two Redlegs joined me in the fighting position as mortars and rockets continued to rain down behind us on all but a completely decimated and destroyed LZ. Somehow, somewhere, they both had managed to acquire M-16s, though God only knows where because, when they crawled into my hooch, they had entered it empty-handed.

Dodging the incoming, Lt. Hill spoke to each man and exhorted him to live — to get Charlie. He treated us all for shock, and indeed we needed it. He truly deserved to receive the DSC (Distinguished Service Cross) for his efforts that night. Whether or not he ever received anything is unknown to me. Since he was on LTC Lewis's shit list, I doubt if Lewis would have approved any award for Lt. Hill. All the same, he deserved better than what he got. The courage, determination, and guts that he showed that night will not be soon forgotten. In part, we owe our lives to him too.

The three remaining men in my bunker were badly hurt. "Hillbilly" Kelly, my good friend, had a crushed chest. He had only twenty-three days left in Vietnam and had not received so much as a scratch until that night. He would see the world a little sooner now. "Red" Rohner had facial wounds. He had ninety-seven days left and had not been wounded until this point. Rocky, the cherry from New Jersey, who was with me in the fighting position when the attack commenced, had facial and eye injuries. I was sure he would lose at least one eye. He had what we called a "Million-Dollar Wound," and would be going back to the World after a little more than a month in Vietnam.

Finally, the NVA's bombardment stopped. Partially deafened, my ears continued to ring from the concussion of the explosions. Now it was our turn to react. Puff the Magic Dragon, a Douglas C-47 cargo plane mounted with three General Electric 7.62-mm Gatling-type mini-guns and illumination flares, circled overhead throwing down deadly rounds of lead. Cobra gunships (a.k.a. Blue Max) hovered overhead, continuously firing into the wood line. Somewhere out there were our LPs and I wondered how they were managing to survive. Amazingly enough, they would all stagger in the next day without a scratch. The LZ landing pad, located directly in front of my bunker, was in flames that lit up the entire area around our position and over half of the LZ because the fifty-five-gallon drums of oil, gas, and diesel fuel that had been stored there were now burning out of control. In the barrage they had somehow been ignited. We now had light so that we could repel any ground attack, but we were so completely illuminated that we were nothing more than sitting ducks. Death and destruction rained down from on high. We would see the tracers leaving Puff's gun ports as it circled high above us. Cobra after Cobra unloaded itself into the nearby wood line.

At my position, I was soon joined by the cooks and clerks. Our end of the LZ had taken the brunt of the attack. There was not much left to defend. Medics had arrived to patch up the wounded and carry them to the other side of the LZ to be medevaced. The dead they left. There was nothing they could do for them — others needed their ministrations.

It was a long, long time before daylight. We had the light from the burning oil drums, and we finally had illumination. Not until it was daylight did I fully realize that I was the only one left at my position. The rest were dead or wounded. Mercifully Frank's body had been dragged away, but a huge, sticky pool of congealed blood remained to soak into LZ Becky's black dirt. The rest of my platoon had also been badly hurt. Our new platoon sergeant, who had been assigned to us only five days prior to the LZ attack, was wounded. Franklin Keeney, a soul brother and good friend, from Miami, Florida, was hit. Every person in Blackfoot had been hit, some seriously, some minimally. Chief had a scratch. Jackson Winter, a soul brother and good buddy, received a cut. Sgt. Elia had a cut. I had a shrapnel wound in my right leg — one inch long and about an eighth of an inch deep. I hid it. Most of us did not even bother to get treated or report our wounds. We all felt that we just did our job and wanted no Purple Heart or other medals for performing our duty. We had paid dearly with our blood and our lives.

A strange occurrence, which happened to me several times in Vietnam, continues to haunt me to this day. During this attack, and subsequent firefights, I felt no fear at all. Not once did I feel afraid for myself during these battles. Only when the fighting was over did I have time to think about what had happened. It was at that point that I became afraid. I almost freaked out. It was as if I awakened from a bad dream.

About 0700 hours, as the sun peaked through the treetops to reveal the carnage that had been perpetrated upon LZ Becky, Jackson Winter spotted two gooks near the wire. A few guys immediately ran out and shot at them. Meanwhile, alerted to the enemy's presence, we all stood on the berm yelling and exhorting the kill team:

"Kill the son of a bitch!"

"Kill the bastards!"

"Grease the motherfucker's ass!"

"Don't let him *Chieu Hoi!*"

Believe me, had I been on the reaction team, I would have killed them even if they had been trying to surrender. At that point there was absolutely no doubt in my mind I would have enjoyed killing them both. After what we had just experienced, I felt that they did not deserve mercy.

Lt. Hill, ever present, however, prevented the reaction team from killing one man. Upon being roughly dragged in, the POW revealed some startling information to an interpreter. There had been, he told us, approximately 750 NVA poised to overrun the LZ. We could not have withstood an onslaught of that size. We had blown their attack wide open because, just as they were poised to swarm all over us (on my end of the LZ, no less!), we had instituted a mad minute. Our mad minute had killed 60–70 NVA and thrown them into confusion. Hence, they decided to rely on their rockets and mortars, which, if the truth be told, had done a pretty good job of annihilating us. The POW told us that Puff the Magic Dragon, our Cobras, and artillery fire from other firebases had killed a lot more Charlies. He also revealed that this was the largest force ever assembled by the NVA for launching an attack on a LZ. Had we not had our mad minute at just the right time, we would have been overrun. Our artillery, prior to the attack, had fired beehive rounds into the wood line. Each beehive round contained, I was told, 9000 barbed arrow-like fléchettes, which, upon impact, were propelled in all directions. Those beehive rounds were probably directly responsible for saving our lives. Thank God, for once, a mad minute paid off. Never again would I look at them in terms of wasted money.

Daylight revealed the technical details of Charlie's handiwork. The change was so stark, so ... unbelievable. We could hardly fathom the change. Every bunker on our end of the LZ was either totally destroyed or extensively damaged. Rocket craters, like craters on the moon, some five feet in diameter, dotted the landscape in great profusion. Incoming mortar holes pockmarked the earth everywhere. The TOC had been blown up. Fires dotted the landscape and raged out of control. Such massive and comprehensive destruction was mentally difficult to accept. We walked around

8/12/69: LZ Becky lies devastated after the NVA attack.

like zombies. Because LZ Becky had never used nighttime illumination, the NVA had been able to zero in on every vital position and either knock it out or destroy it. Mortar pits no longer looked like mortar pits. Matériel was strewn everywhere.

In all, there were 22 KIAs, 7 MIAs were *never* found (they had been blown to smithereens), and 29 men were sufficiently wounded to warrant evacuation.

The order came down from the Cav's CG, General E. B. Roberts, to abandon LZ Becky. We worked like dogs all day long. Whereas LZ Ike had taken five days to fully abandon, we abandoned Becky in one day. And, guess where all the matériel and salvageable equipment was sent? To LZ Ike! The Cav was forced to reoccupy Ike after having dismantled it only three weeks earlier in anticipation of building Becky.

One of the tasks I performed that day was rather gruesome, if not macabre. A Redleg had been in the process of loading one of the 155s when it took a direct hit. His head had been blown off and wedged in the firing chamber of the artillery piece. I helped a medic scoop it out. Somehow, I managed not to vomit. I never did see the rest of the body.

8/12/69: More devastation on LZ Becky.

As we fiercely worked to abandon the LZ, the big guns from Barbara (the 175s), which had to be 15–20 miles away, fired artillery shells into the wood line surrounding Becky. To hear the faraway boom of the long guns gave us an eerie sensation.

By 1800 hours, we accomplished the impossible. We had stripped Becky of everything that was worth saving and shipped it out. I had been up for forty-two hours. Lt. Hill called us together and in a solemn voice informed us that Blackfoot and the platoon from Delta Company, which had been defending Becky along with us, were to go to Tay Ninh for an R & R — courtesy of LTC Lewis. We leapt for joy! We could hardly believe it!

As soon as I arrived in Tay Ninh, I went to the hospital and had a surgeon lance the boil on my neck.

It was at this time that I realized that my rucksack had taken a direct hit while it rested outside my sleeping hooch on LZ Becky. As I went through it, trying to sort everything out, I discovered that a piece of shrapnel had destroyed a pocket containing my Q-tips, foot powder, some of the Chinese insect repellant (which I had been carrying since our base camp discovery earlier in the month), first aid cream, and a phisohex bottle, and had embedded itself in the book, *The Choices We Face* by Lyndon Johnson, that I had been carrying. Luckily, I had finished reading it. Little did I know, after all I had been through, that I was to receive my first combat medal for the actions I had taken to patch up the Redlegs. I later received the Army Commendation Medal with "V" for valor, which read as follows:

> For heroism in connection with military operations against a hostile force in the Republic of Vietnam. Private First Class Wise distinguished himself by valorous action on 13 August 1969, while serving with Company B, 2nd Battalion (Airmobile), 8th Cavalry during an enemy attack on Fire Support Base Becky, Republic of Vietnam. When his unit came under intense rocket, mortar and ground attack from a determined enemy force, Private First Class Wise left the safety of his bunker and moved through the hail of hostile fire administering first aid to the wounded and helping evacuate them to safety. His display of personal bravery and devotion to duty is in keeping with the highest traditions of the military service, and reflects great credit upon himself, his unit, and the United States Army.

8/13/69: E. Tayloe Wise after our R & R in Tay Ninh.

The R & R in Tay Ninh was also a godsend in other ways. I took my first shower in two months (the last having been on LZ Barbara). It felt great to take a bath. I soaked every pore in the cold water. We were also issued new clothes which, on top of the showers, made us feel like human beings again.

Indeed, Tuesday, August 12, 1969, would go down as one of the most significant days of my life. I had survived against overwhelming odds. I had been wounded (as had everyone else) and yet shrugged it off as just part of the job that had to be done. I was lucky. Some had not been so fortunate. A lot of people would cry back in the States when they learned their sons, or loved ones, would not be coming home. For Charlie, this was a

8/13/69: Bill "Doc" Raley, Blackfoot Platoon's medic, in Tay Ninh.

great propaganda victory. He would make much of this, and use our defeat to exhort his troops to further boldness.

Out of all of this, I gained a great sense of comradeship with my fellow soldiers. I now felt much closer to them, and we all gained a sense of togetherness. We felt as if we were part of a cohesive group — a team, and were damn proud of ourselves after this hell because we had survived — we had done our job. Our training had paid off. Becky's abandonment saddened us — because it was a defeat. We had been resoundingly trounced and could not forget that sober fact. We had been humiliated. Our defeat, we also realized, came as much from Charlie's hands, as it had from the policies of our commanders. We had been the bait for a trap. Only someone had forgotten to tell Charlie that he was supposed to lose, and many good men, most of them young teenage boys, had been uselessly sacrificed.

One cannot help but admire the NVA. They had one hell of a lot of guts and courage to do what they did. It took a lot of stamina and willpower to keep up the attack under the fire power that was directed at them by the Cobras, Puff, and other LZs. Charlie got his pound of flesh, but he paid a stiff price for it.

In Tay Ninh that night, after showers, we had a ball. We unwound by drinking untold amounts of beer and had all the Cokes we could guzzle. I finally went to bed after forty-four hours of going without sleep. I was tired — but little did I know how tired I would soon be, for we would have to reconstruct Ike.

The Army had to do something quickly to prop up our sagging morale after the beating we had taken. After only six hours of sleep, we were awakened for a hastily arranged awards ceremony, which took place the morning of the 13th. Major General E. B. Roberts, the Cav's CG, presented thirteen valor awards to the remaining members of Bravo Company for their actions in recent field contact around LZ Ike. (It was too soon to give awards for Becky.) A sergeant in my platoon, Luiz "Larry" Martinez, got

LZ Ike — our bunker with mesh wire in front.

a Silver Star. Jackson Winter, a member of my squad, got a Bronze Star with "V" device. Another good friend, Franklin Keeney, received the Army Commendation Medal with "V" device for his part in the ambush outside of White, when I was in Quan Loi getting glasses. Vic Tenorio also received an Army Commendation Medal with "V" device. Lt. Hill got a Purple Heart with Oak Leaf Cluster. The Army definitely wanted to show its appreciation before it sent us out to LZ Ike and the hell that awaited us there. After the presentation, we were quickly CA'ed to Ike. Our respite in Tay Ninh had not lasted long.

We worked all day on Ike's defenses. Countless sandbags had to be filled, bunkers rebuilt (I wished we had not done such a thorough job at demolition), and sleeping hooches reconstructed. We had a 100 percent alert the first night, and I got only seven hours of sleep. By 2300 hours on the 15th, I had gone ninety hours with only eight hours of sleep. I felt a little punch-drunk. The rest of the guys were also dead tired from the same lack of sleep. Physical exhaustion began to set in and we were all nearing a breaking point.

On our second day at Ike, the 14th, we were sent out on a patrol. As we took a break in the jungle, we heard voices.

Gooks!

We hit the ground. But, because we were so damn tired, so physically exhausted, we made too damn much noise. The gooks didied. Thank God! I do not think any of us were in the mood for a firefight. Physically and mentally, we all were just too strung out. I was so damn tired that I wanted the gooks to stay so we could kill a few and avenge Becky. We probably would have gotten the worst part in that firefight, had it even taken place. Most of us were just too damn tired. We would have made too many mistakes had we joined the battle.

That night I was on LP. LTC Lewis had instituted a new LP policy that we immediately hated. Instead of going out about 100 meters from the last strand of concertina wire, we had to go to the jungle wood line, which was about 150 meters from the LZ's berm, and then we were supposed to penetrate *another* 150 meters of the jungle before we set up our LP. If the LZ came under fire there was no chance we could make it back. We were stuck but good. It was another of LTC Lewis's brilliant ideas. During a mad minute that night we could hear the bullets zipping by our position. Unfortunately, we were all still too tired to protest this new policy and were more intent on catching up on our sleep. This new policy was just one more atrocity perpetrated upon us by our battalion CO. It seemed that Lewis was determined to push us to the limit and use every last ounce of strength we had, mentally and physically, so that he could achieve some nebulous award for kills. It was bad enough having to retreat from Becky, but to make LP a definite candidate for suicide squad was about the limit.

By 1400 hours on the afternoon of August 16th, I was just about ready to collapse from lack of sleep. In 104 hours, I had managed to get only twelve hours of sleep. I felt like a walking zombie and was definitely at the end of my rope. I turned to Lt. Hill, my rifle in hand, and told him:

"Sir, I've just about had it. I'm going in my sleeping hooch and sleeping four hours. If anyone comes in prior to that, I'm going to waste him."

He looked at me a little strangely, shrugged and said nothing. I told one of my buddies to wake me in four hours and not a minute earlier. I also told him if anyone crawled into the hooch any sooner, I would not hesitate to blow him away. I got four uninterrupted hours of sleep. It felt wonderful.

I was really fortunate that day, because, after my four-hour nap, I pulled an LP patrol that night and got ten more hours of sleep. To get this extra sleep, which almost became more precious than water, we would volunteer to go out on an LP patrol. Instead of a regular four-man LP, we had 10–12 men on an LP patrol. We knew that, basically, Charlie did not like to break brush at night, so we would set up in the thickest and heaviest brush we could find. With so many men, we only had to pull one hour of guard duty at the most, and so each of us got at least ten hours of sleep. Of course, that particular night it poured rain and we all got soaking wet with no poncho cover, but I still slept well.

E. Tayloe Wise on LZ Ike.

Driven to the brink, I had somehow managed to pull myself back to the rim. It is difficult to describe what a lack of sleep can do to a person. One becomes a totally different human being. You walk around in a daze, doing things automatically. Your reaction time is way off. What is going on around you becomes more difficult to comprehend. You get to a point where you do not give a damn, and anyone or anything in your way must be pushed aside. Finally, you reach a breaking point. You either get your sleep — or you go nuts. We all like to think we have the stamina and endurance to push our body past its limit. Once past the limit, however, we become less aware of what is happening to us. Often, without sleep, I found myself in a daze — sort of floating outside of my own body. It then became difficult to know what was real and what was imagined. Pushed past the brink of exhaustion, I became a robot whose actions were all in slow motion. That 104-hour stretch was one of the worst experiences I had ever undergone. Mentally, I knew I was spaced out. I could not think straight, or even talk coherently. Physically, my whole body had begun to shut down on itself. While there was no pain, there was great weakness— an inability to perform simple tasks. I found I had to mentally ask, command, order my legs to move, my arms to carry things. Thank God sleep was finally made available to me. I don't think I would have lasted much longer. All of us suffered from loss of sleep. My actions and thoughts were basically the same as the men who worked with me. We were the walking dead, awaiting the Greek god Lethe to come take us by the hand.

One night on LZ Ike, I will not forget. Three other guys and I were sent out on LP for the night. Rain poured down as we left the LZ and moved to a position some 500 meters from the LZ. We were all a little shook up by having to go so far out, but those were our orders. Reaching the spot where we were to set up, we discovered that our radio did not work. Joe Musgrove and I had time in country and the radio's malfunction did not bother us. But the other two guys were cherries and they freaked out. They wanted to go back in and definitely did not like being 500 meters from the LZ without communication. They had a good point because, had we been discovered, we would have been unable to call in artillery. Joe refused to make up his mind until he knew what the majority wanted. I said, "Stay." The other two men said, "No fucking way!" So, as darkness descended, we hurried back to Ike wondering all the time if we would get shot at by our own troops as we rapidly approached the LZ because we couldn't notify them we were returning. We said more than a few prayers as we neared the LZ.

It was almost dark by the time we got back. I knew they would give us a new radio and send us back out. By the time a spare radio had been found, it was dark. The other three men were scared stiff about returning to the LP position and, going to our new platoon sergeant, who was an E-7 lifer, they told him they were not going back out. I didn't do a thing. I wanted to see the results. I was not about to risk my neck by refusing to go back out, although I was just a trifle bit worried about having to break brush at night. By this time, the NVA, if they were out there, would have started moving towards the LZ. Our chances of running into some would have been good. It was this fear — of encountering gooks — that kept us from going back out. The E-7 told the three that they would go on LP or he would get replacements for them; but, at any rate, an LP would go out. We did not want to go. The other three decided to hide in an empty bunker, and it was not long before our platoon sergeant realized we had not left. He came looking for us.

He called out to us, and I yelled out that we were heading out, but could not find the gate. About thirty seconds later he walked right up to us. Needless to say, he was slightly pissed. So were we. By this time, all of us had made up our minds that we were not going back out.

"Sarge, it's a suicide mission."

"You guys get off your asses and head out, NOW!" he ordered.

"Fuck your asshole — get somebody else!" someone said.

In the ensuing deadly silence, we all heard the distinct sound of a round being chambered in an M-16. One of us was preparing to blow the man away.

I knew if I said I would go, the three others just might follow, but I was in no mood to get my ass shot off.

We were stalemated.

Just then, 1st Lt. John K. Kauhaihao, from Honaunau, Hawaii, appeared from out of the darkness. Since we could not pronounce his long Hawaiian name, we all called him Lt. K. He was Cheyenne Platoon's lieutenant and had overheard us tell the sarge to go take a flying fuck.

"Hey guys," said Lt. K, "if I take you out past the barbed wire and go 200 meters with you, will you go?"

All four of us answered yes in unison. Lt. K was the type of leader whom you could follow anywhere he decided to go. I never knew the man well, because he was not my platoon officer. But he had guts— no, he had balls. He was the kind of officer you would follow into battle without question because you knew he was a man to be trusted. Lt. K was one of those rare individuals whom you only meet once in life and know that it was both an honor and a privilege to serve with him.

True to his word, Lt. K took us past the strands of concertina wire and 200 meters out towards the jungle. We then took 45 minutes to inch our way along in the darkness to where we could set up. It was a hell of a trip. Behind every tree and grass clump lay a gook just waiting to jump out and waste us. Believe me, none of us ever expected to see daylight again. Walking out to that LP was more frightening than my night on Becky.

What it boiled down to was that we were nothing more than a suicide squad. We all knew that if we got into trouble, if we blew our position, or Charlie stumbled upon us, we were all dead ducks—goners. It was a hell of a thing to realize that the officers who ran the show could do this to us because we were expendable. It ticked me off, and I am sure it pissed off a lot of other guys also. The sad thing about all this was that most grunts did not have the education or intelligence to realize what was being done to them. The brass counted on the infantryman's inability either to think independently or to balk at questionable orders. The Army did not appreciate individuals, such as myself, who were in the lower ranks and had a college education. We were dangerous because we would not roll over and play the game. We questioned the orders. It never ceased to irritate the hell out of me to see grunts meekly accept what was dished out to them because they did not know any better. They were being taken advantage of in the crudest way. These men put their trust in their leaders and in the Army, both of which they blindly obeyed. The thought that the Army would needlessly sacrifice them never crossed their minds. They simply and honestly believed that the Army would protect and would never expend them. If they got wounded or killed, they were, they believed, just unlucky. That Uncle Sam would throw away their lives was alien to everything they had been taught or knew about the service. Yet many men were uselessly led, like sheep to the slaughter, down a no-win trail filled with betrayal. It was all so damn sad. On August 24, I wrote to my parents and said:

> Officers ought to realize that they too are expendable, and I can guarantee you, if a man (be he officer or platoon sergeant) gets too bossy over here, he doesn't last long because we wait for a firefight to straighten him out.

It would not be long before this statement turned out to be most prophetic. It was as if I had the ability to see into the future and predict what was to be.

On the 19th of August, my duties changed drastically. Our platoon medic, Bill Raley, left to go back to the World. Since there was no medic to replace him, he recommended me for the job. After my small feat on Becky at patching up the Redleg, it appeared I was the logical choice for combat medic. I knew enough about medicine, administering drugs, and first aid, and had confidence I could handle the new responsibility. I was really pleased when Lt. Hill asked me to be Blackfoot's medic. For once, I felt as if I was going to accomplish something in Vietnam. I took the job for selfish reasons also — medics did not have to pull guard duty, so I would get a lot more sleep. At that time, this was only a temporary assignment, but I had talked to other medics on the LZ, and the LZ doctor, who both felt I would have a good chance at being made a permanent medic. Bravo Company's head medic and I were good friends, and he offered to train me in some of the technical stuff. They say you should not volunteer for things in the Army, but this was one time I had to because being a medic made me feel useful. I felt it was my duty to be a medic and there was no one else in my platoon (or Company) with the education or training to shoulder the heavy responsibility of such a job. It was a job I wanted to do. Of course, I would have to carry an extra thirty pounds of medical supplies, which was not exactly thrilling, but it would be well worth it. Now, instead of being a nobody, I was somebody. I had a responsibility to look out for and tend to my fellow grunts.

Being a combat medic was probably one of the most gratifying things I ever did in my entire life. To save life, instead of taking it, made my remaining stay in Vietnam all that more purposeful. It was a great responsibility and I did not intend to let my fellow Skytroopers down.

I was made temporary platoon medic just in time. My first customer turned out to be myself. I came down with chills, was miserable, could not stop shaking, and had an upset stomach and fever. Just as the chills slacked off, I got the green apple quickstep, which forced me to stay within twenty feet of the latrine for about twenty-four hours. The medicines that I self-administered took effect and evidently cured me. It was the only time, to my knowledge, that I had diarrhea while in Vietnam, and I considered myself lucky to have shrugged it off so quickly. Some guys got it, and nearly died from dehydration. We once had a cherry join our Company while we were out in the jungle and, within two days, he came down with dysentery. After treating him for three days, I sent him in to the hospital on log day. That was the last time we ever saw him. He never returned to the field.

On the night of August 24, Charlie decided to harass us a little bit. We were on guard when suddenly about 100 meters in front of our bunker, there were three gigantic explosions— KABOOM! KABOOM! KABOOM!

"Incoming!"

We ran for cover as the shrapnel from the 107s flew past us. One piece of shrapnel sailed by so close to me that I could see its red glow from the heat of the explosion. Then we heard the distinctive pop of an enemy mortar tube. They must have shot at least thirty mortar rounds at us, and not one landed inside the berm. They were notoriously poor shots, and we could not help but laugh at them.

Out on patrol the next morning, we located the launch site of the rockets and mortars. It turned out to be about twenty-five feet from where we had set up our LP post only thirty-six hours previously during our non-functioning radio fiasco! Needless to say, this only proved that walking around in the dark would have disastrous consequences for us.

One of my first chores as medic was to treat almost everyone in my platoon for ringworm. With the exception of two other guys and myself, everyone had it. I doled out pills (finactin or griseofulvin) to everyone with the admonishment that they had to dry out their feet more often. Each day, while in the jungle, I often took my socks off and wrung them out. As a result, I had little trouble with my feet. But others who did not, or would not, take care of their feet had some major foot problems.

While on LZ Ike, I somehow managed to sit on my glasses again. This time, I broke half the frame but not the lens. The extra pair that I had ordered back in June while I was at Quan Loi had never arrived. I had sent messages by two people who went to Quan Loi about needing my extra glasses. This was all to no avail. Now the 2/8 base camp had moved to Tay Ninh, so my requests probably had been lost in the shuffle. I, personally, would have to go to Tay Ninh to get them. That would present me with a major problem because I did not want to leave my buddies without a medic. I decided to wait.

Up to this point in time, I had been writing extremely detailed letters to my parents concerning my Vietnam exploits. On August 25, I received a letter from my father that disturbed me greatly. Evidently, my detailed letters were upsetting my mother. There appeared to be only one solution. In my next letter I told my father:

> ... the story must be told. Therefore, I will write my detailed letters to you at the same time that I write general letters to you and Mom. I'll mail my detailed letters to you at your post office box and you can read [them] and decide whether or not mother should read them. I know that from time to time you've told me in my letters not to leave anything out. Well, I won't be.

As things turned out, he later replied and told me to continue writing detailed letters, explaining that while they enjoyed the content of my letters, it was what I was doing that made my mother fearful for my safety.

While we were on Ike, our Company got a new top sergeant who was an absolutely super guy. David H. McNerney was a Congressional Medal of Honor (CMH) winner. For actions on March 22, 1967, with the 1st Battalion, 8th Infantry, 4th Infantry Division, he had won the highest award any soldier could hope to attain. He did not have to be in Vietnam because CMH winners did not have to go back to combat — he could have had any post he wished. In the service, a CMH man had the world as his oyster. Yet, here was this patriotic man back in the field humping with the rest of us. He and I would become fairly good friends.

At that time, it appeared that I might, with luck, be able to get out of the field in another four months and get a rear job as there were only five grunts in our platoon who were eligible (by having enough time in country) for rear jobs. There was a three-way tie for third and I was one. That tie would soon be broken by the effects of combat.

I made yet another sad discovery while on LZ Ike, which made me sick at heart. I had taken pictures of some special girlfriends with me to Vietnam and had placed them in the waterproof wallet that the Cav issued to us. Somehow, it leaked. My pictures had gotten wet and stuck to the inside of the plastic compartments, which were somewhat similar to a Ziploc bag, but much smaller. Two beautiful pictures of my best friend at TCU, Ingrid Buck, who was more of a friend than a girlfriend to me, were ruined. I could not remove them for fear of damaging them even more. A picture of Nancy Burroughs, another good friend from TCU, was completely ruined. These developments were most upsetting to me. The only picture that remained intact was of my Texas girlfriend, Abby Stern, who had laminated it prior to sending it. It took a little out of me to lose pictures that I had carried for so long. I felt as if a part of me had been lost and was saddened by this unexpected turn of events.

Like all the other LZs, Firebase Ike was not without its rats. One night, a huge one boldly scampered into our bunker while we were playing cards. His size topped them all. He said, "Deal me in," and took $10.00 from us in five hands!

We were all dependent on different-tasting foods and drinks as the blandness of the C's and the staleness of the water really got to us. So, when someone sent us food from the World, it was most appreciated. We really craved different types of Kool-Aid. Someone had sent me some Pillsbury Funny Face Kool-Aid. It was delicious and had a zingy, more tangier taste, and we favored it more than the regular Kool-Aid. On log days we got cocoa with our C's, which I loved. A hot cup of cocoa really did wonders for your soul when you had been humping all day in the rain. It was hell being wet and cocoa was a perfect perker-upper.

On August 23, 1969, my friend John Sivick and I were promoted to Spec. 4. It felt good not to be a private anymore. I was encouraged at having received this promotion because it at least indicated I was doing something right and was keeping my nose clean with my superiors.

We had been on LZ Ike a long time. Rebuilding an LZ was not all fun and games. Besides hating LZ duty (because we got no sleep), I could not stand it for other reasons. LZs were really filthy. Disease had every chance in the world to abound on LZs and Ike was no exception. Stagnant pools of rainwater became breeding pits for all kinds of insects. Mud and dirt were everywhere. Dust was easily stirred up and floated in the air as we trudged back and forth. It got in our hair, eyes, noses and throats, caking everything to which it adhered itself. Our sweat seeped through our clothing and turned the outside layers of dust to mud. The only time grunts used the latrine was to take a shit. Otherwise, we pissed wherever we pleased, and when the earth we urinated on dried, in the hot, sultry South Vietnamese sun, it, too, turned into dust again, which we inhaled into our nostrils, throats and lungs. We lived in absolute squalor. As a medic, it was my responsibility to dispose of the shit every day by burning it. The latrine was nothing more than a one-holer. One sat on the wooden seat and deposited his excrement into half sections of fifty-five-gallon oil drums that had been placed beneath each toilet seat. Each morning we would pull the half drums out, douse the shit in diesel fuel, kerosene, or gasoline, light it, and burn it. The burning feces exuded an incredibly foul odor, and we had to stand far back from it. At times, our LZ was nothing more than a pigsty. It was so much nicer to get back out in the boonies where things were cleaner, more sanitary, and disease did not float through the air. In the boonies we buried our shit instead of burning it. That was much nicer.

The maimed kitten, which we had found at the gook base camp prior to the incineration of Becky, had not been abandoned. We had carried it to Becky, where it had miraculously survived the NVA onslaught, and then on to Ike. It paid for its keep by chasing LZ Ike's rats. Although lame, it was patient and caught a few of the furry monsters.

Thus ended August 1969, one of the longest months of my life and certainly the most harrowing of months while I was in Vietnam.

SEPTEMBER

Firefights

I have seen war.... I hate war.

Franklin Delano Roosevelt (1882–1945)
(Address at Chautauqua, New York, on August 14, 1936)

By August 29 we were back in the boonies. It was a great relief to get off the LZ and return to the jungle. After Becky's destruction, and Ike's rehabilitation, I had no desire to see another LZ for a long, long time. It was safer and healthier out in the boonies. Or so I thought. Fate was soon to prove how bad this presumption was on my part. Although I hated humping the extra weight, it was worth it. I figured that my 110-pound body was now carrying about 85 pounds. Another benefit to being a medic was that I got to choose where to walk in the file (line of march). I usually walked in the last third of the file as we broke trail. That way, if we got hit, I probably wouldn't take the first blast from Charlie and could hurry forward to give aid.

Unfortunately, this time out we were not to be so lucky. This trip to the boonies would be the last for many men. The brass certainly must have known what they were doing because they landed us right in a hornet's nest.

By this time, I had been involved in major enemy assault attacks where we had been in entrenched positions. I had prayed both to be in a firefight and not to be in one. After four months in country, I got my wish, and more, for a firefight. What I underwent those last days of August and the first week of September 1969 was to test my mettle most severely. Almost everyone I knew, who were my friends, would be gone by the end of the first week in September.

I wanted my taste of hell, and I got a mouthful. It was sickening in its own way. I was to meet death and get to know him rather well. For death and I worked hand in hand with him a winner more than ever. Becky and Quan Loi were to become a piece of cake, compared to the decimation our Company experienced over the next several days. How we all kept our sanity is another story. There is something different about a man who has faced death. It is something intangible on which one cannot put his finger. It follows you for the rest of your life and brands you indelibly. You will never be able to describe to anyone what it is really like. What matters—what is most important—is that you survived. When you see so much killing, so much destruction, it numbs you to life. You grow extremely callous and remote from your fellow man. You learn that it is best not to form any close relationships with anyone because tomorrow they (or you) probably will not be around. I learned how to be hardened—unfeeling—towards my fellow man and my friends. It was not worth the emotional involvement. Upon returning to the World, I carried this remoteness with me as, I am sure, have many others. You became detached from what was happening around you. It was difficult for me to form relationships with people upon reentry to the civilized world. I was a loner before Nam, and much more of one after it. People have found it difficult to get close to me and I to them. I think, in part, it is because of what happened to me when I left Ike.

On August 29, we were CA'ed to an LZ about five miles from Ike. The next day, August 30, we walked all day through tall elephant grass, setting up that night along a well-used trotter, near the edge of a jungle clearing, where the bright green elephant grass grew chest high. As the afternoon waned, four NVA came down the trotter and walked right into our trap. We blew claymores and threw frags. The gooks didied. We sent out a reaction team that did not go far as it was fast becoming dark. We had missed them. Now our shit was in deep trouble. We all knew they would be back to get us, either that night or the next morning. Joe and I pulled guard in a foxhole we had dug even deeper after the ambush. That night all was quiet.

Dawn came early for us on August 31. We were up early and, after pulling up our trips and claymores, were ready to move out quickly. Charlie was waiting, and we had to move before he zeroed in on our platoon's position with a mortar. We saddled up and moved out, only to stop three minutes later. The point team found a body about fifty meters from our position. It was one of the NVA who, evidently, had died from our ambush the previous night. We called our CO to let him know we had a kill, as he was with Aztec or Cheyenne, which were located a few hundred yards behind and to the left of our position.

Patrolling an area with elephant grass. Note the defoliated trees from Agent Orange.

We started moving again and had not gone fifty meters when—THUNK! THUNK! A gook mortar tube! We DX'ed (took off) our rucks and hit the ground as all hell broke loose. We came under intense machine gun and AK fire.

The gut-clutching chill of death gripped me in the stomach, and I knew this was my first firefight. This was it! This was what I had been waiting for all these months. Now it was do or die! God, I only hoped and prayed I would survive it.

Shouts of "Medic! Medic! MEEEDICCC!" came from everywhere. I never hesitated. Grabbing my medic aid bag, I started crawling forward. One of my sergeants saw me and yelled, "Hey, stop! Don't go! It's too intense! Get down! GET DOWN!!"

"To hell with that!" I replied, "I'm going, I'm needed up there!"

As I crawled, I could hear the pop of the AK rounds as they sped past over my head. I crawled like an ant—close to the ground. Bullets were landing in front of and beside me, kicking up dirt.

Dan Webster, a grunt in my squad, was the first man I reached. He had been hit by a bullet in the left ankle. I felt for an exit wound and, by George, out popped the AK-47 round!

"Hey, here's a souvenir for you," I said as I handed him the round, which he put in his helmet band while grimacing in pain.

To my left came more screams for medic. After quickly bandaging Dan, I crawled toward them as bullets cracked by overhead.

Sgt. Luiz Martinez was next to the body of our new E-7 platoon sergeant, who had been hit in the upper chest and neck. He had two more wounds in the back and had clearly been shot by friendlies. This man had not endeared himself to anyone in Blackfoot Platoon. Now someone may have evened the score — or he had been hit in the crossfire.

"He's dead, Martinez."

"Are you sure?"

"Yeah!"

"Come on, Wise, check him again!"

"He's dead, man, can't ya see, I gotta go!"

I went through the motions of double-checking, but he was dead. Frantic screams of "Medic!" off to my right beckoned me. I crawled towards them.

I was pinned down by AK fire twice as I tried to reach the next man. Evidently the gooks had my number — and tried to zero in on me since I was the only grunt moving. Everyone else was keeping his head down and saying Hail Mary.

The next man I reached was badly wounded. He was a cherry, about nineteen years old, and had only been with us two to three weeks. This was the first time since joining Bravo Company that he had ever been in the jungle. It was to be his last. He had a wound under his right armpit and a wound in the leg. His wounded buddy held him for me as I worked on him. He was conscious and knew who I was. But his glassy eyes told me death was near. I got a bandage on his leg and side, but he died as I worked on him.

Just as he expired, a nearby gook threw a chicom at us that landed about ten feet away. The explosion threw shrapnel everywhere, but missed me.

I then worked on the man who had been holding the dead boy and patched him up when someone ran over to me under intense fire.

"Doc, listen, we need you badly, Chief is hurt."

Chief was my friend — my buddy. I ran in a crouching position, under fire, to where he lay. At this point, we could not have been further than twenty yards from the NVA's forward positions. Chief, who was our machine gunner at this time, had attempted a John Wayne–type move by standing up to fire at the gooks. He wanted so badly to be a hero, but all it got him were three U.S. Army machine gun bullets in the back. He had caught some of Aztec or Cheyenne's covering fire.

Chief was in a bad way. Shock had rendered him almost insane. He became my most difficult assignment so far. This man weighed about 240 pounds and did not want me, or anyone else, to touch him. He was screaming that I was going to kill him, screaming at me, "Get him away from me! Get the medic away, he's not helping me! He wants me to die!"

I grabbed him, shook him, and gave him several backhand slaps across his face — all to no avail. I couldn't get the bandages on him. He tore them off. He was positively insane with fury. I slugged him and screamed for help as AK bullets whistled all around me. Another grunt, along

8/30/69: E. Tayloe Wise as medic working on Joe Musgrove.

with one who had gone in search of me, held him down as another chicom grenade exploded about fifteen feet away, blowing shrapnel in every direction but somehow missing us. I had to do something fast. If I didn't, he would die. Finally, with the help of the other two men, I got the bandages on Chief as he weakened due to the loss of blood and shock.

After working on Chief, I realized that the firefight was over.

I was in charge of the dead and wounded. I directed what was left of Blackfoot to carry the WIAs and the KIAs to a central point for a medevac bird to pick them up. We had eighteen WIA and two KIA. I identified the dead, tagged them, and wrapped them up in their ponchos.

The medevac bird made three trips for the dead and wounded. The dead always went last as there was no rush to get them back to the rear. The only rush they would hear would be that of angels' wings, if there was a heaven in this hell where we were located. By this time, I was exhausted.

One other guy and I were the only medics out there. I had to patch up all the WIAs because the second medic, who was from Aztec or Cheyenne, could not get to our position until the medevac ship arrived.

About 1200 hours, we got ammo resupply, medical supplies and more cherries. Fresh meat for Charlie to chew up and spit out. These cherries wouldn't be virgins for long.

About 1400 hours, Cheyenne, which had hooked up with us after that morning's firefight, pointed out. Charlie was ready and waiting and opened up on them after they had moved about 200 meters. The ensuing firefight lasted all afternoon. It was heavy contact.

The other medic worked up front with Cheyenne while I remained in the rear at the medevac pad to take care of the dead and wounded, who were brought back to me.

About 30–45 minutes after Cheyenne had contact, a guy came running down the trotter to me and said, "Listen, we got a wounded man down here that needs you badly. He's on this trail."

Grabbing my aid bag, I ran 200 meters down the trotter and came upon a grunt who had been literally shot to shreds. I had never seen a guy with so many wounds. He had been left alone by the wayside as Cheyenne moved about 150 meters closer to the NVA positions. He had at least twenty shrapnel wounds all over his body, so I set to work to patch him up. Our position was dangerous because we were in a no-man's-land with Cheyenne about 150 meters away and Blackfoot at least 200 meters back down the trotter. It was a perfect time for a sniper, and we were the most logical targets. It wasn't long before we came under sniper fire, and I had to lay low while working on the guy. It took me at least 30 minutes to patch him up because I had to cut his clothes off to get at the wounds and dodge the sniper bullets at the same time. The other guy, who had originally summoned me, returned the sporadic sniper fire. Somehow, we got the wounded man on a poncho and, under fire, ran back to the medevac pad as we dragged him behind us.

The dead and injured from Cheyenne started to trickle in to the medavac pad. Some grunts carried in two KIAs. Thinking one of them was alive as they brought him in, I rushed over to administer first aid.

"What's wrong? Where's he hit?"

"He's gone, Doc."

Indeed he was. His glassy eyes stared out at me as his bloodstained chest and the dark dried blood on his fatigue shirt indicated where three AK rounds had nailed him. One arm was blown off. Unceremoniously, they dumped the body and moved back to the front lines. In the intensely sweltering heat of the day, I had to run forward some 300–400 meters several times that afternoon to get the wounded. It took six men to carry one grunt. You never know how heavy a man is until you start carrying him. It's all pure dead weight.

When one of the medevac birds came in that afternoon, the prop wash from its rotors blew off my last pair of glasses. Now I was totally without glasses, with no hope of getting another pair anytime soon. They landed somewhere but, try as we might, we were unable to locate them in the tall, thick elephant grass. So, now I really was a blind mouse humping around in the jungle. I put in a rush order for more, but didn't expect any miracles.

Besides getting shot at on the ground, Charlie had to contend with smoke on his ass from jets making napalm air strikes on his positions all afternoon. When the jets weren't pounding the shit out of him, the Cobras were unloading their rockets on his ass. We were making the NVA pay heavily (we hoped) for killing our men. Under this protection, Cheyenne and Aztec were finally able, by dusk, to push into the bunker complex, which the NVA had been defending, and secure it. Blackfoot, after medevacing all the dead and wounded, moved up and joined them to set up for the night.

For me, it had been one hell of a Sunday. It was definitely *no* church picnic. Never in my life had I ever imagined a firefight could be so terrible. Little did I know then that I had earned my first Bronze Star, which read as follows:

> For heroism, not involving participation in aerial flight, in connection with military operations against a hostile force in the Republic of Vietnam. Specialist Four Wise distinguished himself by exceptionally valorous action on 31 August 1969, while serving as a rifleman during reconnaissance mission in the Republic of Vietnam. When his unit came under intense enemy fire by a numerically superior enemy force, in the initial contact several men were seriously wounded and unable to withdraw from the killing zone due to enemy fire. By employing fire and movement, Specialist Four Wise and several members of the gun team were able to move into defensive fighting positions and began placing effective fire on the enemy. He then began to move forward under the intense fire to recover the wounded. As he and the other men returned with the last of the wounded, the enemy attempted to assault their positions, but were repelled by the effective fire put out by Specialist Four Wise. His display of personal bravery and devotion to duty is in keeping with the highest traditions of the military service, and reflects great credit upon himself, his unit, and the United States Army.

Seventy-five percent of this citation was not true, but particular medals had to follow a certain form and style. I was not serving as a rifleman, but as a medic. My MOS, however, had not been changed, so, technically, I was still a rifleman. In no way did I employ any type of fire and movement. I was too damn busy patching up the wounded. We were pinned down, and I was the only one moving around with any regularity. No one else moved forward — they stayed where they were for fear of taking lead. At no time during that battle in the morning had the enemy tried to assault us. One threw a chicom at me. But they certainly didn't try to overrun us.

Unfortunately, my first firefight with Charlie was to turn out to be one long continuous battle that would slowly decimate Bravo Company.

Monday, September 1, dawned early. We were in the heart of Charlie's country. We had pushed him out of a bunker complex that he had heavily defended, and he was determined to kick some ass. Again, Blackfoot was to take the brunt of Charlie's wrath. He was not going to let us off easy. We saddled up and started to move out. Within fifteen seconds of the command to move out, shots rang out and AK bullets cracked by overhead.

Our point man that day was the dark-complexioned man from the island of Guam, Vic Tenorio. Vic, who had black hair, dark skin, and Oriental-type eyes, could have easily passed for an NVA. For some reason, he had his pot (helmet) off and was walking down the trotter about fifteen yards in front of the next grunt when he saw three gooks walking toward him. Thinking he was a gook, they started to wave and yell at him. Vic waved casually, nonchalantly brought his M-16 up to hip level and shot the first gook in the chest, killing him outright.

All hell then broke loose.

"Medic!"

I had DX'ed my pack and started to run forward with my medic bag. Lead was flying everywhere, and I could hear bullets whistling and cracking by my head. The first man I reached had been shot in the shoulder. I stuffed dressings on the wound, bandaged it and assisted him to the rear.

"Doc! CO's down!"

"Damn," I said to myself. "That is some bad shit."

Under extremely intense fire, I ran forward and found Capt. Mooneyham gritting his teeth after taking an AK round in his upper left thigh. I patched up the CO, who grimaced from the pain as he continued to direct his men. Capt. Mooneyham, who had received his commission through a college ROTC program, had been a gentle and good man who thought of his men's safety above all else. Whenever the situation had been a question of safety, Capt. Mooneyham had taken the time to cautiously check it out. I cried inwardly as I bandaged him up. For this would be the last time we would see him. He was out of it now. No one who could equal his compassion would replace him. He would be sorely missed.

I took charge of the wounded and moved them to the rear as artillery rounds came screaming down within twenty-five yards of our positions. Our FO was taking no chances and shrapnel flew everywhere, forcing us to keep our heads low. Somehow, we managed to medevac our wounded men and, afterwards, pulled back into the bunker complex, both for protection and to regroup.

That afternoon, I wrote home:

8/30/69: Vic Tenorio outside his sleeping hooch.

> These firefights were real battles. I mean ... bullets flying ... shrapnel going by ... grenades being thrown. Believe me ... I can't understand it, but I wasn't scared or afraid! I didn't have time to think about that (fear). I was too busy patching men up.

Again, fear had somehow, inexplicably, taken a back seat. I could not explain it then — I cannot explain it now. Fear was the farthest thought from my mind as death zinged by overhead. My total concentration was centered on my buddies, my friends, my commanders. They, and they alone, needed my help. I had to give of myself by aiding my fellow man. That became my main drive and purpose in Nam. If I accomplished nothing else in life, at least I saved human life.

We sat tight in the bunker complex until late afternoon. At that time, we were ordered to push forward another 100 meters into the complex before setting up our night log. We later learned that Charlie Company, which was operating nearby, had discovered an NVA telephone line that connected two NVA companies. The men of Charlie Company were instructed to tap the line and, with the aid of their Vietnamese interpreter, they soon learned that the NVA had Bravo Company's position in the bunker complex zeroed in and that they were going to nail us with mortars. Bravo was alerted in time, hence our 100-meter shift to avert a possible tragedy. As we were setting up, the distinctive sound of an NVA mortar tube assailed our ears from about 200 meters away.

THUNK! THUNK! THUNK!

The NVA fired 15–20 rounds at us. At the time most of us in Bravo Company had no idea that we, specifically, were Charlie's intended victims, but we found his bunkers comfortable to use as hideouts. As usual, the NVA mortar men missed us by a mile. They were such bad shots that we rarely worried about an enemy mortar barrage. We called artillery in on the suspected enemy position, but I am sure that, by the time our calling cards arrived, Charlie had didied because he was famous for shooting his wad and then taking off. I could not blame him. This was guerilla warfare at the basic level — hit and run. The NVA, while poor in aim, employed excellent tactical maneuvers, whereas we were like bird dogs that plod on and on, looking for the fallen victim. Charlie hit fast and vanished by melting away into the surrounding jungle. What he lacked in numbers and supplies, he more than made up for in his ability to choose the field of battle. We were not fighting a stupid enemy. He was cunning, clever, ingenious, and persevering. It is difficult to succeed against such odds, as the British found out in 1776 when they marched against their American foes, who employed guerilla tactics similar to those used by the NVA almost 200 years later. We were fighting Charlie on his terms — not ours. There was no way we could win. How do you fight a ghost? How can you fight someone who strikes and then melts away? You can't. The toll will always be high in such situations. We grunts knew it was a useless endeavor. We were pawns — nothing more. We were the sacrificial goats that the American military machine offered up to the god of death. Charlie fought to gain control of Southeast Asia's breadbasket — the Mekong Delta. We opposed him because the Domino Theory dictated that communism had to be stopped, but all we were really doing was increasing the profits of the American corporations, and enhancing the stature of a military machine that badly needed a little no-name war to polish its image.

I was finding my job of medic to be most rewarding. It gave me a purpose in life. I wrote home,

> Really ... all I'm doing is my job. I can't tell you how happy I am at being a combat medic. The job is physically tiring, but I feel so good being by a man's side and patching him up. For once I've found something I enjoy ... I only hope you won't be worried about me. I'm doing a job that I have to do. I don't think about being wounded as I move to help guys. I'm thinking — what can I do to help them. Saving a human life is a wonderful feeling and I saved a few yesterday. I love you.

The ending to that letter was indicative of the stress I was under. In most of my letters home, I never showed or indicated any emotion toward my parents. Yet death was perched upon my shoulder. That ending, more than any other, showed that I did not expect to survive Nam intact. It told my parents that I wanted them to know, above all else, I had tried. I wanted them to know that, should I die, which I fully expected to happen, I was thankful for what they had done for me in my short life.

It is impossible to describe the feeling one derives from saving human life. If you have never done so, then you cannot possibly envision what it is like. It is as if a light shines down upon you and gives you a power to accomplish something impossible. The knowledge that something you did enabled you to save someone — to give them their life back — can enable you to rise above and beyond the call of duty.

On September 2, Blackfoot led out again for the third day in a row. We were tough — we were ready. We were going to burn Charlie. Only he fucked us before we could light the match. We had another scout dog with us that led off as we glided down another well-traveled trotter. After advancing about 300 meters, the dog smelled NVA as we came to a small clearing.

"Down!"

We hit it as two NVA opened up on us. They missed.

I was in the rear of the file and the oldest man in country. I had a bunch of cherries around me whom I directed, because most of our NCOs were gone. The NVA snipers had missed and there were no calls for "Medic!" Thank God! I was beginning to dread that call.

We decided to cut the crap. We assaulted the NVA in force and they withdrew. We pushed ahead and secured still another bunker complex. Cheyenne and Aztec were then directed to come up, pass us, and forge ahead. We were glad of this development as we were just a little more than tired of taking the brunt of Charlie's efforts to kill us.

While this was happening, one of the guys in our platoon spotted a gook sneaking up on us and opened up on him. Simultaneously, firing from Aztec and Cheyenne erupted to our front. The gook went down from our firing but a real firefight broke out forward as an NVA machine gun position pinned down our men.

Five guys in Blackfoot had seen where the wounded NVA had fallen and, laying down a blanket of fire, they rushed forward towards his position.

"Medic!"

I moved to the rear to find one slightly perforated NVA, with five or six bullet wounds in one leg and a real nice bullet hole in his left ass cheek.

Our men stripped the NVA of every stitch of clothes. We were taking no chances whatsoever of his concealing any hidden weapons. I patched him up, and we dragged him unceremoniously back to our position.

Then I learned some bad news. While I had been working on the NVA, the other forward men in Blackfoot had been fighting. Two more grunts had been killed and a 2nd lieutenant had been shot in the back. He was in bad shape, in lots of pain, and had just been assigned to our Company the previous day, so he did not last long. That was no miracle considering the circumstances of our posture the last few days. One of the KIAs was a man who had been in country nine months. The other, a PFC, had taken a bullet in the head and never knew what hit him. He had only been with us three days. I wondered, as I took charge of wrapping the dead, where my bullet was and when it would find me.

The medevac could not land. We were in extremely thick jungle. So, the bird had to lower a webbed basket-type seat, called a jungle penetrator. We got the 2nd Looey and the wounded NVA onto the medevac ship. The KIA would have to wait. I asked several guys to cut some eight-foot-long poles that would be stout enough to carry the weight of the dead bodies. After tying the dead up in their ponchos, I attached them to the poles. Then other grunts and I placed the poles on our shoulders and carried the bodies. This had a profound effect upon me. I wrote my parents that:

> It was a gruesome task. Today I just got sick. I've seen so much death in the last three days that I'm tired and scared. I want to get out of here. Our company is hurting. In three days, we've been in five firefights. We've lost six KIA and at least 25 WIA. So, we are hurting badly.

Yes, we were hurting badly. Bravo Company rarely fielded more than 90 men — usually we only had 60–75 able-bodied infantrymen. In just three short days, 33 percent of it had been KO'ed. We were down for the count. Life was taking a turn for the worst, with Bravo Company taking the brunt of the fall. For three and a half months (the time I had been with Bravo) we had been lucky. Now friends were losing friends. Cherries took people's places as fast as the eye could blink. It was all so disheartening and demoralizing. Would anything be left of us? We were being added to the fire like kindling.

Struggling under the weight of the bodies, frequently changing places because the poles bit into our shoulders and made them raw, we finally reached a clearing where we set up for the night.

September 3 dawned early for us. It was difficult to find someone familiar to talk to because there were so many new faces— so many cherries. The cherries were being thrown into the fire as fast as the Cav could

9/3/69: Loading dead and wounded on a Huey.

shuffle them off the Freedom Birds. What these new guys must have thought, or felt, is a mystery to me. I am sure most were scared to death. War makes men think most irrational thoughts and do strange things.

That morning, as we waited for the log bird that would resupply us and take the dead bodies off our hands, a lone shot rang out.

"Medic!"

I rushed over and found a young kid who had shot himself in the foot. "What a stupid idiot this guy is," I thought to myself. "He's got to be a damn fool!"

Gritting his teeth in pain, he said, "Well, I was just itching my foot with my rifle, and it went off, but it was on safety."

"Sure, sure," we all said to ourselves.

His foot was shot to shreds. When he asked if he was OK, I lied and told him he was. His foot, however, was completely blasted and he would probably never have full use of it again. That bullet had broken almost every bone in his lower foot. It turned out, however, that he did indeed have a defective M-16. We took his rifle, cleared it, put it on safety, and fired it. It fired easily despite the fact that it was on safety. So, he "probably" had not wounded himself on purpose. The log bird arrived and, after off-loading it, we put him and the two KIAs aboard.

That log bird brought us a new CO, a West Point graduate who had just finished serving a tour in Germany. As far as I was concerned he did not know his ass from a hole in the ground. He demonstrated a complete lack of common sense as far as being a leader, and was insensitive to the health and safety of his men. Vietnam should have taught him something, but it didn't. As was common with military college graduates, he thought and acted as if he was better than everyone else. We were the swine he was in command of, and he was determined to send us to the slaughterhouse.

I will not deny that the military needs leaders. Plus, it needs well-trained college-educated leaders. What it does not need are men who think that, because they are Annapolis, Colorado Springs, or West Point graduates, they are above the *hoi polloi*. Such officers are insensitive to the needs of their men and are arrogantly unwilling to take any kind of advice. These men believe that they know the answer to every problem. In Nam, things just did not work that way. Leaders who fucked over their men, or failed to heed their advice, eventually ended up getting fucked. As a leader in a combat situation, you *cannot* and *must* not be imperious. If you are, then woe be unto you, for you will reap the revenge of your comrades in arms, as had our E-7 platoon sergeant on August 31. A good leader listens to his men and, sometimes, follows their suggestions or advice. Any individual who ignores the safety of his men, who disregards their observations or advice, as our West Pointer did, deserves to die. I do not know if our new West Point CO survived Nam, because I left the field and never saw him again. But he definitely needed to be taken down a peg or two. He thought, because he was a West Pointer, that he was right and everyone else was wrong. He just did not know how to take advice. While this may have been his first combat command, it still did not provide him with the excuse to be so unbending.

On the first day with our new West Point CO, September 4, we humped two and a half klicks to an open field where slicks picked us up and CA'ed us to an LZ about a mile from Ike. It was almost night when we landed, so we found ourselves setting up in the dark.

My second longest day in Vietnam occurred on September 5, 1969. Aztec and Cheyenne moved out independent of Blackfoot. Our job was to sit tight and hope to knock off a few NVA in an ambush. It was to be the last time we would see many of our buddies.

Aztec and Cheyenne were to have the misfortune of walking into an

NVA ambush and, before they knew what had hit them, were almost wiped out by what was later estimated to be several NVA battalions numbering approximately 500–700 men. Our people never had a chance.

Charlie's bunker positions in this area were constructed in a "V" pattern as shown in the following diagram:

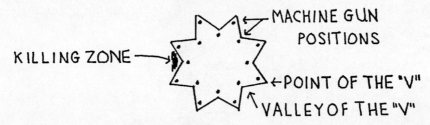

Instead of stumbling onto the point of the "V", Aztec and Cheyenne unsuspectingly entered the valley and were entirely within the killing zone before Charlie opened up. A killing zone is an area that one cannot reasonably expect to enter and leave alive. It is like being hemmed in on all sides and having someone take potshots at you, while you run around in circles. The situation was reminiscent of the Charge of the Light Brigade when the British were decimated at Balaklava during the Crimean War in 1854. Only we were not charging ahead for glory, God and country; we inadvertently happened to stumble upon an entrenched enemy position filled with little yellow men who were ready, willing and able to annihilate us. Our West Point CO would have passed rather easily for the British Earl of Cardigan that day.

Charlie patiently waited until Aztec and Cheyenne were well within the killing zone, almost at his outer perimeter, before he opened fire from well-camouflaged positions.

The Aztec and Cheyenne grunts never stood a chance. Our men never knew, or had any inkling, that they were so near an NVA complex. When the NVA opened up on our men with everything they had — AKs, machine guns, etc. — three grunts died in the initial burst of fire. Our guys DX'ed their rucksacks and hugged the ground. Everyone was pinned down. The new West Pointer lost control — he did not know what to do. Two quick-thinking sergeants yelled for everyone to crawl out and retreat.

As the men crawled out, the captain ordered them to do a flanking maneuver (movement to one side or the other). Charlie had anticipated such and was waiting. The remaining men crawled right into another ambush that the NVA had set up to their rear. One grunt took a bullet to the head and, with his brains strewn over the ground, died instantly.

What was left of Aztec and Cheyenne, after such a devastating attack, pulled back even more. The ambush was so intense, so fierce and heavy, that our men had been forced to abandon everything they had. All they had left were their M-16s and clips of ammo. All their food, water, claymores, extra ammo, radios, etc., lay back in the killing zone alongside the three dead. The battleground is outlined below:

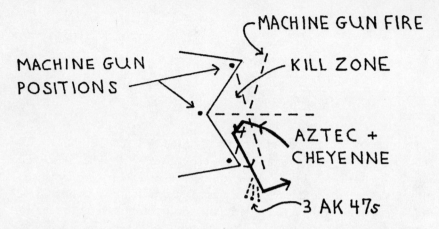

Our new Company commander was totally freaked out. So massive had the devastation been to his command, that I doubt he ever fully recovered. He was so confused that he probably forgot he still had Blackfoot, which was set up a good klick away, as a reserve force. He was bewildered, in shock, after being almost wiped out. I cannot blame him for this. He, too, was a cherry, and this was only his second day in the field; to put it simply, he got his ass kicked. No one could possibly have expected him to perform well under such circumstances. It was an impossible tragedy that could not be avoided. For anyone to expect otherwise would be a grievous error in judgment. The man never had a chance. How can any leader be expected to perform well under such trying circumstances? Especially since he did not know his officers, NCOs, or grunts, and what they were (or were not) capable of doing. Some might condemn him for losing control, but I cannot. He was placed in an untenable position.

Lt. Hill had been following the action via the Company radio until it fell silent. We did not know why it had gone dead, but figured the radioman was down. Little did we realize that both Aztec's and Cheyenne's platoon radios had been abandoned. So, now we were totally out of touch with the rest of our Company. We knew they were in contact, but had no idea how badly they were getting their asses kicked.

Using his own initiative, Lt. Hill decided to move us up to assist Aztec and Cheyenne.

The inevitable happened.

Prior to abandoning everything they had, Aztec and Cheyenne, while pinned down, had called in artillery and Cobra strikes. The Cobras were working over the area in front of the two beleaguered platoons to try and stifle the intensity of the NVA ambush and protect what was left of Aztec and Cheyenne.

Blackfoot could not communicate with the rest of the Company. We could talk directly with battalion, so we were not totally cut off.

One of the avenging Cobras spotted our movement in the jungle. The pilot, thinking we were NVA, decided to make a run at us. We had no idea what was happening until he opened up on us.

We hit the ground as he made his first pass, firing his machine guns, grenades and rockets. Explosions landed on both sides of us, not twenty feet away. He turned to make another run on us.

Our radioman screamed frantically to battalion to call off the Cobra. Sgt. David H. McNerney, the CMH winner, was about five feet in front of me. As we lay flat on the ground, I can vividly remember the Cobra's machine gun bullets striking the ground in a line every six inches, as they passed right between us when the Cobra made its second run. Miraculously no one in the platoon had been hit. I am sure, had the Cobra made a third run, that our number would have been up, but luckily battalion got through in time.

Approaching the scene of the battle, I saw an unforgettable sight. A medevac had come in to take out some of our wounded. As the medevacs could not land, they had to hover and send down jungle penetrators to hoist up the wounded. With their big red crosses clearly painted on both sides, they were sitting ducks as they hovered above the jungle canopy. Charlie couldn't have cared less that they were medical birds; to him they represented the enemy, and he had no intention of respecting the red cross painted on them. The NVA opened up on the medevac slick and hit it. When we were within sight of this, we could see that the medevac was on fire as a body hung in a jungle penetrator about fifteen feet beneath it. Flames leaped from the wounded bird. The bird was trying to escape, and its gunners were futilely replying to the NVA attack, knowing that, in a few minutes or seconds, when the ship crashed, they all might be dead. The burning ship was trying to get out of the contact area, but we could see it was going down. The pilot tried frantically to make a nearby field. Whether or not he did, I don't know. All I know is that we heard the ship crash and later learned that the body in the sling was Lt. K, the Hawaiian, who had taken three bullets in the chest. He did not survive. Lt. K's death was just another nail in the coffin. It was to discourage us even more.

Now the stark reality of Nam hit us full in the face. If you were wounded, you now knew Charlie was going to try his best to shoot down the medevac evacuating you and your comrades. The little bastard could have cared less about observing international law and respecting a medical mercy ship. What hopes and dreams we had that we would be safely removed from the scene of battle were dashed by this chain of events. It was just one more reason to hate the gooks a little more. We would make Charlie pay whenever we could.

As Blackfoot moved to link up with the other two platoons, our point man found a wounded NVA.

"Medic!"

I hurried forward to treat an NVA who had his entire right arm, between the elbow and the hand, blown off. The hand was just hanging by a thread of flesh. Evidently one of the Cobras had done its job. I applied a tourniquet on the guy and then, because we were pissed as hell about what was happening to us, we forced him to march with us to where we could link up with what remained of our Company. There was no way we were going to carry this son of a bitch. He marched with us, just in front of me. Another grunt sort of held him by his hurt arm and propelled him forward as I covered him from behind with my M-16.

When we linked up with Aztec and Cheyenne, I learned that Roger Pratt, the senior Ben Casey, from Libertyville, Illinois, had been wounded in the leg. Now I was the only medic left in the Company. There were dead NVA everywhere. I saw the body of the fourth KIA, whose brains were oozing out of a gaping hole in the side of what had once been his head. Morale was extremely low. Our men had no food or water and three more grunts lay dead somewhere to our front.

We cut a landing pad for a medevac ship. I was in charge of the POW. After taking care of all the wounded, I waited in a bomb crater with him for the medevac bird to arrive. When it appeared, the NVA, who were extremely close by, opened up on it and on us. Bullets whined by overhead. I flipped my M-16 to rock 'n' roll and placed it against the POW's head. Had the NVA overrun us, I would have died knowing that I took at least one of them with me. The look of sheer terror on his face was a joy to see. I wanted that son of a bitch to know I had no hesitation about shooting his ass to hell.

The medevac chopper hovered about five feet off the ground as the crew chiefs fired over our heads into the wood line. The medevac had to make two or three trips for all the wounded. On the last trip, I pushed the POW forward. He was incredibly eager to get on that bird! Somehow, with all the pain he must have been in, he found the strength to climb aboard the hovering ship. The chopper personnel dragged him in, but he was scrambling in as fast as possible. This time we got our wounded out without losing a ship.

That night, Friday, September 5, was, next to the night on Becky, the longest night of my life. We set up in a perimeter. The situation was tense. We had forty men left in the Company, were fully convinced that we would be overrun, and had been told that there was more than a good possibility that might indeed happen. Word came down that, if we survived a human wave attack, we were to head out on a 240° azimuth until we reached the junction of two streams. We were told to wait no more than eight hours at that point. By that time any stragglers, or survivors, should have made it to the stream junction to regroup. From there, if no one came, we would proceed to LZ Barbara. Our only problem was, how the hell did we know where the 240° azimuth was in the middle of the goddamn jungle? Especially at night! Those who lived probably would not have a compass. Plus, it was so damn easy to get lost in the jungle — not to mention how easy it would have been to stumble upon some NVA and get killed, or worse yet, be taken prisoner.

I can vividly remember looking up at the stars that night and praying to God by saying, "Please God, let me live until tomorrow morning. Please don't let us all die." I had never been much of a religious person for the last ten years or so. I had gone from agnostic to atheistic beliefs. I really did not believe God existed. On the night of September 5, 1969, I started to believe in God again. My faith in Him has never wavered since that night. Somehow, He must have heard my prayer.

I spent that night behind and almost underneath a fallen tree, where I had dug a foxhole. A half hour after I dug in, as the day joined night, when shapes can barely be distinguished, an NVA tried to crawl up to our position right in front of me. One of the nearby men spotted and fragged him. We also let loose with a volley of bullets for good measure. The next morning we found his body about fifteen feet away from our position.

The next morning we were up early. A lot of us were hungry and thirsty because Blackfoot had been forced to share its food and water with the men of Aztec and Cheyenne. We were extremely low on water, and we did not like being low on water in that jungle inferno. We had received ammo and medical resupply, but no food or water. Needless to say, there were a lot of pissed-off grunts. We were sure the LTC was punishing us for getting our asses kicked so badly. We thought that the man was a maniac. All he wanted was more dead Charlies. His unbending philosophy seemed to be, "Fuck how many grunts have died, just get me more kills." I noticed that he never came out in the field anymore, he just flew around in his chopper.

Blackfoot, which had been decimated already and transfused with cherries, was to bear the brunt of the day's work. The powers that be had decided we would attempt to enter the bunker complex at a different point from the one that had been Aztec's and Cheyenne's ill-fated and aborted entrance. For three long, hot, grueling, thirsty hours, we attempted to maneuver ourselves into a position for entry. Finally, after inching forward about 150 meters, we reached the edge of the complex undetected. Now, no sooner had we found a way in, than our cherry CO changed his mind. He told us to turn around and come back out. Boy, were we pissed. Upon linking back up with what remained of our Company, we learned our great and glorious CO had decided to lead the residue of Aztec and Cheyenne back into the area where they had been ambushed the preceding day.

I am sure Charlie was waiting for us with a smirk upon his face.

Aztec and Cheyenne were shot up again. The NVA repulsed them and wounded two more grunts who were not only E-6 sergeants but also platoon leaders; so they pulled back. Cobras, jets, and artillery were called in to soften up the enemy positions. Besides dropping napalm, the jets also dropped tear gas bombs and, as the CS wafted through the jungle, we could faintly smell it.

I moved up to aid the wounded. One of the sergeants had already received an ampule of morphine for the nasty wound on his right elbow from another grunt who, like me, had volunteered to be a medic. I prepared a stretcher, and we moved both men to the rear — one could walk and the other we carried — to await the arrival of a medevac. As we moved the men back to the medevac area, the NVA started firing mortars at us. Luckily, the mortar rounds landed about seventy-five meters away. For some reason, it took a long time for the medevac to arrive. The morphine began to wear off so my charge was in some pain. I was faced with giving my first shot. If you have not been trained how to give a shot, if you hate needles as much as I do, then you can understand my predicament. My stomach was queasy. This was going to hurt me a lot more than him. I stuck the syrette in but the needle only traveled about an eighth of an inch into his arm.

"Sorry 'bout that."

"That's OK, just *jab* it in, Doc!"

"OK."

I withdrew the syrette and then jabbed it hard. The needle went in all the way! I squeezed the morphine out and withdrew the ampule.

Thank goodness, just about dark, the medevac bird arrived. I got him and four more wounded men out on that ship. I did not want to give any more needles!

The day had passed quickly and evening fell as Blackfoot moved away from the medevac area to link up with Aztec and Cheyenne. It was so dark that four NVA tried to slip in and follow behind us. Lt. Hill noticed something was awry and opened up on them. One NVA threw a chicom as another died in his tracks.

The exploding chicom sent shrapnel everywhere. One of our guys took some in the side of his head. I rushed back to find him slightly wounded. He was OK, and I bandaged him up. As the wound was not serious enough to call in a medevac, I made him sleep next to me that night so, if he needed help, I would be nearby.

By the next morning, September 7, we had been without food and water for three days. The powers that be finally relented and sent it to us. We were completely drained. LTC Lewis had flown in ammo resupply but not one drop of water. We drank as much as we could and filled our canteens. After this experience, we were not sure when, if ever, we would receive more water.

Once we were resupplied, Blackfoot saddled up and made ready to push into the bunker complex again. Cheyenne led off because, by this point in time, Aztec Platoon no longer existed — it had, to all intents and purposes, been wiped out. Out of thirty men, only seven remained from Aztec, and those men were taken and divided between Cheyenne and Blackfoot. Aztec had ceased to exist. Why Cheyenne had to bear the brunt of leading off again, when Blackfoot was almost at full strength, is a mystery. Perhaps it was because the three bodies up ahead, which still had to be recovered, were originally men from Cheyenne.

Cheyenne attempted to push into the NVA stronghold only to meet with fierce resistance. The NVA still had at least two machine gun positions, which continued to pin down our men. Under such heavy fire, we had no choice but to withdraw. The CO called in more jets with napalm, artillery, and Blue Max strikes and had more CS bombs dropped. That day Charlie's positions had the shit pounded out of them. We wanted those bodies and were going to recover them no matter what, even if we decimated the rest of the Company to do so. During these strikes, help in the form of Charlie Company arrived. They had been moving steadily toward us for two days and finally linked up on our left flank to support us. They were, indeed, a sight for sore eyes, and we all breathed an inward sigh of relief at this reinforcement because we knew we were in bad shape.

We needed all the help we could possibly get. By now, there was not much left of Bravo Company. We had suffered over 65–70 percent casualties with at least 43 WIA and 11 KIA during the last eight days. There was nothing left of us. Beaten, tired, hungry, demoralized, we could care less about recovering those bodies, or pushing Charlie out of his well-entrenched and fortified position. The relief was welcome because we had taken enough punishment. We did not want any more crap thrown at us by the NVA. Bravo Company had lost so many experienced men that we were coming apart at the seams. The new faces of all the cherries only reminded us of our failure and made us "old-timers" uneasy at having to cope with so many inexperienced grunts. Not knowing these cherries, or their capabilities, made the rest of us old-timers distrust them even more. If you did not know a man, you did not know how much you could depend on him.

In a widely circulated newspaper article by Peter Arnett and Horst Faas, dated September 7, 1969, from LZ Ike, one of the Cav's battalion commanders was quoted as he spoke to some raw recruits who had just arrived on Ike. He told them that they would hate LZ Ike because they were "sitting on a bull's eye" and were evenly matched with the enemy forces opposing them.* What he conveniently "forgot" to mention was the fact that the U.S. Army had just had the shit kicked out of it and had been forced to abandon Firebase Becky. He also neglected to tell them that we were not evenly matched with Charlie. We were playing in Charlie's backyard, and he was stomping the shit out of us on his home turf. While we may have been better supplied and equipped, Charlie still held an ace up his sleeve. He knew where and when to pick a fight and how to melt away into the jungle. He had well-built positions that could withstand anything except B-52 strikes. The loss of men meant little to Charlie because of his philosophy about life. Therefore, mentally, losing men did not affect him like it did us. For that time and place, he was the best fighting man we could have engaged in battle. You never got the best of Charlie. He could retreat, lick his wounds, and fight another day. The NVA were indeed past masters at fighting a guerilla war. The damages they could inflict in a firefight were enough to satisfy them. Charlie fought behind positions that were well constructed, strong, and from which it was impossible to dislodge him. He was a determined foe, and there was absolutely no way, short of an H-bomb on Hanoi, that we would beat him at his own game. This knowledge gnawed away at us. We were being sacrificed by our country—dying in vain.

I have no hesitation in making the statement about our dying in vain. We lost 58,193 men in Vietnam (of which 10,800 were "non-related" war deaths) to a useless cause. The mothers, fathers, wives, etc., of America

---

*Peter Arnett and Horst Faas, "Draftees Receive 'Bull's-Eye' Baptism," *Richmond (VA) Times Dispatch*, 7 September 1969, sec. A, p. 1.

offered up their youth for a lost cause. We bled and died for nothing in Vietnam. We veterans have a right to be bitter. We have a right to expect more from our country because of that sad fact. Our country owes us. We fought in the first war our country resoundingly lost. We got our asses kicked for nothing—and it was all in vain. Yes, the mothers and fathers and leaders of America can take pride in the fact that they sent their young men off to fight in a no-win situation. I know, because of what happened to me in Vietnam, I will **NEVER** lift another gun to defend America as long as I live, unless the United States is physically invaded. I would counsel young men of draft age and young women, if faced with another Vietnam-type situation, to resist — to go to Canada or prison, so that they will not be offered up on the altar of sacrifice for a nation that will not be grateful. We fought and we died, but for what? There is no acceptable reason my country can offer to me for what it perpetrated upon us. I can really empathize with America's black population because of this. They had to put up with slavery and then, upon gaining their hard-won freedom, had to rise to meet the still-present challenges of discrimination. We Vietnam vets were enslaved by our military and political system and then chained to hoe the rice paddies of Southeast Asia. We became American's 20th-century slavery system. It is time for the slaves to rise up and strike down their masters. America's leaders and politicians must have the fear of God put to them. Another travesty must not be foisted upon us ever again. We can be strong, but we do not have to send our young men off to fight someone else's war. We Vietnam veterans owe it to ourselves and our country to ensure that the system does not fuck over America's youth again. We must use the ballot box wisely to elect individuals who will think before they inadvertently place us in another untenable position.

Late on the afternoon of the 7th Charlie Company moved up, pushed into the bunker complex, met no resistance, and secured it. Blackfoot moved up and located the three bodies. The gooks had had plenty of time to search the area and they had taken most of the equipment and ammunition, which our guys had abandoned during the ambush of the 5th.

As senior Ben Casey, I was in charge of taking care of the dead. After three days of lying on the hot, steamy, humid jungle floor, the bodies were rank and emitted an overpowering stench. Bloated, maggot filled, and decomposing, they were almost totally unrecognizable. The stench of the rotting bodies was so powerful that we were forced to wear gas masks that still did not totally wipe out the nauseous smell of decomposition. Maggots crawled out of the eye sockets and filled the mouths. The bodies were so swollen by decomposition that their clothing bulged and appeared ready to burst at the seams and spew forth disease. It was sickening. Several of us vomited as we placed the bloated bodies in ponchos and wrapped them up. I directed several guys to cut some stout poles. We then tied the remains to the poles so that we could carry the dead to a PZ. At this time, I learned that one of the dead men, an infantryman named Joe E. Stevenson, from Atlanta, had been in my basic training company at Fort Benning, when I first joined the Army. I had seen him once or twice prior to his death, but was unsure of his name. Now I knew it. I did not know either of the other two men, but one had the nickname of Pooh Bear.

The onerous task of carrying the bodies to a PZ fell upon us. The pole bearers were forced to wear gas masks and change often because the poles bit deeply into our shoulders and the smell made us all nauseous. It took us all day to move approximately 300 meters. The dead held us down. The dead men's heads were not fully covered and, every so often, we used our insect spray on the heads in a fruitless attempt to kill the thousands of maggots.

That evening we stumbled upon another bunker complex. My platoon sergeant, Luiz Martinez, from California, surprised an NVA who was hiding in one of the bunkers. The NVA didied as Martinez shot at and missed him. The NVA, however, scored with a chicom that exploded, hitting Martinez in the chest and face. We took care of him, and, because his wounds did not appear to be too serious, we did not call for a medevac. All went well until about 2100 hours when Martinez started choking, hemorrhaging, and having convulsions. We were forced to call a medevac. It was raining cats and dogs, and the medevac bird took four hours to find us. When it finally located our position, it hovered overhead and sent down a jungle penetrator. We got Martinez out. Then, with the three bodies lying about five feet away from me — because I was in charge of them — I laid down to sleep after I had once again sprayed each head to kill more maggots. The rotting corpses reeked of decomposition. It was a miserable night. I was bone tired, incredibly wet, and, to top it all off, I had to sleep next to three dead men.

On September 8, we reached a clearing. In the process of getting there, we crossed three rain-swollen streams. Getting the dead across each watercourse proved to be difficult and time consuming because the water came up to our necks, was swift, and tugged at the bodies. As I placed the bodies on the birds, I pitied the poor morticians who would have to prepare the remains for shipment back to the World. How anyone could stand them long enough to positively identify them would be a task in itself. Sadly, those would be closed-coffin funerals.

The slicks CA'ed us to Ike and from there a Chinook carried us to Tay Ninh for a well-deserved two-day R & R on the 8th and 9th. At that time,

I was told that Captain Mooney-ham had recommended me for a Silver Star for rushing to his aid and bandaging him up. I never received it. It did not matter to me because I was not over there for glory or medals, but I now wish I had received it, because I was proud of being a medic. It meant something to me. I had such a great feeling of accomplishment. I loved helping people in pain a hell of a lot. It was, and is, a wonderfully rewarding experience. While in Tay Ninh, my superiors told me that they were trying to have my MOS changed to that of a combat medic, and that I was being nominated for a combat medical badge. I received neither because, by the time the Army got around to doing something about it, I was out of the boonies.

E. Tayloe Wise riding in the doorway of a Huey helicopter.

Tay Ninh provided only a brief respite for our Company. Our hated battalion lieutenant-colonel dropped by to inform our beleaguered Company that we had wiped out two NVA battalions in the last ten days. Since an NVA battalion consisted of about 200 men, I sure wanted to know where the 400 bodies were. We had seen fewer than half a dozen. Charlie could not have carried off that many dead or wounded. The brass was exaggerating again to pump up our morale.

In Tay Ninh, I slept, drank beer, took several showers, and shaved for the first time in ten days. It felt so good to have a clean face. I had not had a haircut since my arrival in Nam back in April, so I took the time to get one along with the usual massage. It was great to unwind. Had I known what awaited me, I probably would not have relaxed so much. All of us were issued new clothes and guys who had lost their equipment on September 5 were issued replacements. On our brief R & R, I received two care packages from my parents. One contained Q-tips (which were desperately needed) and some rum and vodka. Boy, was I ever happy to get that rum. I mixed it with a Coke and drank it right away! I decided to save the vodka for the jungle. Being under so much pressure, seeing so much

9/8/69: E. Tayloe Wise smoking pot while on R & R in Tay Ninh.

death, was getting to me. I loaded up on cigarettes at Tay Ninh's PX. I had started smoking again and was up to half a pack a day. I really did not want to smoke, but all the tension was just too much. My nerves needed calming down and cigarettes helped a little bit. I was also able to purchase another camera at the PX for $25.00 to replace my broken one. Finally, I got another pair of eyeglasses. After two weeks without my spectacles, it was good to be able to see again! Now that I could see properly, I was not as hesitant about returning to the boonies. Perhaps I should have been. On our second, and last, night at Tay Ninh, we all had a pot party and got blown away. It was a perfect ending to a well-earned R & R. For what we were to face, the false courage generated by the marijuana was much needed.

After our two-day sojourn in Tay Ninh, we were CA'ed right back to the same bunker complex where we had fought for three days to recover our dead. Now we knew we were in for some more deep shit. Moving from this complex, on the 10th, we discovered a newly constructed bunker complex not far away. We spent the whole day blowing up those new bunkers. There were so many bunkers that we had to call in the hippies (combat engineers) to blow up the rest. The hippies arrived the next day (the 11th) with a new 2nd lieutenant who was on temporary assignment with us, before going to Charlie Company. While we waited approximately 75 meters down a trotter for the hippies to blow the bunkers, another Company, which was about 400 meters away, walked into the NVA and became engaged in a firefight. We listened to the battle as the nearby bunkers were blown and then received word that we were to return to the demolished bunkers, set up, and act as a blocking force in case Charlie came our way after the firefight. Charlie never showed up. The next day, we still remained in position hoping to spring an ambush.

By this time, Charlie probably knew where we were. That night, the 12th, in the pouring rain, he zeroed in on our position with mortars. For the first time in the jungle, since I had been in Nam, Charlie finally managed to score with his mortars and hit his target. Since he knew the immediate area of the jungle better, this is not surprising. In the pouring rain, we could not hear the THUNK! THUNK! of the rounds exiting the mortar tube. When the first round landed, we paid it scant heed. The second round landed a little closer. All of us laid flat on the ground as the third round came screaming into our position. When it landed, we said, "to hell with it," exited our sleeping hooches, and slithered, in the mud, to our foxholes. Charlie dumped about twenty rounds inside our perimeter, but no one was hurt or even scratched.

I was really pissed, though, at this turn of events. Since I had left Tay Ninh, my poncho liner, which I slept in, had been wet for the last three days. Finally, having sat around all that day in ambush, I had managed to dry it out. When the mortars came in, I inadvertently dragged it part of the way to the foxhole with me. Not only was it wet, but also it was caked with mud. I was mad as hell. After the attack, it poured all night, and I had nothing dry to wrap around me.

Since I was now Blackfoot's medic, I traveled with the CP, which consisted of the platoon officer, if we had one, the RTO (radio-telephone operator), or the platoon sergeant. I no longer had to pull guard duty and thus could sleep more, which presented a problem because, after six hours of sleep each night, I woke up. I just could not sleep longer than six hours without waking. I guess the reason for this was that, because sleep was so sporadic in Nam, you simply got used to less of it and your body adjusted its inner time clock to wake you. Upon awakening after my initial six hours, I would usually lay awake a half hour or so and then sleep for another three or four hours.

I came close to death so many times in Nam that it is hard to pick out when it was closest. September 13, 1969, stands out as a day when I probably tempted fate about as much as it could be tempted. I will never forget that day because I definitely exposed myself to intense enemy fire over an extended period of time. There just must not have been a bullet with my name on it that day. Otherwise, I would not be here now.

On that day, we picked up and moved out. We were moving so slowly and quietly that we walked right down a trotter into a brand-new bunker complex and found a Charlie fast asleep in his bunker. He was awakened and tied up. He had a brand-new SKS rifle that we expropriated. He gave us no resistance and seemed most cooperative in answering the questions put to him by our Kit Carson and our West Point CO, who could also speak Vietnamese. He gave them a lot of helpful information, and Blackfoot got credit for capturing him. Our beloved LTC had been heard to say that he

Interrogating an NVA POW.

wanted a prisoner. Blackfoot obliged him by serving up one, totally un-scratched.

By noon, Aztec (which had been reformed again by the infusion of lots of cherries during our brief R & R) and Cheyenne linked up with us. The POW was turned over to Aztec, which was to take him to a PZ so he could be airlifted out.

Then the shit hit the fan.

Aztec walked into an ambush set up by three NVA who had AKs. One man was wounded. We called in Blue Max and artillery.

I sat in the rear with our new 2nd lieutenant, a man named Roger Brown from Fishkill, New York. I learned he had graduated from college in 1966, and had a master's degree. We chatted a few minutes as we awaited further developments. His last words to me were ones I would never forget.

"Man, this is a groovy war!" he said. Those were the last words I ever heard him speak.

We received orders to saddle up and move out. We were going to attempt to flank the three NVA who had pinned Aztec down.

It was the classic ambush — a perfect trap — and we took the bait — hook, line and sinker. I can remember studying in NCO School about such ambushes. The three AKs were a lure off to our right. To our left was a hidden machine gunner's nest. While the three AKs pinned Aztec down, this position had remained silent — waiting.

One of the perks of being a medic was that I also got to choose where in the file I would position myself. I usually walked about two-thirds of the way back in the file. I reasoned that, if we ever got hit, I would be far enough back to be out of the line of fire, but close enough to go to the aid of the men. For some inexplicable reason, on that day I walked in the extreme rear. It was good that I did, because in the space of fifteen seconds, I lost everyone else I knew.

An earth-shattering explosion rocked our ears. The first ten men in front of me went down like bowling pins. All of them had been hit by a claymore blast. As soon as it detonated, the enemy machine gunner began his searching fire. Men who may have survived the blast died in the withering hail of bullets that followed it.

Cries— no, screams— of "Medic! Medic!" filled the air.

Moans of the dying were drowned out by the incessant bursts of machine gun fire. I moved forward. Whether I crawled or ran, I don't remember. The first grunt I reached had his right elbow blown off. I immediately applied a tourniquet as his blood splattered all over my arm, and sent him back to the rear. By this time, the other medic from Cheyenne reached me, and we moved to aid the wounded.

The next man was my friend, Wyman "Deak" Hensley. He had multiple wounds in the face, stomach, legs and hands. One of the fingers on his left hand was blown off and another was hanging by a thread. My heart went out to him as I worked on him because I knew he had wanted to be a commercial artist. In one quick blow, his career chances had come to an end. He used to draw pictures for us that were really good; now he probably would never draw again.

The other medic worked on a brand-new sergeant whom we had picked up in Tay Ninh. He had taken the full force of the blast and died as the other medic worked to save him. The hail of enemy machine gun bullets flew by overhead and beside us as we gave aid to the wounded. That we medics were not tagged by one is a miracle.

Lt. Brown had moved up to man our machine gun since our gunner was down. As I knelt over Deak to bandage him up, Lt. Brown, lying flat on the ground not four feet away, fired the M-60 machine gun.

Suddenly, the machine gun fell silent.

I turned to see Lt. Brown staring off into space. I moved to him, only to see he had a bullet wound in the throat. He gurgled, rasped a bit and died with his head in my lap. There was nothing more I could do. No blood came from the throat wound. I guessed that the bullet had probably severed the spinal cord in the neck.

"Doc, over here!" someone cried.

I left the 2nd lieutenant, who had died on his second day in the boonies, and moved to another man. He, too, was dead.

Bullets whipped by our heads. As heavy as the enemy firepower directed against us was, I still cannot understand why we both were so lucky in not getting hit. As new men moved up to fire on the hidden machine gunner, we both knelt over the bodies of the wounded and feverishly worked to beat the Grim Reaper. But, that day was his, not ours.

Charlie moved off and we secured the area. I moved the dead and wounded to the rear. I found the man with his elbow blown off calmly talking to "Red"—a grunt from Lancaster, Pennsylvania, who was so named because of his red hair. Red had a tiny shrapnel wound in his left ankle, and was distraught and clearly in shock. It should have been the other way around. My man with the elbow injury was in much worse shape. I talked Red down as we prepared for the medevac.

The medevac bird came in, but as it hovered above us, Charlie shot at it, so it took off. I was most fearful and concerned about the man with the elbow wound. It was almost two hours since I had applied his tourniquet. I knew that he would probably lose his arm below the elbow if the tourniquet remained in place for more than two hours. The medevac could not land. Then word came down. We were to march 300 meters to a field where there would be a PZ. That would take at least another hour. Time had just run out on the elbow case. I did not want him to lose that arm. So, against all I had ever learned, or been taught, I removed the tourniquet. There was a little bleeding, but not much. I was elated — perhaps the artery had not been severed! All the way to the PZ, I walked with him to ensure that the bleeding would not continue. It didn't. I felt so good — I had saved his arm!

Tired, bloodied, and grim, we reached the PZ. It had been a long march because we were carrying both dead and wounded. Three medevac birds landed, and we got our WIAs and KIAs on them. Then, we had to return to the scene of the firefight. Our LTC's insatiable bloodlust evidently dictated that we were to hound Charlie to death. After returning to the scene of our firefight, we pushed forward into yet another bunker complex where we found a huge well. It was six feet square by fifty feet deep. We were amazed by its size and depth, and had to rope it off to prevent anyone from falling in that night. It had been a long day — one of the longest in my life. Little did I know, but I had earned my second Bronze Star, which read as follows:

> For heroism, not involving participation in aerial flight, in connection with military operations against a hostile force in the Republic of Vietnam. Specialist Four Wise distinguished himself by exceptionally valorous action on 13 September 1969, while serving as a rifleman during a ground reconnaissance mission in Tay Ninh Province, Republic of Vietnam. When his company was moving toward an enemy bunker complex, they were engaged by an estimated reinforced company of enemy soldiers. Pinned down by the well entrenched enemy troops, the point element was unable to initially gain fire superiority. Specialist Four Wise immediately along with several other members of his squad moved up to the point of heaviest contact and began to put a heavy base of suppressive fire on the enemy, allowing the wounded to be evacuated, he helped regroup the men and swept through the contact area, driving the enemy out of their positions and securing the area. Almost immediately the enemy counter-attacked, forcing Specialist Four Wise and his fellow soldiers to regroup in a better fighting position, thus repelling the counter-attack. His display of personal bravery and devotion to duty is in keeping with the highest traditions of the military service and reflects great credit upon himself, his unit, and the United States Army.

I was now the second oldest member of Blackfoot Platoon. Somehow, I had managed to survive four and a half months in Nam and remain basically unscratched (except for the minor wound I took on Becky). I was consoled by this fact because I knew I was getting closer to getting a job in the rear. Only one thing stood between that rear job and my getting it — death. I prayed I would get the job before death got to me.

The next day, we lingered in the bunker complex for several hours before moving out. We set up late that afternoon, after moving only 300–400 meters. Just as we were DX'ing our packs, we heard the THUNK! THUNK! of an enemy mortar tube, not 75 meters away. We hit the ground, but were too close to the mortar site for the 15 or more mortars that were fired to hit us. We called in jet strikes, Cobras, and artillery. Word soon came down that the jets were going to drop two 750-pound bombs and for us to stay low. We could hear the jets coming and prayed a hell of a lot that they would drop those 750-pounders in the right place. They did. The explosions were tremendous and, hugging the ground, we could feel the earth vibrate underneath us. The NVA did not try anything that night but we still dug some deep, deep foxholes. It was good we did because later on in the evening we had two men wounded by shrapnel from artillery that we had called in to protect our position. Unfortunately, it came in too close and our men received minor wounds.

Several days later, one of the men in Bravo Company received an emergency leave to go back to the World, so we humped 2400 meters to Ike. I was so high-strung while on Ike that every time a Duper, mortar, M-16, or artillery piece fired, I jumped. I had been in so much contact that any kind of shot freaked me out. I had been burned badly by Charlie and felt I was on the razor's edge. We were all keyed up.

On Ike I received a letter from my father telling me to go ahead and "tell it like it is" in my letters home. Evidently my mother could take all the news, so now I would not have to write two separate letters. That was a great relief to me because a lot of time I could not remember what I had said in the "clean" letter. I hated for my parents to worry, but I just had to tell the real story of Nam. I guess, even then, I contemplated writing a book on Nam someday and my letters home would serve as the basis for that endeavor.

While on Ike, I received a letter from Lyndon B. Johnson — the former President of the United States. My Aunt Katrina had sent him a copy of the letter I had written to her in which I told her how much I had enjoyed LBJ's book, *The Choices We Face*. He sent me another book, *My Hope for America*, which he had personally autographed, "To PFC E. Tayloe Wise with all fond wishes— Lyndon B. Johnson." His letter to me, dated September 2, 1969, read as follows:

Dear Private Wise:

Mrs. Proctor [sic] Thomas sent me a copy of the letter you wrote containing your reaction to *The Choices We Face*. I was delighted that you found in it what I had hoped to convey, and I am grateful for your comments.

Enclosed is another book I hope you will find interesting. It comes with my hope that you will return home safely and my best wishes.

Sincerely,
Lyndon B. Johnson

I was astonished that the former President would take his valuable time to write to me. I was just a bit overcome, overwhelmed, surprised and awed by this unexpected communication. Perhaps, if such a great man could take time to do this, there was some hope for me. I wrote him a nice thank-you letter, but never knew if he received it.

While on Ike, we received news that the 2nd of the 8th was definitely going to Phuoc Vinh to pull perimeter, or palace, guard. The entire 8th

USO show on LZ Ike.

battalion was "supposed" to go there on September 22 and stay three to six weeks. Of course, we were told, if we made a real good showing, we might stay indefinitely. We welcomed this news with skepticism. After all, we had been told this previously. If it was indeed true, it certainly would be a better life for us. PV was in a little safer area and we would probably not be subject to so many firefights. Since there would be less contact, we would, after what had happened to us since Becky, welcome that change in our lives. No man likes to see all of his friends wasted or wounded.

We remained at Ike until the 20th, licking our wounds and pulling odious LZ duty. We were also rebuilding the strength of our devastated Company with more cherries. As soon as we had received enough cannon fodder to place us again at fighting strength, we were CA'ed to an area, which had been hit by a B-52 strike, to check it out. We found tunnels, some of which went to a depth of forty feet and had numerous air vents. We also found a 500-pound bomb that had not detonated upon impact.

Because we found the tunnel, the brass decided to keep us out in the field a few more days to check out everything. This new turn of events was not good for our morale. We knew our battalion was definitely going to PV. Staying out here in the bush was hazardous to our health, and we yearned for the safety that PV had to offer.

Lt. Rodney D. McCormick, IV, of Laurel, Maryland, was our new platoon officer. We called him Lt. Mac. He had been with us since August 31 (when Blackfoot had its first firefight), and had come in on one of the log birds bringing ammo resupply. Although he had been in the Army for six years, he had spent the first four or five as an EM (enlisted man). He had already done a previous tour to Nam as an EM and was definitely an uptight individual who knew his stuff. He always made a point to tell us everything that was going on, so we would know what to expect. Because he went out of his way to communicate with us, we trusted him and life seemed a little easier with him around.

We were also learning a lot about our new West Point captain. He was a little too gung ho for us. He loved to march, which must have come from his West Point days. We were humping much more and moving longer distances. Capt. Mooneyham had given us a ten-minute break every hour. Now we got no breaks. Under Mooneyham we usually moved around 0900 hours, but now we were moving earlier, from 0700 to 0730 hours. Before, we used to set up around 1630 hours, but our new slave driver made us set up at 1830 hours. It was hell on us, but most especially on all the new cherries. We did not have as much time to write letters, and the men really resented not being able to write home. Because we were setting up later, we hardly had time to eat as darkness came early, and we were not permitted to have a cooking fire after dark. Our fine young captain also had another dangerous habit. We would receive an order to march from Point A to Point B. Well, he would march straight from A to B without checking out what was on the way to B. He kept pushing and pushing the point teams to go faster. In other words, his whole attitude was one of fuck-what's-in-between-just-get-there. It was a dangerous attitude and would cost him a lot more men someday, if not his own life. You just did not go from one point to another in the boonies without checking out new trotters or bunkers. Much to our disdain, our new captain ignored this and therefore typified the college-educated officers I saw, or knew in the Army. They were basically insensitive to the needs or advice of their men. They counted on these men to fight, yet did not give them the decent courtesy of admitting that they knew anything. The only good officers I ever knew, like Lt. Hill or Lt. McCormick, were men who had risen from the enlisted ranks. They knew and cared about their men. They respected their men's opinions, and they never made their men feel like they were deliberately putting them in jeopardy. The service academy brass were know-it-alls. Snobs. Stuck-ups. I never met one in training, or in the field, whom I liked. They lacked a certain empathy for the people into whose hands they placed their lives. When an officer as good as told you not to bother about checking out something, he demonstrated his ignorance. For a man who had his entire infantry company take 50 percent casualties on his second day in command, our captain was treading on mighty thin ice.

I firmly believe a major part of our new captain's inability to lead well was a direct result of his training at West Point. Nothing he had ever done before had prepared him for the carnage and chaos that was Nam. It was obvious to some of us that his West Point instructors had emphasized completing the assignment. It did not matter how you did it, as long as you achieved the correct results. He was assigned a mission and, to please his superiors, he did it by the book, and ignored all other outside factors and pertinent data. This was not how things were accomplished in Nam. Thus, completion of the mission (going from A to B) became paramount, and the needs or safety of his men placed a distant second. He believed in achieving goals at any cost, at the risk of destroying the men whose effectiveness he needed to attain victory.

What pissed us off even more at our captain was the fact that, because we were setting up so much later in the day, it was usually raining. So, we were all wet. A wet grunt is not a happy grunt. A wet grunt is a pissed-off grunt. That did not help morale in the least.

Because it was the rainy season, it was becoming more and more difficult to keep anything dry. Since I was the medic, I did not have to participate in any of the tunnel searches or cloverleaf patrols. So on the 20th, while others searched and explored, I had time to dry my poncho, poncho liner, and fatigue shirt. That night we were fortunate. It didn't rain, and I slept warm and dry. I had acquired a plastic bag and wrapped my fatigue shirt in it, which kept it dry during the day, when it rained. But, for the last eight nights, even while on the LZ, it had poured, and we slept wet. As a medic, I was beginning to see more and more of immersion foot, a condition where the foot would shrivel and crack due to all the water it had absorbed. I now made it a point to wring out my socks three times a day. I gave my charges Desenex for their feet and told them to wring out their socks three times a day. Whether or not any of them followed my advice, I did not know. I think they did because my cases of immersion foot slacked off after a few weeks. Many of the men I had to treat did not have any common sense about their own health. Many, I guess, never cared. They had been raised to accept things. I think, because I cared, they appreciated the time I took to help them. I definitely enjoyed playing doctor. It was so rewarding.

Sgt. Dave Elia, the Hawaiian, was still with us. Dave had just made E-6, and we were happy and proud for him. Several days earlier after we left Ike, Dave was involved in an amusing incident. His voice had a definite Hawaiian accent. Blackfoot had been CA'ed separately to the tunnel area, and Dave called our new captain to establish radio contact. The captain, when he head Dave's voice, was suspicious because he was expecting Lt. Mac to call; but Lt. Mac had gone to Tay Ninh unexpectedly. The Captain, thinking Dave was a gook, asked him all kinds of questions before he was sure he wasn't being had. We all had a laugh over that incident!

I was still getting along well with Sgt. McNerney — known as "Top" — our CMH winner. He was still with us, and had survived everything Charlie had managed to unload on us. Sgt. McNerney was a good man. He did not scream or look down on us like most top sergeants. I would share my vodka with him, and he shared his whiskey with me. He was a super individual and got along well with all of us.

By and large, most of the men I served with, or who were in command over me in Nam, were good men. Considering the situation in which we all found ourselves, its amazing someone didn't crack. But, in all the time in Nam, I never saw anyone go off the deep end. The emotional heartbreak was certainly there, but, we all managed, somehow, to keep our sanity. Just the same, the potential to go stark raving mad was there, lying just below the surface. It had to be bridled. We would take our hostility out on Charlie in the firefights and our bitterness out on the World, if and when we returned.

Since we were definitely going to PV, the Army held our mail. The brass told us this, so at least we believed we were going, but we were most unhappy at not receiving our mail. Guys in the field lived for that mail. It always saddened me to see one or two men get little or no mail. How hard it must have been on them not to hear any news at all from home. By this time, the steady flow of letters that I was receiving had begun to slow. I was not receiving half as many letters during my fifth month in Nam as I had in the first four. I was prepared for that, though. I knew people would slack off even though I replied to every letter I received. I was so far away, and going to be gone for so long that bit by bit, people found it convenient to put me on the back burner. This happened to all of us. It was, I suppose, only natural. What surprised me was who, of my so-called friends, had stopped writing. You really learned who your true friends were, in Nam.

My new glasses were not helping me. The prescription was wrong and made my eyes tired after a few hours so I knew something was wrong. I vowed to go directly to an eye doctor when we got to PV and get this mess straightened out, once and for all. I was thankful I had glasses because walking around in the jungle without them had been horrendous. I hated it. Perhaps that is why I never thought about fear during most of the firefights—I couldn't see far enough away to get scared!

I was looking forward to PV for another reason. I desperately wanted to go to a dentist and have my teeth checked because I had not brushed them since arriving in Nam. There was a good reason for this. In the field, we oftentimes received a limited amount of water on log day. Therefore, we hardly had enough to fill our canteens. Had we used this precious water to brush our teeth every day, that would have meant less for consumption. With temperatures of 120–130° on many days, no one could afford to run out of water in the boonies. Water was another commodity that was not shared unless everyone was low, or had run out, or lost it during a hasty retreat in a firefight as had happened to Aztec and Cheyenne on September 5. Therefore, the choice was clear—brush or don't brush.

Looking back now, I wish to God the Army had done something about oral hygiene. Just a little education on the use of toothpicks, and their effectiveness, would have gone a long way. Our dental health, however, was clearly not a priority, as is evidenced by the sloppiness in which my root canal surgery was handled by the Army, prior to my departure to Nam. Since they only did part of the operation, and neglected to tell me that further surgery was necessary, then how could I expect them to give out oral hygiene information? Because I neglected my teeth in Nam, I have now suffered for thirty-four years with tooth and gum problems that I will have for the rest of my life. Just a few words, or lectures from the Army, on the importance of tooth and gum upkeep might have saved me, and thousands of other grunts, further dental problems. Toothpicks could have been included in our 101s with our rations.

Yet, in 1969 we were bodies to throw into the fire. Indian widows committed settee by throwing themselves upon the funeral pyres of their husbands. The Army had much the same approach when it came to good dental care. In September, after five months in Nam, my teeth were, I thought, basically sound. They felt clean, but, below the surface, my gums suffered and paid a terrible price. Plus, the Army only gave a veteran one year from the time he left the service to apply for dental treatment. It took the pyorrhea, which started in Nam, approximately eighteen months to manifest itself in my mouth. By that time, my chance at veteran's dental benefits had passed. I still have all my teeth, but I live in fear of the day when they will begin to loosen and fall out due to gum disease.

I fully realize that I am to blame for this neglect. I do, however, blame the military for not emphasizing the importance of *good dental hygiene* while in Nam, and for not giving us longer to apply for benefits upon termination from the service. *C'est la vie*! as the French would say. You can't win them all! I cannot help but wonder, however, at how many Vietnam vets are walking around today with lost teeth due to poor dental care while in Nam, when all it might have taken to save those teeth was the wise use of a toothpick.

The 22nd of September came and went. Still no trip to PV. By the 23rd, we had been sitting around in the jungle next to the tunnel system, doing absolutely nothing, for several days. Since I was a medic, I did not have to go out on patrol, so time became incredibly boring. On the 22nd, we had cleared an LZ so Dictator Lewis could descend and inspect the situation. El Supremo had decided that our discovery of the tunnels was so important that they had to be explored thoroughly. If the job was performed by our replacement battalion, the 2nd of the 5th Cav, Lewis would not get any glory from it. So, our departure to PV was delayed.

By the 23rd, we were all convinced that some (or most) of the "supposed" air vents that we had discovered were not really air vents at all. Around most of the air vent holes were torn roots and broken trees as if rockets (from Blue Max?) had penetrated the spot. Of course, we did not understand how a rocket could go so deep. Yet each of the entrances to the holes looked as if something violent had hit there and entered. Each hole curved down the same way. We started to dig up several of these holes, some of which emitted a weird smell. We hoped that we would not find anything and we didn't.

Our mail was still being held in anticipation of the move to PV. Nine days without mail was more than enough to put most of us on edge. Morale was not good.

Our first three days in the boonies this time had been beautiful. The rains had abated. The first day, it had drizzled for about thirty minutes; the second day for fifteen minutes; and on the third day, the sun shone forth. We welcomed its rays with open arms. It had not rained at night either, so we slept dry. I was able to sleep with my boots off for the first time in weeks. It felt so good to let the night air caress my feet! So many people take raincoats for granted. When it rains they don them and stay dry. No one can really appreciate the luxuries we Americans have. In Nam, we did not have raincoats. Sure, we had our ponchos—but they did not keep one completely dry. We always had to take them off to make our hooches at night. Plus, if we were setting up late, it was usually raining so we got wet anyway. Sometimes, it poured so much we would start shivering from the cold that came with the rain. We were constantly getting drenched. To be dry is such a wonderful thing. It was hell sleeping in wet clothes, with a wet poncho liner around you, on the wet ground. The uncomfortableness of the jungle was grating on our minds, so we worshiped the sun. Prayed for it. Every single chance we got, we were constantly drying our clothes or poncho liners.

I was also enjoying my role as "Doc." In one respect, I felt I was better than the old Army-trained medic whom I had replaced. He did not bother to treat guys for the little things. I made it a point to treat every health problem, no matter how small, the guys brought to me. The men trusted me — mainly because 98 percent of them were cherries and did not know me when I had been a ground pounder. My hardest problems were boils. I had so many guys with boils and staph infections. I used ichthamnol to draw the core of the boil up and out. When the core came to a head, I had to try and squeeze it out. This was excruciatingly painful and had many guys in tears by the time I had finished. Short of lancing, this was — I had been taught — the most effective method to get rid of the boil. My most successful case at removing a boil was a cherry who acquired one that was about one and a half inches long and at least a half inch deep, right on his coccyx. I managed to cut the boil open, get the core out, and cleanse the area. To do this, I made him stand up against a tree and hold it while I ripped out the yellow tentacles of the boil. This was so painful that he could not help but cry. I cleaned the hole every day and changed the dressings. On the third day of treatment, we received log, and I decided to send him in on the log bird to be checked by the LZ doctor. He went in on the first lift and came back out on the last lift. I was totally surprised to see him. He had gone to the LZ aid station, seen a doctor and been sent back to the field. They had not done anything to him. I felt so good! At least I was doing OK as a medic. I still knew he needed some medical attention and would make sure, upon arrival at PV, that he got better attention.

Since the rains had not descended upon us at night, I started making the guys take their boots off when sleeping. They needed to air those feet out, and I tried to impress upon them the importance of having dry feet.

I was feeling so good about being a medic that, heaven forbid, I considered extending my tour for six more months. After all the hell I had seen and been through, I find it hard to believe I ever considered that thought. My heart went out to men in agony. I wanted to help them so badly. I felt that it was my duty to do so. Being a medic seemed to be in my blood. I had found something I could do, and do well. For the first time in my life, I was somebody. I wanted to continue doing it even if that meant staying longer in Nam. I told this to my parents in a letter home, and I am sure it terrified them. I wanted to be where the action was—patching up people. Well, I am not patching up today, but for eighteen years I took my love for emergency medicine home to the World and was a first aid and CPR instructor for the American Red Cross. I taught people how to render first aid, which gave me the same gratifying and fulfilling feeling that I had when I was in Nam. Because I was able to aid my fellow platoon mates, I really felt as if I had accomplished something worthwhile in my life. This is my mark upon the world, and I sincerely feel that I have contributed something of merit to mankind. I firmly believe that we all owe something back to the society in which we live. God put us here for a purpose, and I feel that I have contributed some of my share towards that goal.

One of my hooch partners was a guy named John Bailey from Daytona Beach, Florida. John, age twenty-four, was a soul brother and an all-around nice guy. He was Sgt. Elia's RTO, and had been with us since August 31, when Blackfoot stepped in the shit. John and I were compatible and enjoyed each other's company.

My good friend, John Sivick, had survived all the firefights. He was, however, no longer with Bravo Company. He had been partially deaf when he came to Nam, and his deafness increased due to all the artillery firing that took place while he was on the LZs. He got a permanent profile and landed a rear job. He was the only guy I came to Nam with who managed to return with me on the Freedom Bird to the World. We were the lucky ones—we survived. Little did I know then that one of the causes of John's deafness would also affect me at a later date. The explosions on Becky and the burst of artillery fire on other LZs later took their toll on my own hearing. My hearing loss, however, would not begin to manifest itself until two or three years after I left the service. It took that long for me to notice a significant loss in my hearing ability. My high-frequency hearing is now shot, and I find it difficult to hear anyone speaking to me outside a radius of five feet when there is other noise being emitted from a radio, TV, CD player, or other people. This is just another small price we grunts had to pay to fight in the wasted war. My hearing loss, and the hearing loss of other uncounted, unknown numbers of grunts, is part of a disability with which we will have to live, and we can thank our government for this little extra bonus.

The world was indeed a small place. As we waited for log by the tunnel complex, Gene LeFrance, an old friend from New Orleans, Louisiana, stepped off one of the log birds. Gene and I had met in AIT School at Fort Polk, and had been in the same platoon in both AIT and NCO School. Now he was assigned to Blackfoot. I greeted him warmly and pumped him about the guys in NCO School whom we had known. We talked a while and reminisced.

Because of the terror I had experienced, and the hell I had seen, I had become a real believer in God. After the 5th of September debacle, I knew there had to be a God. He had let me live when we expected to be overrun. I prayed every night to Him. One of my girlfriends, Linda Beasley, had sent me a miniature New Testament, which I got out and read in times of solitude. I found myself praying a lot to God — hoping to live just one more day. God had shown me my purpose in life — being a combat medic — and I felt so happy and more at ease now, doing my "thing." I knew God existed and that He was with me, watching over and guiding me. I knew He had to be with me after all the times I had exposed myself to enemy fire. He was with me to help aid the wounded, and I knew this beyond a shadow of a doubt, which made me inwardly happy and content.

I finally finished LBJ's book, *My Hope for America*, which I really enjoyed. He wrote in such a clear, yet simple, style that anyone could understand the message he wished to convey. LBJ tried to explain to his readers why America is great, and why it can be even greater. Using beautiful rhetoric, he discussed what we can accomplish with all the material resources we have at our disposal. He clearly explained why we were in NATO, the Alliance for Progress, and other world organizations. LBJ managed to convey the idea of why we should be proud to be Americans and tried to explain why America has grown and what we should want to do for underprivileged people, not only in the United States but also abroad. Upon finishing the book, I could not help but feel proud to be an American. I had enjoyed LBJ's treatise and felt it went a long way toward explaining, in simplistic terms, our role in domestic and world affairs. I was glad he had sent it to me, for I had learned a little more about our political system, and its effect upon the world.

Yet, tragedy continued to relentlessly stalk Blackfoot Platoon. We had been CA'ed to Ike prior to our pending departure to PV on the 24th. On the eve of our departure, death struck swiftly. I knew something like this would occur, and it finally did. At night, LPs were always sent out from the LZs to be an early warning system if Charlie tried to penetrate the area. When an LP left the LZ perimeter the men were "supposed" to follow a certain azimuth for a specified distance. Too often, the members of an LP not only ignored following the correct azimuth but also they disregarded the proper distance they should travel before setting up for the night. After all, most of us in the infantry firmly believed that LP was nothing more than a suicide squad. We did not believe in taking any more risks than necessary. I was just as guilty as the rest in not going far enough away from an LZ. After all, if you were detected, you wanted to be able to pull back to the LZ as quickly as possible.

Having followed the correct azimuth and traveled the prescribed distance, an LP was supposed to let the mortars on the LZ bracket their position for support. Prior to becoming a medic, I loved LP because I would carry the radio and really call the mortars in close to fix our position. One time, while on LP, I called the mortars in almost on top of our position. One landed about fifteen meters away. Boy, did the guys with me ever freak out. Yet, I always insisted on extremely tight bracketing. I wanted help if we got hit, and I wanted those mortars on top of us. But most LPs were lackadaisical about bracketing. They would radio in that they were bracketed even though the mortars were exploding 100 or more meters from their position.

As a result of this nonchalant attitude, many LPs set up in the wrong position and left themselves wide open to injury from the LZ's artillery or mortar fire.

I was awakened about 0030 hours on the 25th.

"Doc! Doc! Hey Doc, wake up!"

"Ugh! What ...?"

"Redlegs just blew away our LP."

"Oh shit!"

"Yeah! Me too, we gotta go get 'em!"

"How many's hurt?"

"Three wounded, one unscratched."

I dressed, got my medical bag, and met the rest. Lt. Mac was going to lead us out. There were seven grunts and three medics. We moved out slowly — after all, Charlie was probably out there. One of the LPs, who had not been wounded, met us just outside the perimeter at the gate to guide us back to the spot.

He quickly became confused and lost. We soon realized that this LP had not gone on the right azimuth to set up for the night. We were about 200 meters out from the LZ where the tree shadows of the jungle wood line loomed ominously upon us. We were nervous as hell that we would stumble upon some gooks who, once they spotted us, would lay back and take potshots at us. As the minutes ticked by, we became more tense and uptight. Finally, by radio, we got the remaining LPs to fire shots. They were about 100 meters off to our left. At 0330 hours we finally reached them. They had set up their LP 20° off the correct azimuth and about 150 meters short. One man was dead, one badly wounded, one lightly wounded, and the unscratched one had met us. A 105-mm artillery shell had landed within seven feet of their position. The KIA was a point man for one of our platoons and had been on his second tour in Nam. It was his last. I was furious to learn he had been put on LP, because point men were usually exempt from OP and LP.

As we headed back to the LZ with the dead and wounded, one of our guys hit a trip flare. Like greased lightning, we hit the ground and froze. The damn trip flare lit up the whole area like day. We were scared shitless some gook would zero in on us. Or, worse yet, some trigger-happy grunt on the LZ would blow us away.

We finally made it back to the LZ. It had been a long night, and I got little sleep, but the dawn brought a new world of hope to us. For on that day, we were to catch a Chinook to Tay Ninh and fly by C-130 to Phuoc Vinh. It was a day to anticipate and look forward to, and by nightfall we were sleeping in Phuoc Vinh. It had taken a little over two months for the Army to make good on its word to transfer us to PV. In that short span of time, Becky had been annihilated, my Company decimated, and all my friends killed or wounded.

An excerpt from the September 26, 1969, issue of *The Stony Mountain Work Horse*, which was the 2nd of the 8th Battalion's command newsletter, summed up August and September as follows:

> After the brilliant defense of FSB Carolyn (which has been recommended for the Valorous Unit Award), we fought from FSB Becky from 9 July 1969 to 12 August 1969. During this period the Battalion killed 230 NVA and captured 1 POW. We killed 23 percent of all the NVA killed in the entire 1st Cavalry Division...
>
> In the period 13 August 1969 to 17 September 1969, this battalion in 39 contacts killed 322 NVA and captured 6 POW's. For this time period, we killed 15 percent of all the NVA killed in the 1st Calvary Division and captured 35 percent of the POW's...
>
> Some of our friends and fellow troopers paid the supreme sacrifice, that man could be free from tyranny.*

Sadly, what this newsletter does not indicate is the fact that LZ Becky got the hell beat out of it and had to be abandoned on August 12, 1969. What it also does not say is that our losses in lives probably equaled at least half of the NVA losses due to LTC Felix T. Lewis's kill-all-gooks-at-any-cost policy.

It had been the longest month of my life. I hoped PV would be a little more peaceful. It was. Life on the Phuoc Vinh perimeter proved to be rather easy. On the last day in September, I found myself in a clearing with the CO, Lt. Mac, and the FO playing bridge.

All we did at PV was sit around all day in the blistering sun and send out cloverleaf-type patrols from Bravo Company's main body. Several days

*"Command Message," *The Stony Mountain Work Horse 2/8 Command Newsletter*, Vol. 2, No. 2, 26 September 1969, 1.

prior to this Lt. Mac decided to teach me how to play bridge. So, on the 30th, I played bridge for four and a half hours with Lt. Mac as my partner, and we got through three rubbers! Since I was a novice, we only won one game. I had learned a hell of a lot and found bridge a most enjoyable game.

The terrain around PV was entirely different from the jungle north of Tay Ninh. Surrounding PV were big open fields with trees and high elephant grass. We could travel 200 meters in five minutes, whereas in Tay Ninh it would take one and a half hours to do the same. At PV, we could move 1400 meters easily in two hours, but in Tay Ninh Province the same distance could easily take three or more days. One of our first CAs at PV was to find a VC mortar position. Intelligence thought it might be in a swamp area. The birds CA'ed us to the area and hovered about five feet above the water. Out we jumped, thinking it was only knee deep. We were fortunate that no one drowned. We were in over our heads and had to swim toward shore with fully loaded rucksacks. Had Charlie been there, we would have been sitting ducks. The heavy, water-laden packs dragged us down, but we made it to land like wet rats. We never did find the mortar position.

My camera was being fixed in PV, so I missed an interesting picture of some bird's nests in the swamp area, which were most unusual. They appeared to be woven like clothes, and hung in strands from the bamboo. Looking closely at them, it appeared as if human hands had taken the grass and intricately woven it into the bamboo shoots that supported the nest.

On September 30, a Catholic chaplain flew out to the field to hold a church service. I had not attended church in over ten years, but I availed myself of the opportunity this presented. The Father held mass with Communion, which I took. I wasn't a Catholic, but I didn't care. Out there, God was God and one didn't bother about religious affiliations. It meant a lot to me to worship God again in a religious service, after having not attended church for such a long while. Perhaps attending a religious service in the last days of September was a good omen. Perhaps things would begin to look up for me. With worship of the Creator came hope.

OCTOBER

Freedom!

Nothing in life is so exhilarating as to be shot at without result.

Winston Churchill (1874–1965)
(*The Malakand Field Force*, 1898)

At Phuoc Vinh we operated in an area directly beneath the flight path of the Freedom Birds that took off from Bien Hoa. Every day we would hear the high-pitched thrust of the jet engines as three or four birds climbed into the eastern sky. Seeing those planes made all of us a little homesick. I had served five months in Nam, and it seemed like five years of hell. Although they had passed quickly, I had seen too much carnage, destruction, and death and wondered how long it would take some bullet to find me. Over there it seemed, at times, inevitable that we would all die in Nam.

After getting our asses kicked around so much in Tay Ninh, our battalion went overboard to be nice and generous to us. During our October 1 log, we received a beer ration, the first time we had been given suds in the field, and so we were really surprised. We were also taken aback when we received chocolate milk and chocolate ice cream, but gulped them down before they soured or melted. I managed to acquire six beers and stored them all in my ruck. My pack was heavy, but I was determined to savor my beer. We had a lot of non–beer drinkers in Blackfoot, so I would trade my Cokes for beer. Even though the beer was warm by the time I got around to drinking it, it was delicious. I soon discovered that, if I placed it in my rucksack next to the small of my back, the sweat from that area of my body seeped through the ruck and kept one or two beers reasonably cool. I also found that I could drink beer in Nam a hell of a lot faster than I ever could back in the World. Perhaps this was because I was a lot thirstier!

This was a rebuilding time for Bravo Company. We used it to train all the cherries we had recently received. Blackfoot needed at least twenty more men. Even there, outside of Phuoc Vinh, tragedy followed us. While on patrol, one of Blackfoot's squads had stopped to rest. As they got up to move on, a grunt used his M-16 to pull himself up. His M-16 was not on safety, and, as he rose, his finger pulled the trigger. The bullet caught a young kid from Cincinnati, dead center in the chest. The young man never knew what hit him, and died instantly. The guilty culprit was a cherry. This was just another example of the useless waste of life that occurred on a daily basis in Nam.

By now, I was the oldest man with time in country in Blackfoot Platoon. Lt. Mac was soon going to be our Company XO (Executive Officer), and a company clerk's job was coming up. I asked him to consider me for the position. I now had the officers in the Company on my side. They trusted me so much that they preferred me as their medic over the other Army-trained medics who had been assigned to us.

As medic, I had access to lots of drugs and pills. Griseofulvin tablets were great for ringworm, which was usually gone after three days of medication. The Benadryl pills, for insect bites and stings, were super and so relaxing that a person could get hooked on them with little trouble. I began to worry, since I was so used to taking medicines for my ills with absolutely no trouble in acquiring them, that I would be in a bind when I returned to the World because most of these pills had to be dispensed by prescription. I was glad that I did not get hooked on drugs in Nam because I might have been in trouble when I returned to the States. Drugs could do so much to ease the pain of remembering the hell you had to experience in Nam. Oddly enough, though, I never had any of my medicines stolen, or had any guys pop pills to survive the rigors of Nam. By and large most of us were fairly straight. As far as I knew, with the exception of marijuana usage, drug abuse was non-existent in Bravo Company.

I was getting my money's worth out of the Army with my glasses and the problems I had with them. On October 2, I set my glasses down on top of my pack where I felt they were secure and would not fall off. One of the guys in my squad brushed against my pack, knocked the glasses to the ground and then stepped on them. That was the third pair of specs that I had broken. Luckily, this time I had a spare pair in my pack. But I was down to my last pair again. With my luck, I felt sure it would not be long before I broke those. I was thankful that the Army supplied glasses to its men free of charge because, if I had to pay for them, I would have been broke most of the time.

While pulling palace guard outside PV, our CO had a good idea for rewarding the outstanding men in each platoon. The exceptional individual in each platoon would be given a Company R & R once a month. He would go in for a period between logs, three or four days, and goof off in the rear. In effect, he got some "sham" time. When you got out of the field, even for a few days, you took what was known as sham time. No matter what the excuse, even if you were wounded, or if you stayed in the rear, it counted as sham time. I had sham time myself when I had gone to Quan Loi to pick up my glasses. There were legitimate shammers—those who were wounded or became ill, which was OK. But someone who deliberately avoided the field was considered a shammer and was not respected by anyone.

On October 4, Lt. Mac consulted with eight guys in my platoon who were unanimous in choosing me to receive the first Company R & R. I protested this decision.

"Lt. Mac, others deserve it more than I."

"No, they don't!"

"But, you need a medic!"

"Not for one log."

"Suppose I refuse. I don't want to go."

"You'll go and that's a direct order!"

So we set up to receive the next log. It looked as if I was going to be forced to take my mini vacation despite my protests to the contrary. The place where we had set up to receive log had two large bomb craters, which were located along the edge of a stream. Several grunts descended upon this man-made swimming hole and within minutes they were swimming in their birthday suits, splashing around and having a good time. I did not join them, but I wished I had my camera. There, outside of Phuoc Vinh, one could physically see the tension fade and dissolve from the faces of the beleaguered grunts of Bravo Company as they frolicked, swam, and acted like the kids at heart they really were deep down inside. Of course, most of them were not veterans of the last month's hell. Back in Tay Ninh we never would have thought about swimming in a bomb crater in the jungle. It just would not have been safe.

The log bird arrived and brought two surprises with it. The first was a pair of sunglasses that I had ordered several months past. The second occurred while I was reading my mail because I received an urgent call to go to the main CP. Lt. Mac informed me that another grunt and I had been chosen to represent Bravo Company in an interview that might possibility lead to being assigned as a personal aide to Major General E. B. Roberts, the CG of the 1st Air Cav. I almost fainted. We had been chosen to see LTC Lewis for the preliminary interview. I was flabbergasted because this was my chance of a lifetime and seemed so unreal. Hastily, I gathered my equipment, hurriedly bid my comrades good-bye (they all wished me luck), and caught the log bird for Phuoc Vinh and destiny. The other grunt and I reported to the Company Orderly Room where we were fitted with brand-new clothes and boots—after all, we both had to look our best. We had showered and dressed when Lt. Hill, now the Company XO, walked in and informed us:

"Guys, there was a time limit to this competition. You were supposed to be in by twelve yesterday. It's too late now."

Our hopes, our dreams, our visions of a rear echelon job plummeted and were dashed upon the wooden barracks floor on which we stood. We were really mad. As it turned out, however, half of the battalion companies had not been informed in time to send representatives. Only three grunts from other companies had made the deadline.

Our Company got in touch with the CG's sergeant major to talk to him about the deadline. About 2100 hours that evening, Lt. Hill arrived at the aid station where I was staying.

"Hey, Wise! Break starch!"

"What for?"

"Colonel wants to interview you!"

"You mean it's on?"

"Yep!"

"When?"

"Now!"

"Whoopee! What happened?"

"CG's sergeant major gave the go-ahead."

"Fantastic."

The lieutenant colonel was going to interview us after all. The other guy had been steadily drinking since 1700 hours. I had had only two beers, so I was in good shape for the interview.

This was the first and last time I ever met LTC Lewis. This was the man I had detested, hated, wished dead, wanted to shoot out of the sky, and now he held my fate in the palm of his hand. How ironic that, ultimately, it came down to an interview with this man as to whether or not I got a rear echelon job. Had he known how much I had inwardly cursed him, and how much I hated him and his policies, I doubt I would have stood a chance.

We both were ushered into his dimly lit office. It was late. A small tabletop light illuminated the desk and his chest from the neck down. His face was partially veiled in shadows. Perhaps he did not want us to see the deeply drawn lines of worry that etched and creased his face. We were all tired. The interview lasted an hour, and I cannot remember one single question that he asked. All I knew was that I had to beat the other grunt. I had to come out on top. I had to get out of the field! This would be my one and only chance. I would not blow it. Most of his questions were standard ones, but he also tried to explain the recent September fighting that had decimated Bravo Company so badly. It was more of a debriefing session than an interview. I think he was trying to justify his actions. He took us for common foot soldiers—grunts—and, I think, wanted to impress us with his tactics. I wasn't impressed. All I wanted was a chance at that rear job. I felt I had come out on top. We learned from LTC Lewis that he would choose two men to represent the battalion. Those two men would then be in competition with grunts from other division battalions. LTC Lewis's interview was like the quarterfinals.

I knew I had a slim chance of winning, but at least there was a chance. I could hardly believe all this was really happening to me. After all I had been in, and undergone, now here I was attempting to win a competition to be a general's aide. I had to be in a dream — this was too unreal. Even if I was not chosen, I at least got an R & R and sham time.

The next day, October 5, I reported to the Company sergeant major to ascertain who had been picked. Five men in the battalion had interviewed with LTC Lewis. Only two of those men would be interviewed by the Division Chief of Staff. I made it! I was in the semifinals now! In two days, I was told, the Division Chief of Staff, a full-bird colonel by the name of Joseph P. Kingston, would interview us. To say the least, I was overjoyed. This was my one big chance, and I wasn't about to blow it.

October 7 was one of the happiest days of my life in Nam. That evening, as I sat in Bravo Company's Orderly Room and listened to one of the Company sergeants from Texas play his guitar and sing western songs and ballads, rain beat down upon the tin roof of the barracks and lent an unreal atmosphere to the situation in which I found myself. There was gaiety and celebration in the air. For me, there was a special meaning to that night. It was to be the last night in Nam that I was to spend as a member of Bravo Company. My days in the field had ended at 1600 hours that afternoon. I was no longer a grunt! No longer a medic. No longer would I be called "Doc." Those days were past. I was now a member of Headquarters Company, Division HQ of the 1st Air Cav Division (AM).

That day eight other men and I had gone for the fateful interview with Colonel Joseph P. Kingston, 1st Air Cavalry Division, Chief of Staff. When we arrived, we were told three men were needed as waiters in the CG's Mess. Colonel Kingston did not interview any of us, but sent us straight to the CG's Mess.

All eight of us were interviewed as a group by the head waiter, Sergeant (E-5) Larry Busch, from Davenport, Iowa, who was to choose three of us. I asked all kinds of questions to learn about the job. Then each of us had a private interview with Larry and the Mess sergeant.

During my interview, they asked if the waiter's job appealed to me. I honestly told them that it did interest me; but, after some probing questions, they learned not only about my job as medic, but also that I felt I could accomplish more by remaining a medic. I told them, however, that the waiter's job was a job and, if chosen, I would do my best in it as I had at being a medic. I thought I had blown my chance at a rear job. At that time, none of us knew that the five men who were not chosen would still get a job with Division HQ. It was do or die then. We thought the five men who were not chosen would return to their battalions and then the field. I could just see myself humping again. It was not a pleasant thought, but at least I had been honest with them and myself.

I was chosen as one of the three new waiters for the CG's Mess. The rest were then told that they, too, had rear jobs.

Larry Busch gave me a note written on a napkin, to take back to Bravo Company, which read as follows:

Sp/4 Wise has been accepted in a position at the CG's Mess Hall. We have sent him back to you so that he may clear battalion. Thank you.

Sgt. Larry Busch, NCOIC, CG's Mess

Carrying that note back to Bravo Company, I felt like a condemned prisoner on death row who has just received the governor's reprieve minutes before the trapdoor was to drop on the gallows I had just ascended. October 7, 1969, was indeed one of the happiest days of my life in Nam. I was FREE! I was out of the bush! No more fucking rucksack to shoulder! No one, unless they have experienced what I have described so far, can begin to comprehend the joy and ecstasy that coursed through my mind and body. I was now out of Dante's Inferno and on my way to freedom. Now I know what the slaves must have felt when they learned of Lincoln's 1863 Emancipation Proclamation. "Free at last! Free at last! Thank God Almighty, we are free at last!" is what Martin Luther King said in his "I Have a Dream" speech on August 28, 1963. I voiced his thoughts in my mind that day. How sweet it was to be out of the jungle. After five months of hell, I had my rear job!

So now I was out of the bush. Just when you had managed to adapt yourself to the jungle, when you felt confident, you left, and some other poor sucker, green to the gills, who didn't know shit, took your place as someone would eventually take his place. It was all insane. The world had turned upside down — just like the song that the British Army had played at their surrender to American forces in 1781 at Yorktown. No wonder we never got close to winning the war, or establishing any kind of a permanent beachhead. Purely and simply, Vietnam boiled down to survival. Serve your time and fuck everything else. There was no deep sense of responsibility or commitment in anyone I knew, not even the high-ranking officers or, for that matter, my own self. All we had to do was get in, serve our time, like prison, and be safely extracted in one piece. We were nothing more than a temporary buffer between the dynamic North and the corrupt South. It would only be a matter of time before Saigon would fall, and we were nothing more than a holding force giving the rich and corrupt South Vietnamese time to transfer their gold out of South Vietnam.

We were told that the waiter's job would be easy. We would work from 0700 to 0900, 1100 to 1300, and 1800 to 2030 hours. The hours were not bad! Of course, I had to spit shine my boots and break starch every day, but that would not be too bad, or inconvenient. We were also told that we would get every fifth or sixth day off. The hours turned out to be a little longer, but after what I had been through, I didn't mind, and we did get every fifth or sixth day off. I was, however, the world's worst at spit shining. I never could get it right and failed to improve my skills while I was at the CG's Mess.

While clearing battalion, I discovered that my duffel bag, which contained my personal property, had definitely taken a beating. Initially, it had been stored in Quan Loi before being transported to PV. Someone had broken into it and stolen several items. My tape recorder was one of the missing items. I was a little pissed, but there was not much I could do, and there was no way the thief could ever be traced or caught. I submitted a claim to the Army and eventually received compensation for my loss.

October 7 also brought one more tidbit of good news. I went to an eye doctor, was examined, and received a new prescription for eyeglasses. It took no more than ten minutes to grind the lenses, and I had new glasses. The new lenses were so much better than the old ones. I could see more distinctly and my eyes did not tire. What a relief it was to see properly again!

As I cleared battalion, I stopped by the Bravo Company Orderly Room to chat one last time with people I knew. An extraordinary thing occurred that really shook me up. The Company had an adorable little puppy that had been born on Ike and brought down to PV when we moved. Everyone played with the dog and loved him. As I held the dog and played with him, he began to shake. Suddenly he jerked and went rigid. I set him down as he appeared to be paralyzed. He then had a fit, foamed at the mouth, and seemed to choke to death. Everyone was shocked and we all watched in horror as this small tragedy unfolded. One of the sergeants took him outside and dispatched him with a .45. I was scared stiff because I thought the dog either had rabies or distemper. We all went to a vet, who told us that unless the dog had bitten someone, nothing could be done. Everyone had fondled the puppy and had been licked by him — even me! I was sweating like hell. I thought for sure I could have been infected, so I questioned the vet at length about the possibility of contracting something. He assured me that no harm would come to me, but I still worried. So on that sad note, I left Bravo Company for good, and entered the world of the CG's Mess.

Indeed the realm of the CG's Mess was something else. The headquarters compound was a city within a city within a city. Our compound was fenced off from the surrounding Army base by high fences of wire mesh and concertina wire. The surrounding Army base was, in turn, fenced off from the village of Phuoc Vinh. The Division HQ had green grass everywhere, a badminton court, and a basketball and/or volleyball area. Officers sat around sunning themselves or exercised to lose the flab from lolling around on their tails too long! Life in the HQ seemed at a standstill. It was so totally unreal — a veritable Shangri-La right out of William Hudson's *Green Mansions*.

My first day (October 8) in the CG's compound was mind blowing. We ate in the CG's Mess prior to the officers' arriving for dinner. The food was unbelievable. We had veal, mashed potatoes and gravy, carrots and peas, watermelon, butterscotch pudding with whipped cream, salad (there were three different kinds), pre-sweetened tea, and a choice of either chocolate or white milk. I gorged myself. It sure beat C-rations!

We waiters had our own private recreation room with tables, chairs, magazines, and a refrigerator for our beer. The beer cost 15¢ a can and we could drink the cold suds any time of day that we wanted.

I talked a lot that first day with the Mess steward (an E-7) and other waiters, who were all super guys. The field, I learned, was a "taboo" subject, so to speak. We were out of it. That era of our lives was past and the past was to be forgotten. I learned that General Roberts only chose grunts for these jobs— so we all had something in common.

The only negative part of the job was that to get it, I had to shave off my mustache. To give up that little idiosyncrasy was easy. I would have done almost anything to get a rear job! So this infringement on my personal freedom did not bother me in the least.

We had our own private sleeping barracks and access to *real* bathrooms that had hot and cold running water for the sinks, showers and toilets. The main latrine, which the officers used, was about 150 meters away, but we also had our own private showers right outside our sleeping hooch. All this was mind boggling. I almost couldn't comprehend, or believe, my good fortune. I wanted to pinch myself to make sure all of this wasn't just a dream. It was so nice to have the modern conveniences of home again.

It is hard for me to describe the transition from grunt to waiter. It was like taking someone out of a nasty, vile and dirty life of squalor in the world's worst slum and making him an instant millionaire. I had lived in circumstances akin to abject poverty for five

Phuoc Vinh — Entrance to General Roberts' Mess.

months, and now I was working and living in the Ritz. Prior to the CG's Mess, I carried everything vital to my survival on my back. I slept dirty and wet under a poncho that usually leaked. Now I not only had my own bed with a mattress and springs, but also I had my own footlocker where I could store my stuff more securely. I did not have to go out and dig a hole to take a crap; now I had real toilets at my disposal. I had only taken two showers in five months; now I could shower every day in *hot* water. The food was out of this world: from C-rations to meals like those at the famous 21 Club. It was all too much to believe. It was almost too horrible to contemplate. How one part of the Army could be working, living and dying in the jungle not two miles distant while another lived in baronial splendor in its own castle was difficult to comprehend. No wonder, when the 2/8 first came to PV, they called it palace guard! The stark reality of this facet of Army life was most disturbing to me. That this type of living existed while men bled and died in the jungles close by was upsetting to me. I was truly thankful that I had been blessed to receive this job. After all, it was an honor and a privilege to attain such a coveted position. Only it really wasn't coveted by most grunts because they knew nothing about its existence. I was overwhelmed by the hypocrisy of the position in which I found myself. On the one hand, I abhorred rank and privilege, and on the other I had become a part of it, while others died in the dusty jungles of Vietnam. I was ecstatic to get the job and knew I was going to like it, but memories of what I had undergone to attain it still haunted me.

Achieving this position reinforced my belief in the system. If you were good, you were rewarded. The only way to succeed, to be someone, was to be good at something. Those who fought, and survived, were rewarded. It was like playing King of the Mountain. Some of us made it to the top of the heap. I had been one. I was thankful for the opportunity, but regretted leaving my comrades behind. I was, in reality, no better than them. We had all fought, ate, and slept together. I guess I was fortunate to become a combat medic for such a brief while. God had guided me to go out and help people in need. I *never* shirked or avoided my medic's responsibility to my fellow grunts. When they needed me, I went unhesitatingly. I did my job to the best of my ability, but I did not feel this made me any better than the rest. It was merely a job, someone had to do it, and I felt, at that time and place, it was my duty to be a medic.

What I had done as a medic had taken courage. Or was it insanity? Are not courage and insanity the same thing? Under extreme stress we either succeed or we crack. If we succeed, we are called courageous. But aren't we really insane? Thinking logically, would a sane person do the things I did? I doubt it. So now, I was out of the jungle and living in a fairly safe area. Nam's insanity was over for me. Mentally and emotionally I was torn inside. It would not take too long to adjust to my new status, but my heart went out to all those grunts who had to continue suffering.

Had someone approached me on October 1 and said, "You're going to have a plush rear job in one week, and be out of the field," I'd have replied, "Bullshit! I ain't believing it till it happens!" Well, it had happened. I was free. My ordeal in the jungle was over. I had run the gauntlet and survived — at least physically — its almost mortal blows. The emotional toll has followed me to the present.

When I joined the CG's Mess, I had to have my uniforms altered. Plus, I had to get the appropriate Cav patches and my rank insignia sewed onto the arms and shoulders of my fatigue jackets. My pants had to be tapered to look good and all my shirts had to have name strips. The cost of alterations to six pairs of pants and four shirts was $18.00, and I still had five more pairs of pants to be altered as we had to "break starch" so often. To break starch meant that we had to put on a clean or new uniform. Even though we were supposed to break starch once a day, I soon realized that twice a day was the norm. The Army did issue small-sized uniforms (my size), but they were so difficult to find that the alterations became an absolute necessity.

During one of my first nights at the CG's Mess, an amusing incident took place that demonstrated how hard it was for me to adjust to civilization again. On the night of October 8, I had to sleep on the Mess sergeant's office floor until a bunk was requisitioned for me. I got an air mattress and blissfully went to sleep with not a care in the world in what was, for me, luxurious comfort. The office, however, was so small that I had to sleep in the walkway that led from the Mess sergeant's room to the front door. About 1300 hours, someone in the kitchen had a problem and came to get the sergeant. Not knowing I would be sleeping in the walkway, he stepped on me. Thinking he was a gook, I grabbed him, and was proceeding to put a fist into him when he yelled and awakened me enough to make me realize what had happened. Mumbling some apologies, I went back to sleep only to have the same thing happen about an hour later with another person. I had never been so scared in my life. I really thought a gook had gotten to me. My thought processes had not adjusted sufficiently to make me realize I was really out of the field.

For the first few days, I could not believe I was eating the food that was available to us. On October 9, I had French toast, bacon, and sausage for breakfast and for lunch I ate egg sandwiches and pea soup. For dinner we had turkey so tender you could cut it with a fork. The asparagus was so succulent, you felt it had to have been picked from a garden that day. We could eat all we wanted and the head cook, Morton L. Nelms from Port Townsend, Washington, was without a doubt the best (and nicest) cook I ever knew in the Army.

At night, two or three times a week, after serving dinner, we would clear the tables and then sit back, with the officers, to watch the latest movies. Unfortunately, we could not really clean the Mess until the movie was over around 2230–2300 hours. Once the movie had ended, standard procedure dictated that the Mess floor had to be swept, mopped and buffed. Then we would give everything a final clean down and set up for the morning meal. We usually got to bed by midnight. Two or three times a week, during the afternoons there would be briefings, and one of us served tea and coffee and got to stay for the briefing. In this manner, we learned a lot about how the war was being prosecuted.

One of the waiters, Mike Blair from Midland, Texas, had graduated from Texas Tech. While at TCU, I had known several girls from Midland and asked him if he knew them. Well, he did! Plus, he asked me about several of his acquaintances who had attended TCU and I knew them. It was indeed a small world. One of the other waiters, who had gone back to the World shortly after I arrived at the CG's Mess, was named "Happy." He was from McKinney, Texas, so I had plenty of Texas reminiscing to do.

In PV, the availability of grass was widespread, and we had access to it twenty-four hours a day. The South Vietnamese, who worked within the compound, were our suppliers and, if they did not have any, they could usually get some for you in a matter of hours. We also could go to the village and buy it. Everyone seemed to smoke it. My ideas on grass changed radically while I was in Nam. I could now understand why grunts smoked it so profusely. After what I had experienced — the hell I had undergone — I knew we needed something to take our minds off the blood and gore that we had witnessed. The trips I took while high on marijuana were not bad at all. In fact, they were pleasantly nice. By October 9, I had been in PV five or six days, and had smoked it more than a few times. Nam's grass was the best pot I ever smoked. It made you feel so happy, content, and at ease with the world. It was the high of your day; and the advantage to getting high on grass was that, when you came down, you did not have a hangover.

I knew I could not become an addict. I just did not smoke grass that often and my trips were not all that big, or long. It made me forget the worries of my past in the jungle. I was in total control of myself every time I smoked, plus I had a standing rule — no more than one joint a day. The grass made my days mellow, but unlike some grunts I knew, I was not blown away all the time. I was mature enough to realize the consequences of overindulgence. Where others lacked the willpower, I was able to stop each day after one joint. I had no great craving for it. If it was available, I smoked it. If not, I didn't climb the walls looking for it. I was nowhere close to being a pothead, but, like fine wine, I sure enjoyed it.

I had a job every grunt aspired to have. For me, the war was over. My hell was done. It was stateside-type duty from October onward. Oh, sure, we got a few incoming mortars or rockets, which were not that worrisome. Because we were living within the Division HQ, it seemed as if the war did not exist anymore. We were safe within our own little private cocoon. I was finally out of the deep water and quicksand. I had paid my price to keep America free. Now it was someone else's turn to take up the standard. I could get peacefully high now with little or no worry of endangering myself or anyone else. I was so relieved and felt as if a huge weight had been lifted from my shoulders.

It took only a few days to adjust to the CG's Mess routine. We awakened at 0600 hours; so, if I had not had much sleep the evening before, I would usually crash in the afternoon from 1400 to 1700 hours. Then from

1700 to 1800 hours, I spit shined my boots (or attempted to), showered and shaved since the evening meal was our most important meal. We usually broke starch for this meal. Once a week, every waiter served one day in the kitchen and did not have to wait on the officers. All we had to do was dry coffee cups and saucers, and polish the glasses. It was easier and more relaxing than waiting and wasn't anything like regular Army KP. Plus, we got to know, and bullshit with, the cooks.

The CG's Mess Hall consisted of two main rooms. The largest one was the dining room, which was dominated by a round table where the CG and his immediate staff were seated beneath a huge 1st Air Cav emblem that hung on the wall and overshadowed the table. There were two smaller rectangular tables where the lieutenant colonels and majors sat. The junior officers, about six in all, consisting of captains and lieutenants, sat in the back. They, of course, were always the last ones served and always griped the loudest about the service, like hogs in a trough looking for more slops.

The second room was a carpeted bar, which had lounge chairs, sofas and a mahogany bar where the officers were served by their own private bartender, a guy named David M. Dawson from Flint, Michigan, who was also a grunt. Prior to the evening meal, the officers would come in and socialize for a half hour or so before eating. On a shelf on one wall of this room was a TV, so they could sit back and enjoy reruns of old TV shows and get the day's latest news. The CG (General Roberts) was always the first man to enter the bar area. He was then followed by the other generals, Colonel Kingston, then the lieutenant colonels, majors and three aides—a captain and two lieutenants.

We used real silverware and china in the Mess. The china plates were all embossed with the 1st Cavalry's emblem, and two stars, symbolizing that this was a two-star generals' Mess, were located on the black stripe that diagonally crossed the yellow Cavalry patch.

One of the advantages to being a waiter was that we did not have to be kitchen KPs. In the CG's compound, all menial labor was done by the South Vietnamese. Two women worked in the kitchen. If they liked you, you were "Numbah One," which meant you were OK. If you pissed them off, however, they would say "GI Numbah Ten," which meant you were an asshole. If we ever called one of the South Vietnamese women a "Numbah Ten," we had to be prepared to hear every four-letter word in the alphabet, spoken in English and in Vietnamese. Needless to say we couldn't help but tease these women at times to see what they would say. It spiced up life somewhat.

Knowing that I was going to be in PV for six and a half months, I decided that I would try to learn the fundamentals of a foreign language.

Phuoc Vinh — Head table in General Roberts' Mess. Note: Linen has the symbol of the 1st Cav Division (AM) and a gold horse sits on the stripe.

So, on Thursday, October 13, I went to the education center and, for $5.00, enrolled in a Spanish 1 college-level correspondence course. If I passed it, I would get credit for it. Actually, I planned on studying it so that I could receive a fundamental knowledge of Spanish, which would aid me in getting a master's degree when I returned to the World and entered grad school. I knew that, if I planned on getting a master's, I would have to learn a foreign language. I wanted to go to the University of Texas to get my MA in archeology, so that I could study Indian ruins in the Southwest U.S. and in Mexico, where Spanish was spoken. If I could obtain the basic foundation, then I felt that I would not have as much trouble taking it in grad school.

On October 14, 1969, I received a letter from my parents informing me that my uncle, Thorton "Thornie" Tayloe, my mother's stepbrother, had died. He was a quiet, scholarly man whom I met at family functions and grew to know as a fine gentleman. Although I did not know him as

Phuoc Vinh — General Roberts' bar.

well as I knew his two children, Virginia and Dickie, who were my age, I liked and respected this distinguished southern aristocrat, whom cancer had taken. I wrote the following letter of condolence to my Aunt Virginia, which I feel epitomized my feelings toward death that I had grown to know so intimately those last few months:

> I have just learned of Uncle Thornie's death. I want to extend to you my most profound sympathy. I pray that you are all right and that you are bearing up after the strain you have been under. I know that the last few months have been most difficult for you. I can only hope and pray that you will continue to have the courage and fortitude that you've evidenced in the past. I know that anything I can write or say is inadequate. Yet I do want you to know that I am praying for you in your time of sorrow. Believe me, I know how you feel because I have seen men die over here, some as I worked to save their life. I know that Virginia and Dickie are nearby to help and comfort you. I pray that they will aid and support you in this most sad time of all times. I know that you both had a

wonderful life together and perhaps life seems empty for you now. Just
remember that you have many years left and two wonderful children to
share those years with. You have been very brave and courageous, and I
want you to know I admire the strength of mind that you've evidenced.
Please excuse my meager condolences. I felt tho' that I must write and let
you know that I feel deeply for you in your loss. Please take care and
remember that we all admire you. When you have a chance, please feel
free to write. I have a new job.

That letter says a lot not only to my aunt but also about the way that
life forced us to live and bear up under the strain imposed on us by outside
forces. In effect, it summed up my own feelings toward life as I saw it in
the context of the war, which then surrounded me. No one can understand
someone else's feelings at the loss of a loved one. Neither can they comprehend the loss that we feel at being forced to participate in a war in which
all or most of our friends are taken from us. Death is cruel. War is immoral.
Death takes and leaves you with mostly the remembrance of things good.
War imbues one's mind with the sights and smells of death and destruction.
We live. We die. It is far better, I think, to die of old age and sickness than
to be sacrificed to appease your nation's image in the world.

Death is everywhere and plays no favorites. We can dodge meeting it
only so long before it comes and walks hand in hand with us to meet the
unknown. The tragedy of Nam was that so many, so young, had to die. In
Nam, I lost many buddies and some childhood friends. Death robbed them
all of a happy and perhaps productive life. Our country did that to us. Our
country must not be forgiven for that sin. Our leaders must be constantly
reminded about the follies of war. We must not let them forget lest they
be tempted to begin a new war for another hopeless cause. The blood of
America's young men and women must not, cannot, be shed in vain ever
again. Otherwise, oblivion, obscurity and death await us at the end of the
tunnel.

The next day, October 15, proved to be another upsetting day. On that
day, I received a telegram from my father that said, "Get out of General's
Mess. Return to the field." I was incensed that he would have the temerity to send me such a message. Somehow, in his convoluted thinking, he
felt I was lowering myself by becoming a waiter. I am sure he sincerely felt
I should have continued to be a medic. All my detailed letters home of
Bravo Company's extermination in September had evidently not been
effective enough to convince him that my health would be a lot better if I
was out of the boonies. After everything I had experienced, there was no
way I was ever going to return to the jungle. How my father ever thought
that I would even remotely consider going back out there to be killed, or

wounded, is a mystery to me. I just wasn't that stupid. I know I did a good job as a medic, and I missed being a medic, but there are times in everyone's life when they reach a crossroads and have to decide which road to follow. I was one who was not willing to tempt fate. I was not going to place my life in further danger, no matter what.

My parents wrote a few follow-up letters concerning this matter, which arrived a couple of days later. Their main bone of contention seemed to be that I was a Wise — that no man with the name of Wise ever lowered himself or bent a knee to do a menial job for people who (my parents thought) were beneath them. Basically, my parents were old-line traditionalists who believed, albeit mistakenly, that chivalry still existed. According to their way of thinking, a man of good name and upbringing *never* lowered himself to do menial tasks. It all got back to the "do what is expected of you" syndrome. Because I had always had that horseshit crammed down my throat, I just didn't believe in it. It was an honor to be a member of an old-line family whose roots went back to the settling of Virginia in the 1630s, but I never considered it as a privilege, and I never looked at it as being better than someone else. My parents believed that one simply did not associate with someone because his father drove a delivery truck, or one did not date Miss X because her father was a common laborer. All my life, I had been raised with that type of Dark Ages, Neanderthal thinking. I was so glad to get away from that type of social consciousness when I went to college in Texas. It's fun to break with tradition, and I did it gladly at TCU. Parents who force antiquated ideals on their children's social life will also fail. Children resent being told how to live their lives because "it's what is expected of you." I had so much old-line tradition crammed down my throat as a child that I rebelled. It was such a joy to freely associate with people whom I chose to know, and it was nice to date girls from all walks of life. Parents who raise children and imbue them with a social class tradition are only perpetrating a special kind of slavery. Eventually the slaves rebel. I have no regret that I shrugged off the mantle of the "do what is expected of you" mentality. I have been much happier and better adjusted by not conforming to my parents' preconceived notions of propriety. When anyone attempts to make you conform to their ideals and beliefs, they are proselytizing. They think they are doing it for your own good but, in reality, they are only doing it for their own personal self-satisfaction and gratification, because they are unsure of their own position in life. I have always resented anyone's attempts of making me do or believe thus and so because "it's the right thing to do." When it's "the right thing to do" you can almost bet your last dollar that it isn't. All they are attempting to do is make you conform. I refuse to conform and, after what happened to me in Vietnam, I have every reason **NEVER** to conform —**NEVER** to do what is expected of me because "it's the right thing to do." Vietnam made me a radical — or more so, a revolutionary in my thinking. I will probably always retain that Don Quixote attitude of challenging the windmill. I have and will champion lost causes because they go against the grain. I may never change much of society or the establishment in my lifetime, but I shall never let it walk over me without putting up a good fight. Woe be it unto anyone who attempts to push me into a corner to make me concede, because I will come out of that corner any way possible and they will ultimately regret their rash attempt to tree me.

As a result of my experiences in Nam, I abhor people telling me what to do. No one tells me what to do. No one gives me an order to do something. Now, if they ask me to do something, that is a whole new ball game. But I came out of Nam with a deep hatred for authority, and people who attempt to enforce their brand of it. People who show off their authority and swagger about with it need to be pulled off their high horse. The best example of this is found in the lower echelons of our local, state and federal governments. These people think they have all kinds of authority, and that they are going to make you conform. Bullshit. We pay them (with our tax money); they should do what we want. Unfortunately, most bureaucrats are too goddamn smug because they know they cannot lose their jobs unless they really fuck up. So they wield their authority unconscionably on people. Most people are afraid of governmental authority and knuckle under. Not me. Fuck 'em! They need to be put in their place and, after Vietnam, I'm certainly not afraid of fighting city hall — whether it be government or the establishment.

So, here I was, fighting city hall (my parents) because they were trying to tell me what to do. I resented their intrusion, especially since they wanted me to go back to the boonies. In their misguided eyes, had I returned to the boonies, as a medic, and been killed, they could have accepted my death with few qualms. I would have died doing what they expected of me. I had no intention, however, of adding my name to a long list of unsung heroes and forgotten warriors by going back out in the field and getting my ass shot off. No fuckin' way, Jack! Only the best grunts were chosen as the CG's aides. I was not lowering myself. I was being smart. I had even given the head waiter and Mess sergeant a chance to reject me by telling them in the initial interview that I felt I was accomplishing more by continuing to be a medic. Had I gotten any other rear job with Bravo Company in Phuoc Vinh, I would have had to pull guard duty and KP, etc., etc. No way was I going to set myself up for that kind of a job. I had bested some damn good men to get where I was and knew a good thing when I saw it.

Besides being a nonconformist, a revolutionary, and a radical, I am also an opportunist. If something good comes along, grab it because hindsight sure won't help you later. I was in fat city now, and I intended to stay despite what my parents thought. So, I wrote them a rather explicit letter telling them why I had no fucking intention of ever returning to the field and, if they didn't like it, tough shit. That ended that, but it made my relations with my parents even more strained. To this day, even though my father is now dead, I cannot forgive him for sending that telegram which, in effect, told me that he wanted me to go back out to the jungle and risk getting killed to uphold the honor of my family name. I couldn't blame my father for this medieval thinking. It really wasn't his fault. I couldn't forgive him, though. He was too deeply rooted in Victorian values, which were leftovers from the dark ages of the early 20th century. The saddest part of all this was, upon my return from Nam, he steadfastly refused to back off and admit that he was wrong or had erred in sending that telegram. When a child realizes that a parent is willing for that child to die, then, to all intents and purposes, the parent-child relationship is over. The child has every right to reject that parent. No parent should tell, or intimate to, their offspring that they should place themselves in a position where the odds are that they will be killed. That is wrong. I often wonder how many other parents did the same thing as mine did. How many other parents wanted to bask in the glory of having a son who was a fallen hero in the most unjust, illegal, and immoral folly in which the United States has ever been involved? Parents who try to project their hopes and dreams of military glory and honor onto their children strive for an impossible goal. The dreams of yesterday, if followed, are tomorrow's dead. In the final analysis, my father was an incredible hypocrite. During World War II he had been a personal aide to General George C. Marshall, the U.S. Army Chief of Staff who was the Supreme Commander of Allied Forces. As an aide to General Marshall my father's job was similar to mine in that he, too, was waiting on bended knee! I am sure he never saw the similarity in our Army positions.

I had no intention of being a dead hero. Like the rat that looks for a hole when the cat's after him, I intended to stay alive as long as I could. I didn't particularly care for the lead sandwiches that Charlie was apt to hand out unexpectedly. They just didn't digest well. The cuisine in the CG's Mess was a whole hell of a lot better and more appetizing. There was just no way I was going to turn it down.

The guys I associated with in the CG's Mess were, as I have already pointed out, a cut above the normal grunt. Most were better educated and had a good head upon their shoulders. Larry Busch, the head waiter, was a short, stocky, curly, black-haired guy from Davenport, Iowa, who had two years of junior college. Marvin M. "Mac" McKeone, from Redmond, Utah, was a medium-tall, blondish, quiet guy who had a degree in forestry from the University of Utah. Joe Rinehart, from Minnesota, was a short, affable guy with three and a half years of college. Mike Blair had a laugh and sense of humor that wouldn't quit. I liked Mike, and we got along well. The bartender, David M. Dawson, a graduate of Central Michigan State, was a tall, well-built taciturn individual who took his job seriously. Bart Renoir, from California, was a smug, cocky, blond-haired guy whom I liked, but found difficult to get along with, for some unexplainable reason. Juan Gonzales, from Puerto Rico, was a permanent KP along with the South Vietnamese women. I found it interesting that the Army assigned a minority individual in a permanent KP-type position along with the mama-sans.

One night, soon after I arrived, we had a floor show in the HQ compound. It was an all-girl Oriental band that consisted of three guitarists, a drummer, a singer, and a dancer. The lead guitarist did not look Oriental at all, but she had nice tits and was a fine guitar picker. It was a great evening. I got somewhat mellow on the 15¢ beer and then had to go clean the Mess and set up for the morning meal. It took me a lot longer to clean and set up the Mess but, when beer was 15¢ a can, one couldn't resist getting loaded.

The 15th of October was memorable in one other way. The Mess officer came by and asked us if anyone wanted to interview to be an aide to General Creighton W. Abrams, a four-star general in Saigon, who was the Commander of the Military Assistance Command, Vietnam (MACV) from 1968 to 1972. MACV was in charge of all U.S. military activities in Vietnam. I turned it down because I felt I would be better off in PV, plus, I figured that the competition to be a four-star general's aide would be intense.

We also heard about the famous moratorium held in the States on October 15. It upset me because I saw it as harmful toward the efforts of grunts to win in Vietnam. I wrote to my parents on October 16 and expressed my concern over this nationwide peace demonstration:

> I'm so furious and upset over that damn moratorium that I feel that I have to speak up. Here we are over here, sweating like hell to win a war, and there has to be this huge peace demonstration. Result — Congress cuts back on funds to supply us. You know what it's like when you're lying out

there, bullets whizzing by, and you have to wait for 2 firebases to fire artillery shells because both don't have enough to fire your mission. I'm so sick to see those damn college presidents giving in to these punks and letting classes out for one day. Believe you me, were I a student at a college and they closed classes for such an inane reason, I would, if I had the money, sue the college for violation of my rights to get an education. I feel every student who didn't get to go to class on that day is having his rights to receive an education violated. Why doesn't the older generation have the backbone to stand up and be counted? What's wrong with the oldsters? Are they afraid that the minority should rule? What's happening to America? What happened to the Constitution's clause that the minority should obey the will of the majority? I tell you this—when America gets to the point where the majority no longer rule and the minority controls them, we might as well hang it up. We'll no longer be a nation. Can the U.S. be turning into a nation of weak-willed men? If that's the way America is going I certainly hate to be around to see its fall. I'm tired of being over here fighting for my country and reading about some little punk, a group of Negroes, or student protesters influencing Congress to make us get out of this war so that they don't have to get drafted and fight over here. My rights are being violated. If I have to serve my country, then those people back there better do the same and not weasel out. I could have refused to come over here and gone to jail, but I didn't. It was my duty to come. Why can't you adults instill a sense of duty, or honor, in the young? What's wrong with you? So what if 50% of the U.S. population is under 25 and 75% is under 29? How many of our youth actually vote? It's you older people. Why can't you stand up and be counted? You know I really hate to think what I might do the first time I see a protester when I return to the States. They are no better than I. If I have to serve over here, then they should. You know I never realized how privileged we Americans are with freedom of speech, assembly, religion, etc. until I joined the Army and came over here. Now I know it was well worth 2 yrs. of my life to give up so I could serve my country. I think that *everyone* (male and female) owes their country service. In order to have our democracy everyone should be willing to pay a small price for it, and 2 yrs. isn't much to pay. We young take too much in our democracy for granted. It is a pity this is so. I wish somehow, I could tell this and make the young of America realize that freedom is not without its sacrifices.

As I read those words today, I do not see how I could have ever written them. Not only was I naive but also I was still clearly under the influence of my parents' ultrapatriotic thinking. I was too blind to see what the anti-war protestors were trying to achieve. I still believed, to some extent, in the old adage of "my country right or wrong," even though I knew we were getting our asses kicked in Nam. I had graduated from TCU in May

1968 and entered the Army four weeks later, which was just prior to the seething discontent that exploded across the nation's campuses. The protest movement surged forward to make its impact upon our nation. The protesters may have been no better than myself, but they sure had their shit together a lot better than I did. I am ashamed that I did not have the courage to join them upon my return to the World.

Our youth were right to protest this illegal and immoral war. I was seeing, first hand, why this war was so insane, and why it had to be brought to a standstill. I don't regret serving two years in the Army. I matured a lot, and it made me realize how fortunate I was to live in America. Yet, I also learned that, when you fight with one hand tied behind your back, your military leaders will do, or try, anything to achieve victory, including sacrificing scores of troops to attain some nebulous decoration to pin on their chest. I still believe we owe our country some type of service — but we should never be forced to participate in an unholy war. It is just not right.

Out of all the movies that I saw in the CG's Mess, one stands out. On October 19, we were all watching *Bandelero* with James Stewart, Dean Martin and Raquel Welch. The climax was fast approaching when lightning struck the compound's generator and out went all the electricity. We never got to see the ending of the movie, and it was only when VCRs became popular in the late 1980s that I was able to view the entire movie again and see who ended up with Raquel Welch!

On October 20, we served lunch to Admiral John S. McCain, Jr., who had four stars and was the Commander in Chief, Pacific Command (CINPAC) from 1968 to 1972. MP bodyguards were everywhere, and I was really nervous waiting on a man with so many stars on his shoulder. He was short and thin, and little did I know, at that time, of the personal strain he was under because his son, John S. McCain, III, was a POW in Hanoi. He was a gentleman and most complimentary toward us waiters. He knew how to treat enlisted men and was easy to serve. I am glad his son, John, who had not only attended the same prep school as I had in Alexandria, Virginia, but also later became a U.S. Senator from Arizona, returned home safely from Hanoi in 1973.

October 21 was my 24th birthday. In the week leading up to it, I had received twenty-five birthday cards from friends, my parents, their friends, and others. The CG allowed us to have the day off on our birthday, and I planned to loll around, sleep, and drink. My Texas girlfriend, Abby, had sent a tin with homemade fudge cookies which, although they arrived early, I had saved until the 21st. My mother had been sending small two-ounce bottles of vodka, and I had four bottles waiting to be consumed. She also sent a cake, which didn't last long. It was a mellow day highlighted by a floor show that night after dinner.

Again, the floor show consisted of an all-girl combo. One versatile girl played the electric organ, accordion, and a steel guitar. She also played a mean polka, which I enjoyed tremendously. There was a girl magician who, despite the fact that she wore a bathing suit with no sleeves, was exceedingly good at making small objects pop out of thin air. All of us were most impressed. The band played a lot of American pop songs. As they played, the rains descended. We stayed and got drenched watching them perform on the covered stage. Their last song was "God Bless America," which brought all of us to our feet as we sang along with the band. Then I went back to my hooch and slept. It had been a good birthday, and I was thankful I was in PV to celebrate it rather than out in the boonies.

Although I had been in the CG's Mess about three weeks, I had not recovered from the experiences of the jungle. On October 22, while I was waiting on some officers in the bar, there was a storm with lots of lightning. About 100 meters from the Mess was a tall command tower. I had just set some drinks down on the bar when lightning struck the tower. Through the window, I saw the resulting flash and found myself flat on the floor. The few officers present got a good laugh out of my reaction. I was chagrined, to say the least, because I had not gotten over sudden sounds or flashes. To this day, some thirty-four years later, I still jump at sudden sharp sounds. This is part of the legacy of Vietnam, which I expect to take with me to the grave. Car backfires are the worst sounds and still scare the hell out of me. Every sudden and unexpected loud sound provides me with an indelible, instantaneous flashback to Nam. It is a cross that many of us Vietnam vets continue to bear.

That night another explosion of different sorts also occurred. There was a small, private mess hall for the six or seven sergeant majors (SMs— the highest enlisted grade one could attain) who lived and worked in the Cav compound. This mess had a refrigerator where the SMs and waiters stored things. About two weeks prior to that night, Rick Hall, a waiter whom I have not previously mentioned, had placed a used whiskey bottle full of tomato juice in the refrigerator, which had been emitting a strange smell for several days. That night, it was my turn to mop the floor of the SM's Mess and, as I mopped, I head a dull pop. I opened the refrigerator door and saw that the bottle had exploded. Glass and tomato juice were splattered all over the refrigerator, which I had to clean. I never could figure out what happened. Perhaps there was some residue of liquor in the bottle that had caused the juice to ferment. I did not, however, appreciate having to clean it up.

Later that evening I went to the day room to relax and watch the Texas–Oklahoma football game on our TV. I say our TV because 10–15 of us had pitched in and purchased it at the PX for $115.00. We had a lot of free time, so we needed to amuse ourselves somehow. As I watched TV, Larry Busch came in and flash! I had my picture taken. Not to be outdone, I quickly got my camera and flashbulbs and went to his hooch. Flash! Everyone had a camera, so, before long, we all had a flashcube battle. It was a lot of fun as all six of us shot at each other with flashes. We had a blast and all of us were partially blinded from so many flashes. It relieved the tension of a long day. I had not had so much fun since I had joined the Army and found that it was a relief to act zany and crazy for just a little while.

On the 23rd, I heard some good news. As I served supper to the officers, I overheard the CG talking about my old battalion commander, LTC Lewis. He had relieved Lewis of command! I could not believe what I was hearing. I overheard General Roberts say that the main reason he relieved Lewis was because he got too many grunts killed. I could have screamed, "Hallelujah!" I know a lot of guys in the 2/8 would be happy to hear that good news. Any officer who is willing to sacrifice his men solely to get enemy kills is no officer in my book. It is a pity that the man was not relieved after Becky's demise. A whole hell of a lot of American lives might have been spared.

It did not take long to adjust to the life of leisure. At the CG's Mess, time certainly didn't drag — at least at first. In fact, I often ran out of it. I was spending four or five hours a day, between meals, writing letters. In the evenings, I saw movies in the CG's Mess, or watched TV. After the movies were over and we had prepared the Mess for the breakfast meal, I would get at least six hours of sleep. It was so good to get six hours of uninterrupted sleep in a warm, dry bed. The novelty, or shock, of my changed circumstances had just not worn off yet.

About this time, I received a long letter from Dr. Alfred Chanutin, a close personal friend of my parents whom I called "Dr. Chan." In his letter was much food for thought, but these parts of one paragraph stood out:

> You have … a distinguished war record, and you have learned to live with your comrades under the most trying conditions. I have seen so many boys who have become men overnight and I think that you have made this very important step. If you have learned and appreciated the word "humility," you will find that your life will be productive and happy. What about your future? I can tell you that … when you move from tumult to comparative quiet, the shock is sometimes not easy to understand. It will take time for you to equilibrate to such a change.

How right he was. It was extremely difficult to adjust to my new surroundings in PV. What was even more painstakingly difficult was my adjustment to life back in the United States, when I returned in April 1970. I was safe, but I was not sound. I don't claim to be unique in that respect. There are thousands of Vietnam vets who probably had the same problems of transitional readjustment. Only I, like many others, probably didn't adjust — inside. Outside, outwardly, I am adjusted. Inwardly, I seethe, burn, and am saddened at what was done to me and hundreds like me. The shock that he referred to in his letter is not gone. It will never be gone. How can anyone live in a sane society after participating in such madness? The old expression, "You can take the boy out of the country, but you can't take the country out of the boy" is most applicable in my, and many others', situation. You just cannot justify allowing someone to participate in murder and mayhem, and then expect him to be the same person prior to his involvement in such acts. We Vietnam vets carry a large hidden wound and an even deeper scar in our hearts and minds. We were not welcomed home by our government or by our neighbors. We didn't lose! We, individually, **DID NOT LOSE**. Our government, with its hands-off policy, forced us as a nation to lose. In turn, some parts of our nation took out their frustrations on the returning men. We became convenient scapegoats. I am extremely bitter at my country and my government for allowing this to occur, and it's about time the people of this nation got off their asses and placed some of the blame upon their own shoulders.

Outwardly, I made the transition. Inwardly, I became a radical and a revolutionary. When government imposes upon its people, government must be changed. When unjust laws are forced upon people that are detrimental to their health, welfare, and ability to conduct business, those laws must be changed, repealed or blatantly disobeyed. Laws that force a majority of people to do something against their will must be violated. Bad laws should, and must, be disobeyed, and political bodies that refuse to change those laws must be thrown out of office or removed by whatever means necessary. The laws of our nation forced its young Vietnam veterans into involuntary servitude and then served them up as sacrifices on a silver platter to Charlie. The individuals who write our laws probably believe that they are right, meet and just and must be obeyed without question.

"If the law supposes that, the law is an ass, an idiot," wrote Charles Dickens in *Oliver Twist*. Laws that force us to go against our will are wrong. As Edward Gibbon wrote, "The laws of a nation form the most instructive part of their history." It was the misfortune of our nation's youth to be drafted by a law that gave them no choice but to fight, be wounded, die, or go to prison. That is not justice. It is tyranny. We Vietnam vets have a sacred duty to ensure that tyranny has had its day forever. Never again should our young men be forced to participate in an unjust cause and have to undergo another gauntlet like Vietnam.

I replied to Dr. Chan's letter with some of the following thoughts:

> You said in your letter—"if you have learned and appreciate the word humility you will find that your life will be productive and happy." Well, Dr. Chan, I don't think I'd ever have learned it had I not been in the service and come over here. We all need to be humble in order to realize just what life is all about. I'm proud, but at the same time I'm humble ... I've learned a lot from being over here. I've grown up ... I'm no longer the son of wealthy parents who's been sheltered all his life and protected from the horrors of the outside world. I've grown into my own self. I know what I want to do. I'm not afraid to try things. I'm not afraid to admit I'm not always right. I know when to admit I'm wrong. I stand on my own two legs. I can't always justify my actions, but at least I did them. I'm to blame if something goes wrong. I'm a lot older now mentally than I was six short months ago, when I came home.... You mentioned the moratorium. We did read about it over here in the *Stars & Stripes*.... I personally think that the people who participated in it are doing America a great disservice. If they only knew how much this is helping the Communists. We all know over here that Nixon is doing his best. We all also know that when we leave from here that the Communists are going to take over. Right now, the enemy is infiltrating into the country. He is avoiding contact and hiding. He's not moving. He's waiting. He's massing in Cambodia. In 2 days he can march from Cambodia to Saigon. He's just sitting back now like a cat waiting for the mouse to come out. When we leave here, he'll sweep in one big gigantic move to the Delta and Saigon and seize control before anyone knows what's hit. The NVA in hiding will emerge and strike swiftly. That's what will happen when we leave because the S. Viets are not capable of dealing with the Commies. They have neither the energy nor the desire. No small wonder the Communists applaud our moratorium. America divided is what they want. It nearly killed me to read about all those weak yellow-bellied college presidents who gave in to the demands of the students and dismissed classes for a day. When America gets to the point where her leaders won't stand up and fight we are lost. When America lets itself be ruled by the minority, we are lost. When respected and learned men can no longer cope with the problems we face, we are lost. When, or once the people see that the only way they can get something is to riot or protest, then we are lost. There is much ill in America today, Dr. Chan, and we see it over here.... Rome was corrupted from within before it fell. Is this to be America's fate?

I had grown up a lot while in Nam. Vietnam made me realize that life was a bitter pill, and that you had to grab it and hang on for the ride. At that time, I already knew the war was a hopeless cause. Yet, I was torn between the old concept of "my country right or wrong" and the grim, gray, stark realities of this most unjust war. My thinking back then had been influenced by my parents' method of seeing life from an Olympian vantage point. Longhairs, hippies, and protesters were automatically wrong. All my life, I had been brainwashed by my parents to believe in high principles and ideals. Now that is not wrong. They had every right to raise me the way they felt was best. Things went wrong because they were not able to adjust their beliefs to tolerate free and independent thoughts. They were hopelessly mired in their own Victorian beliefs. The situation was either black or white — there was no room for a gray area. If you disagreed with their preconceived beliefs, you did it mildly — never crossing them. This was wrong. It hurt them and it hurt me. It didn't encourage a child to think. Hence, I was torn by my new knowledge, and how it varied sharply with my parents' outlook on life. To my parents, something was either right or wrong, good or bad. It is terribly difficult to break the thoughts and beliefs of your parents. At that time, I still had not been able to do so, as is evidenced by my reply to Dr. Chan.

To point out how my thinking had not let go of the parental influence, I had written a letter to *The Skiff*, TCU's student newspaper, concerning the moratorium, which had incensed me because I still believed in the old adage of "my country right or wrong." My rather long tirade against the moratorium, printed in *The Skiff* on November 21, 1969, follows in its entirety:

> I receive *The Skiff* over here in Vietnam and have read with much interest about the Moratorium as it was conducted at TCU. I now feel that I must speak up for the thousands of GIs who are over here risking and giving their lives because of immature students who think it's "the thing to do" to protest this war by screaming for peace. It is unfortunate that these few — a minority to be sure — must hold the center of attention in recent *Skiff* issues and U.S. news media.
>
> Such idiots fail to realize why men like myself are over here fighting and giving our blood. I myself saw heavy combat as a combat medic and was wounded twice in two weeks. The children, who call themselves students at TCU, protest this war because they lack the insight to know what the war is all about. They persist in protesting and screaming for peace which aids the Communists and not Nixon's peace efforts. Such stupid peace demonstrations spur the Communists on to new attacks and more atrocities.
>
> Before students scream for peace again let them come over here and see what it's like. Let them see a GI with his legs blown off. Let them see the cold blooded murder of men, women, and children all because they desired freedom.

Such atrocities will not cease until the NVA are driven from this country. If we leave, thousands more innocents will die at the brutal hands of the Communists. What young people fail to realize is that we are over here to give the South Vietnamese freedom so that they may choose the way they want to live (in peace) and be governed.

We are not dying in vain. We are not bleeding in vain. Young people today are spoiled. They want all the privileges of freedom given us by the U.S. Constitution, yet they are unwilling to give up this luxury of freedom for a while to insure that they, and others will be free.

I noticed quite a few pictures taken of students involved with running the TCU Moratorium. Most had long hair and looked unshaven. These unfortunately are the nonconformists of our society. They are the ones who want something for nothing. They are the ones who are unwilling to put their life on the line as I have had to do.

What these misguided unfortunates seek is not peace, but a way to escape the draft and the obligation that they owe their country. Their country gave them freedom, all it asks in return is for them to help preserve that freedom not only for themselves and others, but for those who cannot fight sufficiently for their freedom.

Let the peace protesters come over here and see how much their idiotic Moratorium has helped the Communists. Let them come over here and see a young 19 year old GI die because the NVA has used the dissent in our country to be bolder in their attacks.

Freedom isn't free. We all must pay the price for it. Some of us pay the supreme price while some dirty, unshaven, long-haired idiot dishonors the Vietnam dead by reading their names in front of the TCU Student Center.

I didn't want to come to Vietnam, but I knew I owed my country an obligation to preserve freedom — not just in the U.S. but anywhere it was threatened so that we all may live in peace.

Now I've had to put my life on the line while some dodo protests for peace and brings dissent. Because of your protests for peace more GIs died this week in an offensive that the North Vietnamese incurred so that more protests would be raised in the U.S.

America does not stand to gain by your protests but Charlie does. I hope the students at TCU can be proud of knowing that their peace protests led to the death of more GIs. That's what you peaceniks have to live with — you caused more GIs to die.

We cannot leave this country (Vietnam) until we are absolutely sure that they can stand on their own feet. If we pull out now, all our efforts, all our combat deaths will have been in vain. I'm sure the majority of Americans don't want to happen.

When Communist infiltration can be stopped and the South Vietnamese are allowed to govern without the threat of murder and violence, then and only then can we pull out.

I urge all loyal TCU students to support President Nixon — to disregard the cries of the minority who wish to bring disunity and discord so that they may profit at the expense of dead GIs. I've put my life on the line over here and I will gladly do it again.

But, if I die, I don't want to die for the immature fools who are aiding the Communists with their peace protests.

It wasn't immature students who were protesting. They were part of a nation fed up with war and young boys dying for nothing. I, the letter writer, had not matured in my thinking. Upon reflection, I am sure that it is true that the peace protests protracted the war and aided the communist cause. The North Vietnamese counted on our protesters to stir up enough discontent that would drag the war out until America gave up.

Remember, the North Vietnamese were incredibly patient people. They had been fighting a war more than twenty years. To someone who had fought so long and so hard, what were another few years of war? Nothing. Hanoi played on the American people's minds to the hilt. Pham Van Dong, Prime Minister of the Democratic Republic of Vietnam, explained to *New York Times* reporter Harrison Salisbury why Hanoi was confident of winning the war. Dong "stressed again and again that North Vietnam was prepared to fight 10 years, 20 years, or any number of years in support of its sovereignty and independence in its 'sacred war.'"[*] Hanoi knew we were an impatient people and that sooner or later we would have to get out of Nam to save face. I am sure they timed and launched their attacks to obtain the maximum amount of media effect upon the U.S. people. They used our protests to their sole advantage, and in the end, their strategy worked.

We were in Nam, I believe, to give South Vietnam freedom. Yet we did not understand, or had no concept of, their way of life. They wanted our money and our military equipment to fight a war that had really been lost at Dien Ben Phu in 1954. Their way of life dictated that many would die — after all, there were too many hungry mouths to feed. So what if Charlie killed off a whole village. That meant more food for the masses. The VC and NVA controlled Vietnam far more than we ever realized and corruption in the Saigon government controlled the rest of it.

I do not think that America gained anything by Vietnam. Vietnam soured the minds of the spoiled and pampered children who were the result of the World War II baby boom. I was one of those spoiled children. World War II was horrible and deeply affected our parents' thinking. They had given us everything and then sent us off to die in rice paddies. It was

---

[*]Harrison E. Salisbury, "Hanoi Premier Tells View; Some in U.S. Detect a Shift," *New York Times*, 4 January 1967, p. 2, column 4; See also Harrison E. Salisbury, *Behind the Lines — Hanoi December 23, 1966–January 7, 1967* (New York: Harper & Row, 1967), Chapter 18.

too much for the baby boomers to take and they rebelled. This was the right thing to do on their part. The disillusionment with government and the older generation that we see today can be traced, in part, I am sure, to the war in Nam. The spoiled generation was entitled to stand up and protest. They had no other choice. Those of us, like myself, who had been raised in the atmosphere of "my country right or wrong" were torn individuals. Our hidden scars were deeper and it would take us a few more years to reconcile our upbringing with reality. The reality was that the spoiled generation of World War II babies had been lied to and sold down the river. What our parents and our country did to us was inexcusable if not downright criminal. That our leaders, after the greatest period of prosperity and growth our nation has ever witnessed, could do this to us is unpardonable. Our country will feel the effects of this war a long, long time.

On October 28, I got my own personal laundress and shoe shine girl. I was sitting in the Mess sergeant's hooch studying Spanish when his hooch maid entered. She sat at the table and started shining his shoes, so, naturally, we started talking. She offered to do my laundry and I accepted. As it was, she offered to do it cheaper (by 5¢) per set of fatigues than the village laundry which I had been patronizing. Next, she offered to shine my boots. This was an offer I couldn't turn down! I hated spit shining my boots. I was really bad at it and knew she could do it a whole lot better than I ever could. We chatted awhile because she wasn't too proficient in English. She was 28, but looked 38, and was not pretty — in fact, she was downright ugly, yet her ugliness made her beautiful in some strange way.

"GI marry?"

"No, but I have a girlfriend."

"GI got girlfriend village?" (Meaning, I guess, did I patronize the local whores.)

"No!" I said, and shook my head vigorously, for emphasis.

"GI Numbah One."

It was a nice compliment. Later on, she was to do my laundry and boots for free. She came to me one day and offered to do them for free if I would buy her cartons of cigarettes at the PX. Although this was illegal, I didn't give a damn. She even gave me the money to buy the cigarettes! I'm sure she made a fortune on the black market. Plus, I'm sure that when I was paying her to do my laundry, she probably knew someone who would do it for free. So she made out like a thief both ways. It was a way of life for them. Although what I was doing was illegal, I was, in a way, supporting her and helping her live a little better. I have no regrets about doing what I did. Everyone else did it, so why shouldn't I have benefited too, and saved some money?

So the month of October 1969 drew to a close and with its ending, I reached the halfway mark in Nam. I was now a short-timer with six months, or less, left in country. It would be an easy six months, but a long, boring wait. There were not many grunts with the MOS of 11B10 who made it through six months in Nam without getting hurt, killed, or badly wounded. Thank goodness, I had.

On the last night of October, while I served the evening meal, I heard about a coup that Charlie had scored that day that made me all the more thankful I had a rear job. The NVA had shot down a Charley Charley (C & C) bird. A C & C bird was the Air Mobile Command Post chopper, used by a battalion commander when one of his companies was making a CA. The 1/12 Cav C & C bird got hit and went down. All aboard — the battalion commander, the battalion sergeant-major, the CO of the infantry company making the CA, two pilots, and two door gunners — were killed. That was a big score for Charlie. It wasn't often that he racked up like that. It was such a pity that all those men had to die, but this incident made me all the more aware of how really lucky I was to be out of the field.

NOVEMBER TO APRIL

Phuoc Vinh, Hawaii, Bangkok, Home Free

What did you ever do for us, when we came back? Nothing, I tell you,
nothing! You wrangled about victory! You unveiled war memorials.
You shouted about heroism and you denied your responsibility.

Erich Maria Remarque (1898–1970)
(*The Road Back*, 1931)

The first day of November turned out to be my day off, so I went down
to the airstrip and took pictures of Hueys, LOHs, and C-130s. Planes, especially choppers, fascinated me, and I loved taking pictures of them. When
I returned to my sleeping hooch, I studied Spanish for a while. I was really
gung ho about completing the Spanish course. I wanted to learn as much
as possible so that, when I took it in graduate school, it wouldn't pose too
much of a problem for me. Mike Blair was a great help with pronuncia-
tion, so I found it easy to learn. Of course, with my waiter's job, I had plenty
of time to study.

Being back in the rear did have its own special kind of reward. I was
beginning to unwind after being so tense in the jungle. Now that I was
out of the action, I had given up cigarette smoking. Of course, there was
always some grass around, which I never turned down. Now that I had a
rear job, and slept and ate well, I was not wound up like a clock spring
and had less need to smoke to relieve the tension. What little tension there
was, I relieved during our sporadic pot parties. Pot tasted a whole lot better than cigarettes anyway, and had more salubrious effects. Besides, liquor
gave you a hangover — pot didn't.

212

On November 5 I was sitting in our hooch writing letters to friends when my eyes started watering. One of the waiters, sitting at the same table, had just lit a cigarette, and I thought that was the cause of my watering eyes. But, when I started to cry, I knew that tear gas was the cause of my discomfort. All of us were teargassed out of the hooch. I found a towel and covered my face to breathe. Either by accident or design, someone had popped a CS grenade nearby. It was not pleasant to say the least.

The next night, however, was even more thrilling. The NVA had been intermittently shelling PV with mortars or rockets all during the day of the 6th. There was a siren in our compound that was so damn loud it would wake the dead when it went off to warn us of incoming. It had been whining all day and really hurt our ears. I was watching an interesting TV show with Eric A. Bromberger, one of the cooks, who not only had a master's in English, but also told me he had been an English professor at UCLA for one year before he was drafted and made a grunt. Suddenly, mortars started dropping in, and the siren went off. We hit the floor as they landed closer and closer. It did not take us long to figure out that we would be a whole lot safer in Eric's sleeping hooch, which was also a bunker, so we headed for it and reached it safely. The nearest rounds landed about seventy-five meters away, which wasn't too bad — but, still, they were too damn close for comfort.

For some time, I had been having problems with receiving my monthly pay. After making arrangements with Colonel Kingston, I caught his chopper on Saturday, the 8th (my day off), to Bien Hoa — the location for the Cav's finance department. My trip to Bien Hoa was one of my most memorable chopper flights while in Nam. I had taken my camera along and took one and a half rolls of film. I was able to get pictures of Phuoc Vinh, the nearby rubber plantations, rivers, rice paddies, and a huge area that was pockmarked with thousands of craters from numerous B-52 strikes. Coming into Bien Hoa, the chopper flew at an altitude of about fifty feet. For the first time since being in Nam, I saw rice paddies up close. As we drew closer to the landing pad area, the chopper leapfrogged over clumps of trees and hugged the rice paddies in between them even more. There was no doubt in my mind that we were making ourselves a hard target for Charlie to shoot. I took lots of pictures of the multicolored paddies and their adjoining farms. My stay in Bien Hoa, however, was short, and I was able to straighten out my financial records. The return trip to PV was uneventful.

Life started to drag at Phuoc Vinh as there was not much to do except serve the meals and lie around in between them. It was definitely an adjustment from the perils of the jungle. Mortar and rocket attacks occurred with alarming frequency, and I suspect that I became much more conscious of loud noises at PV than anywhere else. Death from the sky came whistling down randomly. On the morning of the 15th, we were rudely awakened by the explosion of an NVA 122-mm rocket, which not only was supposed to be their most powerful rocket, but also was reputed to be capable of piercing twenty-five layers of sandbags covering four layers of steel. After what had happened to me on LZ Becky, I did not doubt the power of those enemy rockets. The incoming 122 landed about seventy-five meters from our hooch and really shook the daylights out of us. It was my day off and I was sleeping late. The resulting explosion awakened me. I looked around, and went back to sleep. After all, there was nothing I could do. I ended up getting twelve hours of sleep that day — the most I had gotten at one stretch since arriving in Nam.

By November 15, I had decided that I was going to Hawaii for R & R. I wrote and asked my girlfriend, Abby, to fly out from Texas and meet me in Hawaii. I offered to pay her way ($326.00 round trip from Dallas), so she decided to come. It would be a great five days.

As waiters in the CG's Mess, we overheard a lot about the war and picked up lots of tidbits. Plus, by serving coffee or tea at the afternoon briefings, we learned about the war on a day-to-day basis. It was all so interesting, especially for obtaining a wider viewpoint on the tactics of war. In this manner I learned that I had left LZ Ike just in time. For the last three weeks (prior to November 15) Ike had been under intense attack and had been overrun twice by the NVA, who were driven back both times. Boy, was I glad I was out of the hot seat! The grunts on Ike had repulsed 3–4 ground attacks and had 50–60 step-ons, or enemy kills. One morning on Ike our forces found and captured an NVA who was hiding in an empty bunker. He told them that he had slipped into the bunker by 2200 hours the previous night. So much for security! After one attack on Ike, our men found the body of a Mongoloid man who was 6' 2" and weighed about 200 pounds. Most likely, he was an advisor sent by the Chinese. By listening to the officers, we learned that more and more groups of NVA were being spotted in the open. The brass were disturbed by these reports of large enemy troop movements during daylight hours. Our intelligence officers could not figure out what Charlie was up to, as he had never been this bold, or brazen, in the past.

About this time, I noticed a small bump on my right elbow, which I ignored for the first few days. It continued to get larger with each day. By November 15, I was unable to bend my arm and excruciating pain shot up and down it almost continuously. The pain was so bad that I did not sleep at all on the night of the 15. So, the next day, I decided to go down to the clinic. By this point in time, my forearm was three times its normal size, and I was unable to make a fist. The doctor at the clinic had no idea what was causing the problem, so he gave me pain pills that made me feel high for a while, and then put me to sleep. He also gave me some penicillin and put me on bed rest for forty-eight hours. I was indeed in a bad way because I could not even raise my arm to salute officers. Now that I was out of the boonies, I had to salute officers again, so, with my arm in terrible shape, I was dodging brass like the plague.

The pills really doped me up while I was on bed rest. I could not walk straight and after taking a pill I felt as if I was extremely drunk. They also caused me to sleep a lot. Instead of getting better, the pain continued, and I could feel the infection spreading to my armpit. On the 18th, I returned to the clinic and saw the same doctor. He took me off the dope, but continued the penicillin. I begged him to cut on me, but he refused.

The pain continued, so I started taking pain pills again, but they did little to alleviate my suffering. That night, in desperation, I took a triple dose of pain pills to subdue the excruciating agony my arm and the rest of my body was undergoing. The overdose knocked me out cold for sixteen hours. Finally, I had had enough. Somehow I managed to dress and stagger to the clinic on the 19th. There was a new doctor who took one look at my arm and said, "Operate." I was so relieved to hear that word that I could have kissed him. Had I known what lay ahead of me, I might not have been so ecstatic.

They laid me face down on the operating table. For some reason, they could not inject Novocain as my entire elbow area was infected. Instead, they used a spray, which was "supposed" to freeze the skin so the patient would not feel anything. I say "supposed" because the freeze spray did not work. I could feel them making the incision as they sliced open my right elbow. I gritted my teeth as sharp knife-like needles of pain shot up my right arm. The pain was almost too much for me to bear. Fluid pulsated out of the incision and I could feel it leaving my body. But that was not to be the end of my suffering. After most of the fluid had drained, they grabbed the area and squeezed out the rest of the pus and infection. Tears rolled out of my eyes. I struggled and tried to push myself up in a vain attempt to get off the table and leave the OR, but they held me down. I felt as if a red-hot poker had been inserted into my elbow. I wanted to pass out, but the intense pain kept me conscious. I felt as if I were going to go through the roof of the building and up into the sky as they continued to squeeze the afflicted area again and again. Evidently, there was more infection in the elbow than they first thought. They decided to make a second incision. Medics gripped my arms and legs as the scalpel bit into my flesh a second time. The second incision, within the first incision, was deeper and put me into agony because the freeze spray did not work on this more tender area. I do not remember if they used the freeze spray for the second incision. By that point in time I was almost past caring. I didn't pass out, but I sure wanted to rid myself of the excruciating agony that wracked my body. I should have lost consciousness, but I didn't. After making the second incision, they again squeezed the elbow area. I wanted to be unconscious and would have welcomed nirvana with open arms. I prayed for God to let me pass out. He wouldn't. My elbow now had a gaping hole that was approximately ⅞" long by ¼" wide by ½" deep. They packed their miniature excavation in my elbow with a special cloth containing iodine so that infection and pus would drain from the hole. The pain was partially gone. They told me that my elbow's abscess may have been the result of my being hit by a small piece of shrapnel without my realizing it, or a mosquito bite might have been the cause. Whatever the cause, it sure put me in a bind for several weeks.

I returned to the clinic the day after the operation to have the hole repacked. By squeezing around the hole, they removed the drain cloth. I almost fainted, but the cloth popped out along with a lot of pus. Because the drain cloth had a kind of iodine on it, it smarted just a tad bit during repacking. This procedure would have to be repeated every day for the next week or so. The hole was huge, about the size of a small tunnel that Mack trucks might enter. In reality, it was about the size of a dime and as deep as four or five dimes stacked on top of each other. I just could not believe how much cloth they could repack in the hole.

On the second day after my operation (the 21st), complications developed. Shortly after returning from having my arm repacked, I began to feel intense pain. At first, it was nothing more than a dull ache, or throb, and then it proceeded to get worse. I took the pain as long as I could stand it, and then returned to the clinic, late in the day. They took the dressing off my wound, pulled the drain out of the hole, and told me to bend my arm. I couldn't move my arm because they had tightly wrapped it with an ace bandage and left the arm in a straight position. It had gotten stiff from the reduced circulation caused by the elastic wrapping.

The doctor took my arm and bent it back and forth several times. I wanted to blast off for the moon, but instead, I nearly passed out from the excruciating pain. After that, I still could not bend it on my own, so they used heat treatment to loosen the arm muscles before they rewrapped the limb. After that session I was able to bend the arm a little bit. For some reason, it took two to three times longer for sores and open wounds, such as small cuts and scratches, to heal in Nam. Because it was so dusty and dirty, especially in the rear echelon areas, the medical people had to be careful that my elbow did not become infected; hence my dressing had to be changed every day.

Five days after my operation, I was so bored that I was ready to climb the walls. I couldn't work at all and my Mess sergeant would hear nothing about my doing the slightest thing. I felt bad about being in this condition because my absence forced the other guys to work in my place during time that they normally would have had off. All I did was read and write, which was somewhat tedious, especially since all the books I had at that time were Westerns.

On the night of the 22nd, a grunt who had gone into the village of Phuoc Vinh went bananas. He opened up with his M-16 on some South Vietnamese and started chucking grenades at people. Before he finished, sixteen South Vietnamese had been wounded — one seriously. Nam had gotten to him — poor soul. That same night in the adjacent Army compound, a mysterious fire leveled a Company Mess Hall, and another Company Orderly Room got fragged and two lieutenants were wounded. Vietnam was definitely hazardous to our health, even from our own men. Perhaps the moon just happened to be in an unusual phase that night.

Bit by bit, Nam's environment slowly gnawed away at one's sanity. Our precarious balance between reason and insanity eroded ever so slowly during our 365-day tour until we were stripped bare. Some of us made it out of Nam before we involuntarily shredded that final façade that held our sanity in place, but others were not so lucky. They became the living dead — those who returned home and reached a final breaking point. Many of them not only destroyed themselves, but also dragged other innocent souls into their Vietnam-induced nightmare. Even sadder is the fact that in the 1970s and 1980s our mental health professionals were ill prepared at identifying some of those forlorn souls in time to avert a tragedy. Many Vietnam vets became walking time bombs— preprogrammed to explode at an unpredictable moment when everything just snaps. It does not take much to set them off, and, now, over a quarter of a century since the war's end, they still suffer from the ravages of post-traumatic stress disorder (PTSD). This is what America did to its young men. I can only hope and pray that those lost souls have gotten the help they need before their self-destruct button is pushed. Unfortunately, the last thirty years have shown that far too many of these Vietnam veterans were unable to obtain the proper psychiatric help before going over the edge.

On the 24th the drain was removed from my arm, and the doctor did not replace it. I was finally on my way to recovery! They told me that, if there was no pus drainage from it in twenty-four hours, then they would let the hole start closing up on its own. The next day, however, I still had a pus flow, so they took a sample, looked at it under a microscope, doubled my penicillin dosage from four to eight pills a day, and packed a new iodine drain in the hole. It turned out to be the last drain I was to need. The penicillin finally took hold and the next day all was well.

After almost two weeks off the job, I went back to work on Thanksgiving. We really decorated the CG's Mess for the holiday. We unpacked cutouts of pilgrims and Indians and taped them to the Mess Hall walls. We also placed turkey cutouts along with orange paper pumpkins on each table. We hung a long, orange garland from the bar. The food for Thanksgiving was superb! The officers were fed well, and we waiters dined in luxury after we had served the main meal to the officers. Colonel Kingston was so pleased with our efforts that he sent the following letter of appreciation to every waiter and cook:

> 1. On behalf of the Commanding General and the members of the Commanding General's Mess, I want to extend our appreciation for the magnificent meal on Thanksgiving evening.
> 2. The effort and care put into the preparation of the meal was self-evident. The food was cooked to perfection and aesthetically arranged and served in a most pleasing manner.
> 3. The members of the mess are most appreciative of your efforts on our behalf. Your efforts were in keeping with the highest standard of the FIRST TEAM.

We were grateful to receive this letter as it showed our efforts were not going by unnoticed. Plus, a copy of this letter went in our 201 file, so it would serve as a reference — if we stayed in the army!

On November 29 we threw a party for our departing Mess Officer, who was a major, and I gorged myself on the food by helping myself to two shrimp cocktails, two helpings of delicious potato salad, three pieces of fried chicken, and two steaks. I was bloated, but that wasn't all bad. What was bad was that I got snockered on only four beers. My resistance to beer was definitely low! I had been in Nam too long when I got to the point that four beers gave me a hangover. I knew I would have to learn how to drink all over again when I returned to the World. It was worth the slight hangover, because we lived like kings and feasted on food that was top-of-the-line chow. I loved the food at the CG's Mess. There was none finer.

My mail on the 29th also brought some good news from Hillbilly Kelly, who wrote to say that, despite having had a crushed chest, he was fine and now out of the Army. I was relieved because he was a good friend, and I had worried about what had happened to him. Although he was out of the Army, I wasn't, and I still had five more months of Nam to endure.

Another buddy from Bravo Company, Jackson Winter, a soul brother, dropped by one day. He had landed a rear job in an office next to the PX, so he and I could easily get together and talk. It was good to have an old buddy and fighting companion nearby. No matter what skin color, religion, etc., a guy has, when you share the same wartime experiences, there is an everlasting bond of friendship between you that can never be broken. While I was friends with the other waiters, my friendship with them was different. Jack and I could talk because we had a common thread that bound us together and made life a little less arduous.

I will never forget the men I fought beside in the jungle. They were super guys, and I often wondered if I would ever meet any of them again. As things turned out, I got to see several of them back in the World. In 1985 I saw Chief, some four years before alcohol would claim his life in 1989. Sadly, he never recovered from his wound or the horrors that had been forced upon us in Vietnam. I saw Dan Webster in 1982 and have continued to see him almost every other year since then. In August 2003, I arranged a reunion at the Vietnam Veterans Memorial — the Wall — in Washington, D.C., with Bill Rohner and Virgil Renfro.

Around December 1 Mike Blair's parents sent him a collapsible eighteen-inch-tall plastic Christmas tree. We had been instructed to tell anyone who might send us Christmas presents that they should send them by November 15 to make sure there was plenty of time for the packages to arrive at Nam's godforsaken outposts. By that time, I already had three packages to put under Mike's tree.

On the night of December 1, we had a real treat in the CG's Mess. Singer Bill Ellis visited the Mess and performed. Four of his songs—"First Cav," "Freedom Bird," "Grunt," and "Firefight"—were well known throughout the Cav. He was exceptionally talented and we enjoyed each of the six songs that he sang. In fact, he had really done well in the Army! As soon as some of the higher-ups in the Cav recognized his singing and songwriting talents, he was pulled out of the boonies of Nam and put in the Special Services branch, where he not only made a record but also toured Nam and the States.

This entertainment put me in the mood to entertain, so I composed the following Christmas poem and sent it to my parents. It reflected my memories of Christmas past and how being away from my family impacted my outlook on the upcoming Christmas season:

Christmas '69

'Tis time to spread the Christmas cheer,
So break out that delicious cold beer,
And sip on your eggnog.
Watch the old man's chin droop and nod
As he dozes off watching the tube.
Ah! Such a sweet interlude!
He's partaken of the turkey feast
And gloated himself like a beast.
Now all he does is snore —
A thing the grandchildren adore.
They long to climb into the old man's lap,
But he'll awaken with a snap,
And give a Ho! Ho!, a smile, a laugh —
For this is Christmas dinner's aftermath.
The embers from the hearth glow,
And the old man goes to the vault below
To break out more Virginia Gentlemen.
While the old lady in church says Amen,
And comes home to burn the bread again!
The green tree droops in sadness—
The year's Christmas is without gladness.
For the family's separated this Yuletide,
And the old folks this fact must abide.
But let's not be sorry or sad —
'Tis really the season to be glad.
Next year we'll be together,
Sharing the joy of cold Christmas weather.
We'll down the eggnog and then some,
And decorate a tree somethin' awesome.
Perhaps there'll be an addition, who knows?
The grandchildren will be all bundled up in clothes,
For the old man'll take 'em sleddin',
Then come inside to his favorite chair's soft beddin' —
Sip his drink, and snore at the TV game.
Yes, then Christmas will truly be the same!
So Merry Christmas to all
From one who can't be there at all!
So I'm sending to you all my love —
Maybe next year we'll see freedom's white dove.

Peace

On December 4, General Creighton W. Abrams, Jr., the chief military commander in Vietnam, flew in on a chopper escorted by two Cobra gunships to visit and eat lunch with General Roberts. There were more CID

(Criminal Investigation Division) men and MPs protecting this four-star general than I had ever seen. In fact, they were worse than the Secret Service, who had protected President Lyndon Johnson when he spoke at my TCU graduation in 1968. Abrams hardly talked during lunch or at an afternoon briefing where we served coffee and iced tea. We were nervous and tried our best not to commit any faux pas around him.

About this time we got a new waiter, Roger Nelson, a soul brother, who, it turned out, was from Montpelier, Virginia, a small whistle-stop about fifty miles from my hometown of Charlottesville. I never thought I would meet someone in the Army who lived so close to my home. The world was indeed a small place.

During this period of time, I had been a waiter off and on in the sergeant-majors' Mess. Actually, I had sort of become their waiter because it was easier than serving in the CG's Mess. It soon became a job that I did not relish as most of these six SMs appeared to be unintelligent and rudely overbearing. On December 6, I asked the head sergeant-major if my R & R to Hawaii had been approved for early January. I was concerned about receiving my R & R in the first week of that month because Abby could only get away from TCU at that time. She would be student teaching from the second week onward, and I had sent her $326.00 to pay for the round-trip airfare from Dallas to Hawaii. The head sergeant-major told me that there were thirty-three R & R applications for that time slot and that only sixteen had been approved. He said, offhandedly, I was not one of those and he was number one on the list. This really upset me, so I got a little drunk that night.

During the week prior to that conversation, I had not been getting along with the sergeant-majors. I resented serving meals to these men because they ate like pigs, were most insensitive, and rudely ordered me around as if I was their house servant. They really bugged me, so I started screwing over them. I would take an extra long time in the kitchen to get them second helpings. I purposely left a fork or knife off the table and had to go get one. While gone, I took an extra long time. This meant someone had to wait and his food got cold. Somehow, I always managed to "run out" of food, tea, or something else. I told them this was all the kitchen had initially given me, which irritated the shit out of them. I did all this on purpose because I despised these morons and I desperately wanted to return to the CG's Mess. The SMs always acted as if they deserved more than the CG's Mess received.

Finally, at lunchtime on December 8, they could stand no more of me and told Larry Busch to send them someone else who would not be so lackadaisical. A few days earlier, I had again pleaded with Larry to please remove

Roger Nelson, one of the CG's Mess waiters.

me from duty in the sergeant-majors' Mess because I was "sick and tired of these sorry sons of bitches." He demurred on my request and told me to "stick it out." At that I decided I was going to get away from those dumb asses as fast as I could manage it. I did, and was back in the CG's Mess where I wanted to be in the first place. That meant a little more work for every meal, but I didn't mind as it cut down on time to be bored. Right after I was "fired," I went down to the Company Orderly Room to see if I had been allotted an R & R, despite what the sergeant-major had said. I scanned the posted R & R list and did not see my name. My hopes plummeted but then, as I reread it more carefully I saw my name! I was elated because I had received R & R for the right time slot. That night I had more than a few rum and Cokes and got pleasantly plastered. While I had been waiting on the sergeant-majors, I did not get every third or sixth day off. I had to serve them breakfast every day, which was a pain in the ass. Now I would be able to sleep late once in a while.

On December 6, I woke up at 0300 hours to listen to the Texas–Arkansas game, which was broadcast live over the Armed Forces Radio Network. The TV would carry the replay in a week or so, and I would watch it then, but I wanted to listen to the live radio broadcast. I wanted Texas to win and they did.

About this time, news stories about the March 16, 1968, My Lai "massacre" were hitting the front pages of U.S. newspapers. I was infuriated by such media hype and wrote the following letter to my parents on December 6:

> You mentioned the My Lai "massacre" in your last letter. Well, let me tell you how sick I am about the whole mess. You see I doubt such a thing occurred. The damn news media are so g. d. [goddamn] hungry for thrilling stories that they'll go to any lengths to blow something out of proportion. As for the "alleged" photos of the massacre — it sickens me to think how stupid some people, including U.S. Senators, can be. You can take a picture over here, anywhere in the boonies, and never be able to

identify the place. You can't tell whether or not (1) those people were killed by VC or NVA, (2) they were killed by artillery, [or] (3) they were killed by G.I.'s. You can't prove how they were killed by photos. It sickens me to think what American justice has come to when a man, or men, can be convicted by photos that show no geographical or identifying landmarks or how the people were killed. I doubt very seriously it was a "massacre." After all they can't convict these men unless they have proof—i.e. 109 bodies. And the S. Viet Gov't says it never happened—that there was no "massacre." They are not even sure where the alleged "massacre" took place. There were 6 villages in that area *all* under VC control. Medina's company, of which Calley's platoon was a part, had lost 33% of their men due to booby traps, etc. while operating around that area. So, perhaps they were justified in getting rid of a village that provided shelter for the VC. What the damn American public fails to realize is that our men ... are taught only one thing in the States—KILL! KILL! KILL! Take no prisoners! Kill! So, now the American people protest because our guys are killers. You can't have your cake and eat it. I'm really terribly disappointed in the American people. They brought this upon themselves. They say it's all right to go out and kill the enemy & take no prisoners; yet they are so willing to believe ill of our troops when something like this occurs. They're all ready to jump to conclusions because the g. d. news media makes such a big thing out of it, and deplores such a "massacre." So what if there was a massacre? The G.I.'s were simply ridding the land of a shelter for the VC and NVA. This is war. We can't be pretty or nice. I tell you this—if either Calley or Medina are convicted, our courts have really sunk low.... I say damn the news media. I also damn that long haired twerp in California who never witnessed the massacre, yet started this investigation. It's sorry people like that guy who cause trouble in our country. Everyone loves to tell war stories and this idiot—this bum—listens to a few war tales and decides it's a "massacre." He has no right to bring this all up. You can't convict people on "war stories." Besides, he was a chopper machine gunner, and he probably gunned down plenty of people himself who were innocent. I really don't know what our country is coming to. Have we sunk so low that we have to get vicarious pleasure out of condemning our own soldiers for doing their job? Over here you kill without question. Everyone is the enemy. Why don't the stupid people in the States realize this? If the villages at My Lai were sheltering VC & NVA and setting booby traps then they were the enemy, & the enemy regardless of what size, shape, form, age, or sex must die. He can't be trusted. If you can't bring the village under your control, it must be eliminated. Believe me, you just don't know how the morale of guys over here is affected by such publicity. People forget that, in every war, there are atrocities on both sides. There always will be. But, why must we condemn our own men? Don't the American people realize the huge, terrific propaganda value Hanoi gets out of this? Hanoi will really whoop it up. Did you know that many NVA are afraid to surrender to Americans or leave dead NVA behind, because

Hanoi has told them that Americans are cannibals and eat humans? This is true. Think of the propaganda they'll get out of My Lai!!! I get so furious at the stupidity of the American public. It's so gullible — ready, eager & willing to believe anything the g. d. news media tells it. I fear America is slowly coming to its downfall …

I, myself, was personally in on a kill of a gook who begged [for] mercy & surrender. We emptied *beaucoup* clips of ammo into him. So, that too is a massacre. Ha! Cow manure!

Although those words were written over thirty-four years ago, I still have many of the same feelings. Due to the NVA, Bravo Company — my infantry company — had lost over 80 percent of its men in September 1969. To us, the only good gook was a dead one. When you teach a man to kill, you cannot expect him to hold back, especially when he continuously sees his friends blown away by NVA or VC snipers, mines, and booby traps. Life, I will agree, is sacred, but the military machine makes men do strange things. You cannot teach a man — KILL! KILL! KILL! and then expect him to lay back and be nonchalantly affected by the horrible deaths of his comrades. Sooner or later the frustration of not being able to prevent your comrade's death or disfigurement will reach a boiling point. The outrage of My Lai as reported in the news media had one purpose in mind — to goad the American public into believing that the American fighting man was an insensitive monster. In part, the media was successful in its portrayal of the American soldier in Vietnam. True, human life didn't mean much to us grunts. After all, we were fighting in an unpopular war, and people weren't exactly falling over themselves to welcome us home with open arms. So why should anyone care if we knocked off a few villagers? The occupants were, as far as we were concerned, collaborators. We may have controlled My Lai by day, but during the nighttime Charlie had them by the balls. How many other My Lai's were there? More than a few, I would conjecture. I cannot condone what 1st Lt. Calley and his men did. It was, indeed, wrong to slaughter innocent men, women, and children. Yet, I can understand, all too well, why My Lai happened.

The floor show we attended on December 9 was notable for one reason. An all–Korean band played country western music and the violin player, we were informed, had a master's degree in violin. He was absolutely superb. The two girl singers were also exceptional. We always enjoyed the floor shows. All of us were horny as hell and would have loved to fuck any of the sexy girl singers who entertained us. The women dressed provocatively and knew how to shake their tits and asses in such a manner as to encourage our latent sexual fantasies. It is a wonder that someone didn't get up on stage and rape one right in front of all of us. We would have applauded such a performance. Yet, I was meeting my girlfriend, Abby, in Hawaii in early January. She and I would end up sleeping in the same bed, but I wouldn't be able to make love with her because she wouldn't let me! I must have been crazy — or should have had my head examined.

To make up for all the days I had missed while my arm was infected, I worked every day from Thanksgiving onward for about two weeks. I was not about to let my buddies down for having to work on their regular days off. Besides, it kept me busy and drove the boredom away, but by December 11, fifteen days after I returned to work, I was just a little more than tired. Thus, I was relieved to hear that five new waiters were being assigned to

Roger Nelson (left) and E. Tayloe Wise (right) relax outside the CG's Mess.

the CG's Mess. These additional men meant that we would definitely get every fifth day off. I really liked that thought!

The 11th turned out to be another long and boring day. *The Sound of Music* played in the CG's Mess that evening. It was a long movie, and started late, so I wrote letters while it played. It did not end until 0030 hours, so we worked until about 0130 hours cleaning up, and then had to get up at 0600 the next morning. I was getting spoiled by the amount of sleep I got in PV. I was making up for all the Zs I had missed while in the jungle. I came to resent any intrusion upon my regular seven hours of sleep. Of course, we could crash in the afternoons too, but I preferred to get all my sleep in one lump.

To relieve the tension, which periodically built up in us, we did some wild and crazy things at times. For each meal, the cooks baked bread rolls. Most of the time there were always a few left, which were inevitably thrown away. For some reason, on the night of the 14th, there were more leftover rolls than usual. After the evening meal, when the officers had departed, someone chucked a roll at one of the cooks. Before we knew what was happening, he chucked one or two back. In a flash, we were engaged in a miniature war—cooks vs. waiters. We threw rolls back and forth fast and furiously, and chased each other around the Mess, the bar, the kitchen and outside. We had a ball and laughed a whole lot at our childish behavior. Somehow, we only managed to break two glasses and one pepper shaker. Just like our flashcube war, this was another example of how we combated the boredom and tedium of PV as we waited for our interminable 365-day tour of duty to end.

Basically, life in the CG's Mess was dull and boring because, other than our serving at meals or briefings, there was little else for us to do except to sleep. We had served our time in hell; now was the time to relax in the gardens of paradise. Although it was a new experience for me to get all the sleep I wanted, sleep in itself can become boring when one only has the choice of reading or writing letters to go along with it. The days dragged, but somehow, we managed to get through them.

On the morning of the 15th, I stumbled out of my hooch at 0545 hours to take a piss. As I reached the halfway point between the hooch and the latrine, I heard a familiar whistling sound. I looked up to see a 107-mm rocket coming in from the west. I hit the earth and watched it speed by, not fifteen feet over my head, and impact seventy-five meters away, in the ARVN compound. I do not know if anyone was hurt, as I never heard anyone in the Mess say anything about it. But Charlie was definitely getting too close for comfort. And Tet was still a few months off.

Oddly enough, by December 17, I had received seventeen Christmas presents. I felt rather self-conscious because I had more presents stashed under my bed than all the cooks and waiters put together. Christmas was a sad time of the year for all of us. We were away from our homes and families—many of us for the first time. Lots of grunts did not have many friends or parents back in the World who really cared about them. This was a lonely time, and it was magnified more so for those guys who had not received a single present or card. It seemed to me that everyone I knew had sent me a Christmas card, and I eventually ended up with Season's Greetings from forty-eight people.

The only time I ever saw Saigon (now Ho Chi Minh City) was just before Christmas, on December 17. I was getting bored as hell in the CG's Mess and wanted to take a little holiday, so I got permission from Colonel Kingston to fly in his chopper to Tan Son Nhut, so that I could shop at the PX there. It had a wider selection of articles than the PV PX, and I even found a book on how to study for the Graduate Record Examination (GRE). I was trying to get into the University of Texas Graduate School and had to take and pass the GRE before I could be considered for admittance. Since I had not studied in almost two years, I was a little worried about being able to pass such a hard test, especially since I was scheduled to take the GRE in a little less than a month.

After visiting the PX, I decided to see if I could go into Saigon. I walked to the main gate and they let me out. I only walked about seventy-five meters from the gate into the square that faced it. The dirt, filth, and squalor of Saigon was readily apparent from just this short distance outside of Tan Son Nhut. I lingered for about fifteen minutes and then scooted back inside the safety of the base. I was just too scared to walk alone down a Saigon street. I felt that I would probably be robbed or stabbed in the back. That was the only time while I was in Vietnam when I was alone on my own, without other grunts to keep me company. I was really freaked out. I could not handle being alone in that strange environment of a Saigon street where everyone, it seemed, was a potential enemy. I immediately missed the protection afforded by my fellow grunts. Being all alone in that square, even though the gate was not that far away, was like leaving the womb. Psychologically, I just could not handle it. I needed the backup of someone's presence. I am amazed that I stayed out 10–15 minutes, as I was terrified the entire time. I desperately wanted to mingle with the crowds and window-shop, but my fear of being knifed in the back was just too strong.

The NVA sent us Christmas greetings during the week prior to the 25th. For two nights in a row our compound came under intense mortar and rocket attack. One night four incoming mortar rounds serenaded us. Fortunately, no one was injured, but the next evening Charlie pulled an even more dastardly deed. Using a recoilless rifle, he destroyed five choppers. Unfortunately, we could not fire back at him because his position was in a no-fire zone. Guess where the no-fire zone was? The village of Phuoc Vinh! Charlie set up his recoilless rifle on the roof of a village hut and fired directly into the Army base. Because he was firing from a position that was occupied by friendlies, we were restrained from returning fire out of fear of hurting some damn "friendly" South Vietnamese who had probably loaned Charlie the ladder to climb up on the hut's roof. That was the god-damned hypocrisy of this stinking war. Our hands were constantly tied. It was like playing chess with an opponent who had three queens. The South Vietnamese were so two-faced. They knew they had us by the balls. We controlled the village by day, but night was Charlie's time. It was all so fruitless. We worked our asses off to help these people and they laid a heavy con job on us. They sucked up to us so that we would give them everything.

From the beginning, the U.S. faced a no-win situation in Vietnam. The hopelessness of that war was made apparent to us, shortly after our arrival in Nam. You cannot expect to win a war with limits—with one hand tied behind your back. Our government hobbled our effectiveness at every turn. All we could do was to try and survive. It was all a great big game. We were not there to win a war or accomplish anything — we were there to run a gauntlet for one whole entire agonizing year. It was as if Vietnam represented our rites of passage. If we survived, we reached manhood. But, if we failed, the penalty was much more severe. We lived with the constant fear of death, dismemberment, or permanent paralysis. We could not afford to fail in Vietnam. The price of failure was just too high. Little incidents like the incoming fire from the village only served to reinforce our desire to detest the South Vietnamese whom we viewed as being corrupt in every walk of life.

These mortar attacks definitely filed my nerves to a raw edge. I soon became known by the way I slept, and my fellow waiters learned to awaken me with care. If anyone touched me while I slept, I had a habit of coming up swinging. Some of the guys got a kick out of awakening me, so they could see me come up swinging, which I did not think was funny at all. I was extremely jumpy and did not like anyone touching me while I slept. My brain seemed to immediately translate someone's touch into the thought of "Gook! Kill!" The guys soon learned it was better to stand nearby and scream at me when they wanted to awaken me. During the week before Christmas, I was snoozing one afternoon when my mama-san entered our hooch with my laundry. Wanting to let me know that it was ready, she grabbed me by the shoulder. I slept on my stomach. Without realizing what I was doing, I came up swinging, turned around, and hit her right below the Adam's apple with a smashing blow before I realized who she was. She was propelled backwards into the wall of the hooch where she landed and started laughing. The waiters in the hooch howled with gales of laughter. Poor mama-san took it all rather well. I was chagrined and apologized profusely, but she shrugged it off and thought the whole incident was all rather funny. I was just another kooky GI. After I returned to the world, it took about five years before I lost my fear of someone touching me as I slept. More than once, in later years, I unintentionally slugged different women with whom I was sleeping because they had touched me while I slept.

At lunch on Christmas Eve, Cardinal Terence James Cooke, who was visiting Vietnam for the holiday season, ate in the CG's Mess. This pious and humble man was so impressive. After the meal, he entered the kitchen and talked to all of us for about five minutes. He was a quiet individual from whom hope and power emanated. I got to shake his hand and felt blessed to have come into contact with this holy man even though I was not a Catholic.

That day, we all received ditty bags that had been sent from Red Cross chapters in the U.S. Every soldier in Nam was supposed to get one and mine came from St. Dorothy's Christian Mothers in Warren, Michigan. The cloth bag contained tape, peanuts, lemon drops, a can opener, ballpoint pen with refill (which I desperately needed), a lighter, small flashlight, Kool-Aid, playing cards, and plastic bags. All of these knickknacks would be most useful and made me really appreciate the efforts of the Red Cross to bridge the gap of loneliness many grunts must have felt at that time of the year. At least someone cared. We appreciated the little things—that's what counted the most.

Christmas Eve was an abrupt departure from the traditional ones I had experienced in the past. That night an airplane circled overhead and broadcast Christmas carols. The NVA must have thought we were all just a tad bit crazy. Then, at midnight, the sky was lit up by hundreds of flares. They were our answer to fireworks and were incredibly beautiful with their green, red, blue and white hues.

The hottest day on record in Nam, at least in my mind, turned out to be Christmas Day 1969, which was the most excruciatingly hot and most uncomfortable day I had ever experienced. It was 125° in the shade! On this long and boring day, we all worked from 0600 hours to 2300 hours. I got little time off and, when I did, it took me over one and a half hours to open the twenty-four Christmas presents I had received. Most of them were either liquor or food. One friend, Mrs. Andrew Cushman—the mother of my second best friend from childhood—sent me a pint of liquor wrapped in bread. It was an unusual way to receive booze, but at least the bottle did not break in transit! My Aunt Katrina and Uncle Preston had individually wrapped twelve different knickknacks. Most of the food that I received, except for Mary Garth Flood's cookies, I gave away because I could never have eaten it all, and I felt truly sorry for the guys who didn't receive many Christmas presents. I received thirteen paperbacks. In letters home, I had been begging people to send me books, which partially combated Nam's boredom. Almost everyone sent me ballpoint pens. I wrote so many letters (over 100 in December alone) that a ballpoint pen usually lasted five days at the most.

For Christmas dinner, we had printed menus that we placed at each setting. The meal was absolutely scrumptious. The appetizer was a shrimp cocktail with crackers. Then came the main, mouthwatering course of roast turkey with turkey gravy, cornbread dressing and cranberry sauce. We served side dishes of mashed potatoes, glazed sweet potatoes, buttered mixed vegetables and peas. Hot rolls with butter were in abundance, and the officers had iced tea with lemon, or milk, to wash this all down. Dessert consisted of fruitcake, mincemeat pie, or pumpkin pie with whipped topping. On each table we had also set out small dishes with assorted nuts, candy, and fresh fruit. It was a king's repast and, after the officers dined, we gorged ourselves on the food. I stuffed down as much of it as possible. We had really worked our tails off that day. It really was not much of a Christmas for us as we did not have time to sit down and open our presents together. It was sort of hit or miss all day.

Since then, Christmas Day has just not been the same for me. I just do not care for Christmas and what it represents. Having lived and worked in the environment of the CG's Mess and seen the hypocrisy of it all, while I knew that grunts were dying not far away in the jungle, numbed me to the spirit of peace. That officers could live like kings while their troops lived in squalor was almost too incredible to comprehend. Here were our military leaders, dining in baronial splendor, while the peasants starved. I hated being a part of it, yet I could not help but thank God I had such a safe rear job. I was conflicted by my part in all this. I could not condone the way they lived, but I was extremely ambivalent about my participation in this facet of the war. I deeply resented the officers' way of life at the expense of the grunts, yet I was entwined in it of my own volition.

On New Year's Eve, red, white and green flares illuminated the sky at 2355 hours and continued to be shot into the air for over thirty minutes. They were spectacular, but even more notable was the fact that the grunts on the green line opened up with their M-16s and M-60s at the same time and blanketed the sky with red tracers that arced upward and disappeared into the darkness. What a memorable sight! This firepower display continued for over half an hour as everyone on the outside perimeter tried to outdo the next person. The ARVNs in the compound across the road from our hooch had some AKs and opened up with them, which sent chills down my spine when I again heard that eerie sound. What a fantastic way to bring in a new year! I hoped I would survive Charlie's irregular mortars and rocket attacks on our compound and make it home to the World. Only time would tell.

On January 3, I flew by C-130 to Bien Hoa where I caught a bus to the R & R center. My stomach was in knots, and I was hyped up — I was escaping from Nam, albeit for only a short period. I was issued a khaki uniform to wear on R & R and received orders for the military ribbons that I was authorized to display on the left side of my chest. A Bronze Star with "V" Device and Oak Leaf Cluster, National Defense Ribbon, Vietnamese Defense Ribbon, Vietnamese Campaign Ribbon with two stars (for two campaigns), Air Medal, Army Commendation Medal, the Vietnamese Cross of Gallantry, the Presidential Citation Ribbons, the Unit Citation Ribbon, plus my CIB, all weighted down my chest. I looked like a hero, but sure did not feel like one. After all, the honor and privilege of wearing these decorations had come only at the expense of someone's death.

It was extremely monotonous at the R & R center. For two days I had nothing to do or read, until, finally, we were bussed to Camp Alpha in Saigon on the 5th. Our plane was supposed to leave at 1630 hours, but it had been delayed in Guam. After taking off from that far-flung island in the Pacific Ocean, it had been forced to return to Guam due to engine problems. After a three-hour delay, the plane finally arrived. After boarding, we took off from Tan Son Nhut at 2230 hours on the 5th. We flew east across the international date line and gained a day. We landed in Guam to refuel, and then flew on to Hawaii where we landed at 1600 hours on the 5th, after a 12 to 13-hour flight from Saigon. It felt odd to leave during the night of such and such a day, fly for only about half a day, and arrive late in the afternoon of that same day. I felt as if I had been in a time machine, or something.

As my seat was toward the rear of the plane, I was one of the last grunts off as I boarded the bus that would take us to the R & R center located at Fort DeRussy. For some unknown reason, the bus waited another twenty minutes at the plane before pulling off slowly for the R & R center. I thought Abby would be wearing her favorite color — orange — but she fooled me and wore blue. As I got off of the bus, my eyes wandered over the crowd and missed seeing her. Finally, I spotted her and, after eight long months, I got to kiss a girl again. The drought was over! Our embrace was long, passionate, and lingering, after which she placed a lei around my neck. We had to attend a fifteen-minute orientation and were then free to depart. We took a taxi to our hotel, the Princess Kaiulani, also known as the Princess K, or PK.

My first night on R & R was like a dream because I just could not believe that I was actually in Hawaii with my girl. It felt so strange and unreal to be back in civilization. We went to the International Market Place for dinner, and I bought a pizza. I had not eaten pizza since leaving the States, and it could have been the absolute worst pizza in the world, but I would not have cared one iota. I tore into it and wolfed it down. After eating, Abby and I wandered back to the PK's bar and drank mai tais. We then returned to our room (2618) and talked until 0400 hours.

During our discussion in those early morning hours, I did what I had vowed not to do. I proposed marriage and she accepted. Before leaving Nam, I had promised myself that I would not talk about marriage, or our getting married; but here I was, less than twelve hours in Hawaii, and I had popped the big question. Events and circumstances were definitely moving too fast for me. I don't believe any other person would have reacted much differently, given the same set of circumstances. After all I had been through, it was probably somewhat predictable that I would react in this manner. I was so desperate for a woman — any woman — that, more than likely, I would have proposed to any girl who had flown out to meet me. I desperately wanted someone to call my own — someone to share my life and be a part of me, after the hell of combat that I had experienced. I needed the security that Abby, as a woman, represented. I made a bad mistake by taking this tack and, I know full well, I hurt Abby deeply when I broke the engagement within two months of my returning from Nam.

But, unfortunately, we were caught up in events beyond our control, and I could not be responsible, at that time, for my mental state. To this day, I still find it incredibly hard to believe that we stayed in the same room, slept in the same bed for six nights, and did not once make love. I wanted to, but she did not. Back then, still a little unsure of myself sexually, I respected women when they said no and tried not to push myself upon them. After Nam, my whole approach to women changed radically. I chased everything in skirts and took every girl I could to bed. But this was Hawaii, and I was still the knight in shining armor and she the damsel in the tower.

The next day, we went to the Ala Moana Shopping Center. Having never seen a shopping mall, I was enthralled by the number of stores (150+) under one roof. We went to Hallmark Jewelers and chose a $375.00 diamond ring that we could pick up in two days, after it had been sized correctly. Later, we wandered through the shopping center, then returned to the PK where we spent the afternoon talking and making out. That evening we went to a beautiful Japanese restaurant called the Pagoda. Outside of the entrance was an artificial pond containing ferns, rocks, and the biggest goldfish I had ever seen. Inside, the waiters offered us a choice of eating utensils — silverware or chopsticks. Having never eaten with chopsticks, I elected to try them. Abby chickened out. I became a chopstick expert — it was either that, or starve! How odd that I had left the Orient, only to find myself eating in a Far Eastern establishment in Hawaii.

During our second full day on Oahu, we decided to lease a car and drive around the island. I rented a Ford Maverick and found that driving, after eight months, was a novelty. I felt like an alien creature who had descended from his spacecraft only to find that mankind still used primitive inventions called cars for transportation. I never could adjust to the sounds of traffic and the honking cars. Every time I heard a car toot, I wanted to crawl under the front seat. We drove east from Honolulu, past Diamond Head. Compared to the jungles of Tay Ninh, and the blandness of Phuoc Vinh, Oahu was beauty personified. We stopped at every scenic spot along Route 72. At the beaches where we paused, we waded and walked arm in arm in the surf. I felt like a prisoner who has been released from jail. It was so good to be free again and not have to account for my time to anyone. On the northeast side of the island, we stopped at Laie to visit the Polynesian Cultural Center, which the Mormons had erected in connection with their Church College of Hawaii. This cultural center was vastly interesting in that it depicted life on the Pacific Islands (such as the Fiji Islands, Tonga and Tahiti) prior to the white man's invasion. The students of the nearby Mormon college worked here and were most proficient in demonstrating the different native island dances in a show that we saw. We toured the center, which consisted of several different types of villages that were found in the pre–Cook Pacific.

From Laie, we drove up and along the north coast of Oahu. Words are too inadequate to describe the massive beauty of Oahu's north coast. The full force of the Pacific had made its indelible mark upon this coastline, and the raw, untamed beauty of the land it buffeted was most evident. It was a stark coast filled with wind and fury. The waves on the beaches where we stopped seemed much larger than those at Waikiki and came crashing in upon the miles of sand. I loved this area of Oahu more than any other part of the island. From the north coast, we drove back through the middle of the island, which was impressive in its lushness and the thousands of pineapple trees on plantations that stretched from the Koolau Range in the east to the Waianae Range in the west. Truly, we were in a melting pot of the Pacific. We drove by Pearl Harbor and Schofield Barracks but did not stop. I had had enough of war and had no desire to see where so many, so young, had died.

That evening, we dined at The Top of the I, an all-glass restaurant overlooking Honolulu, which was perched on top of the Ilikai Hotel. We entered a glass elevator on the outside of the hotel and, as we ascended in the darkness, the elevator lights shut off so that we could view the city spreading out before us. It was a perfect time to indulge in kissing and, being alone in the glass cage, we availed ourselves of that opportunity as the elevator rose majestically toward the "I." We had an excellent meal in this romantic spot and then went to a local discotheque where we danced until the wee hours of the morning. I was cramming every bit of life I could into those few days. I had to. I felt as if I had been unchained from shackles of bondage. It was so good to be free that I hated the thought of having to return to Vietnam. Oddly enough, during my Hawaiian sojourn, I never once considered not getting back on the plane for Nam.

On our third day (the 8th), we went shopping in the morning and then met a friend of mine from TCU, Lyzette Healani Chenoweth, who lived in Waialua on the north coast. She was home for Christmas break and was doing graduate work in the TCU Spanish Department. Although Lyzette didn't know it, I had told my parents that Abby was staying with her. Had my parents known that Abby and I stayed in the same room while we were in Hawaii, they would have been extremely upset. Being prim and proper Virginians, they would have looked upon my fiancée as a fallen woman, and this act of defiance would not have been the most auspicious of signs for beginning a marriage. I was sensitive to this, because for much of my life, my parents had tried to control my social life — who I dated — by word or action. I cannot blame them for being so socially conscious because that was the way they were raised. Yet, I belonged to that generation that came of age in the 1960s and discarded the old taboos. Sleeping with a girl was not a sin, and just because you make love with someone does not make them, or you, bad.

It was good to see an old friend after those long, lonely months in Nam. I had known Lyzette for several years, and we all drank a lot of mai tais for lunch. When she left to go shopping, Abby and I ambled over to Waikiki Beach, which was only 100 meters from the Princess K. We laid in the sand in front of the Royal Hawaiian Hotel. It was all so peaceful and beautiful. Our view of Diamond Head was absolutely superb, and the gentle waves made catamaran sailing look easy.

That evening we ate at the Willows, an Indian restaurant. The curry was delicious, and I gorged myself. One thing that I was determined to do while in Hawaii was to dine out in fine restaurants and drink as much as I could. I believe I accomplished my objective because I dropped over $1,200.00 into the local economy during my six-day stay. After the meal, we drove out to the jewelers where I picked up the ring. Abby was extremely excited and wanted to see it, but I kept it hidden. We returned to the hotel where, after two hours of heavy making out, I slipped the ring onto her finger.

Now we were officially engaged. When I look back upon this, I do not understand how I could have been so stupid to go that far. The pain and sorrow I was to bring upon this girl, when I broke the engagement, was just not right. It was unfair. Indeed we were ill-fated lovers caught up in the romance of Hawaii during an interlude from the war. I am sure that she is still bitter about my cold-hearted method of cutting off this romance, but I could not help it. Upon returning from Nam, I was just not emotionally ready to handle marriage. I was too mixed up. After all, anyone who walked around with a fully loaded pistol for four months after his return from Nam, as I did, was in no way ready to settle down. Abby was a good girl who, I feel, deserved much better. Had we married, I feel sure that we would have gotten divorced rather quickly.

We Vietnam veterans went over as babes in the wood, lambs for the slaughter, and returned as bitter and mixed-up young men, disillusioned with our country and its system of government. My heart goes out to all those women whose lives were affected by the divorces that they had to endure and suffer through when their men returned home from Vietnam. We have to thank our all wise and far-seeing government for fucking up the married lives of untold thousands of Vietnam veterans. I know that many women still blame themselves for the failures of their marriages to Viet vets; but they shouldn't because our country is wholly to blame. It took us away from our homes and families, chewed us up, and then spit us out. We were creatures of the black lagoon returning to claim our brides and girlfriends. Inwardly, we changed dramatically in that lost year. Outwardly, we appeared to be the same. To impose ourselves upon our wives and girlfriends after so much trauma, blood and horror was just too much. We were, and are, the walking dead.

In Nam, we learned — oh, how we learned — not to make close friends. We grunts wanted lasting friendships, but when buddy after buddy after buddy got blown away, we hardened to the rigors of war. We shut the world out and refused to let anyone close to us break that shell. We developed a survivor mentality. If we could stay alive for one year, we would survive. Those of us lucky enough to survive were not so lucky after all. We brought home our hardened shell and refused to let anyone get near us. Closeness became death. And death had to be shut out — avoided. We survived Nam, but now we have to survive life. There is no question in my mind that it has been extremely difficult for many of us to adapt. For some, it has been impossible. The innocent victims of this war became our wives, children, parents and girlfriends.

We were unwillingly forced to endure an agonizing detoxification period when we all returned to the reality of the World. Most people could not understand this stage that we vets had to undergo. Bam! Upon returning from Nam, most of us were immediately discharged from the service. We had no transition period from war to civilian life. It was like getting kicked out of the house for the first time. We were all alone on the nation's streets as we were alone on the battlefields of Nam. The name of the game once again was survival. We couldn't stand being close to anyone — our parents, wives, girlfriends, etc. We had been used and then discarded. So, in revenge, we used and discarded others. It was only a natural happenstance of Nam. We were unprepared to face the reality of life. The armed services should not have allowed its personnel to DEROS (Date Eligible Return from Overseas) and leave the service at the same time. A transition time, perhaps up to six weeks, was needed. In that time, a man could have the opportunity to adjust; and lectures, combined with counseling, would have eased his reentry into civilian life. But, we were disgorged by the thousands at Oakland, processed out, and left to wander home from the airport in San Francisco. I wonder how many men never went home once they were put out on the streets of Frisco.

So, this is what our women had to look forward to—hardened men with whom they couldn't even communicate. How does one communicate with a killer? How does one talk to someone who has seen his buddies blown away day after day? How does someone get close to a person who wants no more entangling relationships? We were the ice men—cold and forbidding. If we encountered resistance, we reacted violently. We, too, had been brainwashed. We couldn't back down. We took our trained violence out upon those near and dear to us. We had to because we didn't have any other choice. Unwittingly, we were trying to make someone pay for what had been done to us. Too often, the wrong people suffered at our hands.

In Al Santoli's book, *Everything We Had*, Gayle Smith, an Army nurse at the 3rd Surgical Hospital in Binh Thuy, Vietnam, summed up the feelings of countless veterans:

> I was beginning to realize that the problem was I didn't feel anything about anybody anymore. I had no feelings, no feelings of love or hate or anything. Just nothing. And I didn't know why. I guess it was because I was emotionally exhausted. I had been through the highs and the lows and the fears and the hatred and the caring for a year and I had nothing left to give anymore. There was nothing that could compare with what had happened to me.*

Within me, to this day, lie the seeds of violence. At times, I feel like a tiger in a cage. Many Vietnam veterans have this unleashed capacity for violence that is stored deep within our recesses waiting to explode. Over twenty years ago, one of my tenants, who was a wino, entered my office and started calling me a son of a bitch because I had terminated his lease. After 10–15 "SOBs" he invited me out on the street. Having reached a point of no return and taken enough verbal abuse, I walked outside. Letting him throw the first punch, I nailed him against the wall. Then, I knew I wanted to kill him, but I didn't want to do it outside where people could see me. I started to drag him back inside where I could finish him off. Thank God, we never made it, because he would be dead today and I in jail for murder. I wanted to kill him — had instantly made up my mind to do so. But he,

---

*Al Santoli, *Everything We Had: An Oral History of the Vietnam War By Thirty-three American Soldiers Who Fought It* (New York: Random House, 1981), 146.

perhaps, in his alcoholic stupor, realized that death was at hand, and managed to break away from my grip. He was lucky — someone else may not be so lucky. So I, and hundreds of other vets, live with the fear of exploding uncontrollably and venting our rage upon an innocent bystander. We are walking time bombs and must be diffused. Many of us cry out for help. But there is no one to help. The Veterans Administration is too indifferent, while the American Legion and Veterans of Foreign Wars don't want us. The only organization that seemed to care, the Disabled American Veterans (DAV), has actively worked to aid the Viet vets. They care, and I am sure they will help a lot of people.

So, I gave Abby the ill-fated diamond engagement ring, and we went out to a night club, the Canton Puka in the International Market Place, to watch a comedy routine put on by a remarkable band. I had never seen this type of entertainment and found it most amusing. The performers kept us in stitches, so that we could hardly stop laughing. It was absolutely delightful and made tears come to my eyes.

We spent the entire fourth day (the 9th) at the beach. Abby swam some, but I, not caring to swim, merely lolled around and waded in the surf. That evening, we went to J. B.'s, a disco where the jet set hung out — or was it just another tourist trap? When we finished dancing, we walked back to the hotel, along the beach. The crashing waves, the cool wet sand, the offshore breeze, and full moon all lent romance to this hourglass situation in which we found ourselves entwined. Time was running too fast for both of us. Time was running out for me.

On our last day, we awoke late and went shopping at the International Market Place. Abby was quite a good seamstress and made most of her clothes, so she wanted some material to make a dress. We found two yards of a nice pattern that we purchased for $6.50. After we left the fabric shop, we browsed next door and saw a dress, with the same material and pattern, for $23.00! So she had saved a bundle of money.

From there, we went to the Honolulu zoo and stayed for three hours. The bird collection was nice, but I was not impressed with the aquarium. It was wonderful, though, to just be with someone and wander around because my holiday from the war would soon come to an end. We walked back to the hotel, changed, and then went out to the Captain's Galley Restaurant in the Moana Hotel, which faced Waikiki Beach, where we ate on a terrace that overlooked a small tropical garden. I splurged because it was my last night and the midsummer night's dream would end in the morning, when I would turn into a forgotten warrior. We ate chateaubriand, which was delicious. It was the best steak I had ever had the pleasure of devouring. Later we went dancing at a place called the Moon. It was not a lot of fun, so we returned to the Princess K where we drank a hell of a lot of mai tais.

On the 11th, we were up at 0500 hours and caught a cab to the airport. Abby watched me board the plane, and I thought I could detect some tears in her eyes—perhaps it was my imagination. The plane took off at 0730 hours, and I had an uneventful trip to Guam and then Saigon. My time warp was over. I was back in Charlie's land with four more months of hell and boredom to survive. I hoped I would make it.

We had arrived in Saigon at 1630 hours. The last bus to the Cav center had left at 1400 hours, so we had to stay at Camp Alpha, which turned out to be overcrowded. We were then bussed to a Bachelor Enlisted Quarters (BEQ) hotel in downtown Saigon. We rode in Army busses that had wire mesh screens over the windows to ward off a grenade from being thrown into the bus. After all, Charlie stalked the streets of Saigon and wasn't beyond blowing up a bus. I didn't pay much attention to Saigon. The road appeared to be one continuous armed camp with barbed wire everywhere along with numerous military checkpoints. The BEQ was like an armed fortress. I stayed in a room with another grunt, and we slept the sleep of exhaustion. Too much partying in Hawaii had finally caught up to me. The next morning, the men who were sent to awaken us barely knocked on our doors. Not hearing the wakeup knock, we overslept and missed the bus. Fortunately, some other guys had also missed the morning chimes, so at 0700 hours the army sent another bus to pick us up and return us to Camp Alpha. At 1400 hours we caught the bus for the Cav center in Bien Hoa and spent the night there. At least I had been able to uselessly waste another day in Nam. On the 14th, we were bussed to the airport at 0700 hours, and I had to wait until 1530 hours to catch a C-130 to Phuoc Vinh. I was exhausted when I stumbled back to my barracks. It had been a long trip, and I wasn't glad to be back. The prospect of four more months of grueling boredom grated at my heart, mind and soul.

Awaiting me was a letter from Dr. Chanutin that chilled me to the bone. My mother had previously written to me that my father had undergone an operation. She intimated it was for a hernia, and that I should not be concerned. Dr. Chan's letter, however, stated the truth:

> You have probably been informed about your father's operation. He has been in and out of the hospital and will begin a course of radiotherapy. Fortunately, the tumor was well localized and should be amenable to therapy.

I knew damn well a person did not have radiotherapy for a hernia — and I had never heard of a hernia being called a tumor. I knew Dr. Chan was telling me the truth, and that my parents were hiding something. Writing home, I informed them that I was upset that they hadn't told me the truth. I wanted the truth. I got it. Cancer. It killed my father four and a half years later. I was keenly disappointed that my parents had not told me the truth from the beginning, but I can understand now why they didn't. It was just one more story that they wanted to protect me from hearing. I had grown up in Nam, however, and was immune to pain, trouble, and worry. Perhaps they were trying to deny the cancerous presence of death that not only hung over my father, but also sat with me as long as I stayed in Nam.

I was back in Phuoc Vinh only two days before I left again and caught a bird down to Long Binh on the 17th, to take the GRE. My mother had sent me a second GRE study book that greatly worried me because its sample GRE tests were much more difficult when compared to the first GRE study book that I had purchased. I was really nervous that I would blow the GRE because I had only one other chance, in June, to take and pass it so that I might be able to get into grad school for the 1970 fall semester. On the 18th, I took both the GRE and the anthropology aptitude test. The GRE was easy, but the anthro test was atrocious, and I knew I had scored low on it. Later on, I would receive a letter from UT telling me more about this test.

On January 20, 1970, I became a "Two Digit Midget," a term that referred to soldiers who had 99 days or less left in country. That meant I was "short." I was now, officially, a short-timer — and short-timers got exceedingly nervous toward the end of their enforced incarceration in Nam.

The closer one got to DEROS, the more jumpy he became. You began to feel that death was waiting to tap you on the shoulder; and, as you turned, it crooked a finger and beckoned you to join him. We all feared we wouldn't make it. Life became more intense — more demanding. We had to avoid death. Charlie brought death. Charlie was to be avoided. The closer we got to leaving country, the more difficult life became. Each day a short-timer endured in that hell became ONE LESS DAY. We prayed for Charlie's mortar attacks to be less accurate. It was like playing in the Super Bowl. You were ahead with two minutes to go, but would the other team unload on your ass? You knew they would. Therefore you took no unnecessary chances, exposed yourself less and less. Those last 100 days were a special kind of hell themselves. It was all a game called SURVIVAL.

Tet, the Vietnamese Lunar New Year holiday, was rapidly approaching. It was Vietnam's most important holiday and would fall on February 6–8 this year. I had been serving at a lot of top-secret briefings prior to that time, and had learned that the enemy would not be able to launch any big, or even widespread attacks. This was comforting to know, because I wanted to be as safe as possible.

The news of my engagement had reached home and, as I suspected, my parents were not too receptive to the idea. My mother wrote that she

> was not surprised Abby joined you, as I had suspected you had some such plan in mind all the time. It is hard for me to realize that your generation do such completely unchaperoned things, but I am trying to be understanding and not get shocked.

I knew from those words that she was shocked and that she disapproved of our meeting in Hawaii. As stated above, nothing sexual, other than kissing, occurred between us, but I never would be able to convince my parents of that fact. Her statement, " ...completely unchaperoned things..." made me realize acutely that I would never be able to change my parents' views. It was a hopeless task. While they were like Puritans who lived in a past on ancient glories, my generation — those of us who came of age in the turbulent 1960s — was different because we dared to be bold. We broke with past traditions and, I think, are much happier and better adjusted for doing so. We didn't believe in being inhibited by tradition. We could (and did) make the break with the past — our parents couldn't. I resented my parents for their puritanical outlook on life, but I understood that they were trapped by the caliber of life in which they were raised. Every generation is different and trapped in one way or another. They could not break with the sexual taboos of the past, whereas my generation could. We had been sold down the river by our parents' generation because of our country's involvement in Vietnam. Therefore, we were primed for revolution, and more casual sexual contact was all part of our rebellion. Trust became a big word in the 1960s. We grew up trusting our parents, who gave us everything; however, they and their generation betrayed that trust by forcing Vietnam upon us. We soon learned trust meant death and disfigurement for no purpose. It was natural that we revolted and "did our own thing." We were the Woodstock generation. Drugs, sex, and booze. We did it all to prove to our parents that we were untrustworthy.

Now my parents were faced with a situation that they could not control. I wasn't living under their roof any more, so they couldn't keep me under their thumb. I had met, and gotten engaged to, a strange girl about whom they knew absolutely nothing. No wonder they were worried; their wayward rebellious child had struck at the heart of their lives. I really wanted to make love with Abby in Hawaii, but didn't. I'm glad I didn't because I proved my parents wrong. When it came to girls, they never trusted me or my two older brothers. Each and every applicant had been jealously screened and vetted. This time the applicant wasn't around to be interviewed, which made them uneasy. Their letters indicated acceptance of my decision but, knowing my parents, I could read between the lines and realized they were royally pissed off. I couldn't blame them for being upset. I would have been concerned also if it had been my child whom I didn't trust. I realized that my parents were tied to another age. They were molded and wedded to something that could never be broken. There is nothing wrong with such a credo, although I never understood why they didn't bend a little bit or soften their stance somewhat. With all the change that occurred in the late 1960s and early 1970s, one would think that somehow our parents would soften their stand on morals, marriage and living together. I am sure some parents changed because they understood the metamorphosis that our generation underwent. Many, such as my parents, remained firmly planted in the past. I wished their attitude could have been such that it "bends with the remover to remove" but "O, No! it is an ever-fixed mark, that looks on tempests, and is never shaken."*

I guess we all try to understand our parents. I really wonder if we ever succeed. The road is difficult and full of pitfalls. We must learn to accept them for what they are, not for what they think. They may be wrong, but we children are never right. The winds of change in the late 1960s were too rapid for them. The fox was out and gone before the farmer knew the chicken coop had been robbed. Trust and respect: we lost them both in the turbulent Vietnam era. That is why we are so cold blooded and callous. Our country deserved better.

To me, the word "chaperon" stood for the sickness that prevailed in the older generation. It meant an unwillingness to trust and reminded me of the Spanish way of courting with the young man seated on one side, the *duenna* in the middle, and the maid on the other side. My parents' generation worried too much about "appearances" and "what would the neighbors or our friends think?" If parents have raised their children properly, they need not worry about their son bringing a whore home for dinner, or their daughter getting pregnant. Trust. It's such a little word, but oh, it means so much. In Nam, I learned the meaning of trust. Over there you had to trust your fellow grunts. We were members of a team — the spokes on a wheel — and depended on each and every individual because it meant your life or his. As a medic, I tried not to fail my men. They trusted me.

---

*The Rev. H. N. Hudson, A.M., ed., *The Works of Shakespeare— The Students' Handy Edition*, rev. ed., Vol. 12 (Boston: Estes and Lauriat, 1871), 185–185. This is from Sonnet 116.

How odd that we would learn from Nam to distrust the older generation for sticking us in that mess, but we learned to trust our own generation.

I hadn't sold my parents out, but their generation had done a number to us. While I didn't intend to cut my family ties, I discounted the comments between the lines of their letters. I'm sure that my parents were upset by the fact that I was going to marry *beneath* myself because Abby came from a lower socio-economic class than mine. I never have been a gregarious person and, while growing up, I did not fit into the crowd that I was supposed to mix with socially. I felt much more comfortable around people who were not upper class. I could communicate with them more easily because I never considered myself an upper-crust snob. I am more down to earth and always will be. I feel at ease with earthy types because we can commune on the same plane of consciousness. I never have been interested in someone's parents or how they support themselves economically. I am interested in the person, regardless of sex, race, age, or social standing. Without help from their parents, many of my generation have risen above their meager beginnings. I have nothing but the highest regard, respect, and admiration for such people. Social status is not important to me, but it was to my parents. It was their security blanket; it provided them with a continuance of the old traditions. I can understand their reasons for believing in this manner, but I am also proud of the fact that my generation has not only managed to break so many old traditions but also has been able to lay aside much of the Victorian morality that permeated our early lives. As long as I can help it, I will *never* put myself in a position of being controlled by other people.

In Nam, I learned that people's feelings did not matter one bit. Not one bit! I couldn't care less what people think. You do what has to be done and fuck everything else. If you step on people to accomplish your purpose, that is OK. You do the job and you do it right. People may hate your guts for stepping on them, but they have to respect you. Our generation certainly has the power to change this country. Having been betrayed by our military, political and corporate leaders, it is our sacred duty to use our power to force significant social and political changes upon our society and its thinking. Our society may not like those changes, but they caused them by bringing Vietnam into our lives.

The days dragged by and, via the mail, Abby and I made plans for our wedding on August 7, 1970, which soon was changed to the 6th and finally the 5th. I spent $88.50 and purchased a complete eight-piece setting (96 pieces all together) of Japanese china by Noritake. I had taken a catalogue to Hawaii, and we had chosen the Duetto pattern. Because I was in the service, I could purchase it at a much steeper discount than a civilian could in the States, so I had the china sent to Abby's parents. I also ordered and paid $50.00 for a twenty-one-inch pearl necklace, which was to be my special wedding gift to Abby. That, too, I sent to her parents with a strict admonishment to Abby not to open that particular box. So, when I broke the engagement, Abby got to keep everything—her ring, the china, the pearls, and seven yards of silk that I later purchased in Thailand. I felt so guilty that I dared not ask for anything to be returned. As it turned out, these were only the first of many expensive presents that I was to give the fair sex over the years, before I finally married several times. Giving presents was my outlet for showing that I cared. It was, and still is, difficult for me to give gifts for anything. Personally, I hate doing so. Any excuse not to do so will suffice. When I give a present, it definitely means I care. That is the only way I can open up to people. This stone-walled manner toward relations with the opposite sex is only another façade that I have to lay at the doorstep of Vietnam.

I had written my best friend, David Stevenson, and asked him to be my best man. He accepted and in his letter proceeded to tell me that class consciousness was, in reality, a social field. The social scene never meant much to him either. He, too, was a rebel like me. It was good to receive some reinforcement from a friend. Via the mail, I also made plans to fly to Texas and be present for an announcement party, to attend Abby's graduation from TCU, and then fly with her to Virginia where we would attend an announcement party my parents planned on giving. It was all so unreal. I find it difficult to lend credence to the fact that I actually planned and participated in such insanity. I was a combat veteran of Vietnam, and I was going to get married upon returning from that hellhole. Impossible! No, it was absurd. Yes, it was. I was too emotionally screwed up. Marriage at that time in my life could have only led to disaster. Thank God, I broke it off. I don't regret doing so, but I deeply regret the imposition I placed upon Abby, her parents, and my parents.

At the same time I was making my wedding plans, I was also planning to attend graduate school at the University of Texas. I wanted to get a Ph.D. in anthropology and had also applied for a $3,000.00 teaching assistantship. I was on pins and needles because, if I didn't get the assistantship, I would have to find a job. The GI Bill would not help too much. Abby had indicated she wanted to work rather than go to school. So, I was already thinking about money and supporting us.

Life moved along at a snail's pace in Phuoc Vinh. On Valentine's Day, I only received seven cards, a much lesser number than my Christmas or birthday count. I took that meager amount as an omen that people were beginning to forget that I was in Southeast Asia fighting a war. Nam was beginning to swallow me. It was like quicksand. The longer I stayed, the more people forgot about me. I had to get out soon, or I would truly be a forgotten warrior.

On February 15, news of my old unit, the 2/8, reached me in PV. It was getting the hell kicked out of it, and Bravo Company seemed to be bearing the brunt of Charlie's wrath. In two days of battle, the NVA had killed ten grunts and wounded over eighty men. It was déjà vu all over again only this time I was out of it. Just like what had happened to me and Bravo Company the previous September, Charlie was again kicking Bravo's ass all over the jungle. General Roberts was in Tay Ninh Province all day on the 15th, looking over the situation. I felt badly about the problems of my old comrades, but secretly breathed a sigh of relief that I was now safely ensconced in a rear echelon area. In fact, since coming to PV, I had become a REMF (Rear Echelon Mother Fucker)— something all of us in the jungle aspired to be if the gods smiled benevolently and granted us a rear job for work well done in the field.

On the 16th, I received a nice letter from the graduate student advisor in UT's anthropology department. He told me that he had been "besieged" with letters of recommendation on my behalf and also said that, "As I would see it, there should be no problem [about your] entering graduate school." I was thankful for making such good grades at TCU. They certainly helped. I had been worried about my score on the GRE Advanced Anthropology test because I knew that I had not done well on it. But, his letter continued, "You may be interested in knowing that the American Anthropological Association has notified us that the advanced anthropology tests on the GRE cannot be answered satisfactorily by any competent anthropologist." Boy, did I ever get a laugh out of that statement! I knew then that I wouldn't have to worry about my score on the exam as it would probably be thrown out. I was relieved because the GRE Anthropology exam had been a bitch. He ended his letter by telling me that the $3,000.00 assistantship looked rather tight, so I should prepare myself in case I did not get it. As it was, I didn't get it and, after I broke my engagement, I decided not to attend UT.

During this period of time, I was having some problems with the new mess officer, Major Dillon K. Mitchell. He and I did not hit it off too well, and it appeared he made a point of going out of his way to be sarcastic to me. Whenever I saw him approaching, I left the area. I lamented in a letter to my parents that any chance I had of making sergeant (E-5) was shot as long as he was our mess officer. He had pissed off a lot of the cooks and waiters, because we were convinced that every time we filled out a promotion list for him, he simply threw it away, or lost it. All the E-4s were mad as hell at him. All of us knew that if Colonel Kingston, or the CG, learned we were getting a raw deal like this, we would have received our promotions quickly. What ticked us off even more was that he promoted his own staff to E-5s, but he failed to promote any cooks or waiters. Finally, I went to the chaplain because I was desperate to talk to someone. After a two and a half hour chat, I felt more at ease. The chaplain's perspective on life was wiser and more mature; I left still hating Mitchell, but I understood myself and my feelings a little better.

The boredom of Phuoc Vinh and Mitchell's oppressiveness were chewing away at my sanity, so I decided to apply for a seven-day leave to Bangkok. My brother's med school roommate, Ted Ruhnke, and his wife, Mary Stewart, were stationed there; and I figured I could visit them. I was going nuts with boredom, so I prayed my leave would be granted because every day was a drag. We did the same old routine day after day. The pattern never changed. I was beginning to hate PV, but not as much as I had hated the jungle. Anything was better than the jungle! The sun revolved across the clear, blue, hot, sultry sky, never changing, and, at sunset, another obscure day came to pass, leaving nothing but more and more boredom piling up for tomorrow's yet unborn day.

Part of the tedium of PV was caused by the fact that we were understaffed. Several guys had DEROSed, which left only four of us as waiters. We put in long, boring hours. The dullness of life was gnawing away at my sanity and dragging me down. I would be so glad not only to get out of that godforsaken, dirty, little country but also away from all the slant-eyed SOBs who were more interested in the GI dollar than they were in winning the war. I was fed up with our having to fight someone else's war. Let them do their own fighting. On February 22, I wrote to my friend Mary Garth Flood:

> We're in a war fighting a war we can't win. We're fighting with one arm tied behind our backs. Let these bastards fight their own God damn war. Right now, I could care less if the commies take over here — which, eventually, they will do. I'll be glad to see the last American soldier go home. I'm sick and tired of it all.

I was not depressed when I wrote that letter, but little did I realize how prophetic my thoughts were concerning the future of Vietnam. I was beginning to see through the façade that our government had erected. I was also getting "short" and bored with this farce called Nam. All I could think about was getting out of the service. Nothing else mattered. I counted the days until I could go back to the world and leave the U.S. Army. Our involvement in Nam was such a waste of time, money, and manpower. It was all for naught. I am still surprised that the American people let it continue as long as it did. Richard Nixon had been elected President in 1968 because he had a secret plan for terminating the war in Vietnam. Unfortunately, no one realized the President's strategy would lead to a further loss of 25,000+ American lives — almost half the number of men killed during the entire conflict.

Besides my leading such a boring life in PV, my mail had tapered off to practically nothing. I guess this was due to the fact I had been gone so long, and people didn't really care to keep up such a long-distance correspondence. Also, I believed my correspondents probably thought that since I had been in Nam for ten months, it was useless to write because I would be coming home in two months. In two months, I could have been dead. Only my close friends, like Mary Garth Flood, continued to write. Their letters bolstered my spirits and morale and kept me going. Yet, it was so hard to believe that there were some grunts who did not receive any mail at all during the year they spent in Nam. One whole year without mail! That was incredible. I would have gone stark raving mad.

Roger Nelson and I were beginning to get royally pissed at Major Mitchell. Everyone who was eligible for promotion in the CG's Mess had been promoted except us. Roger had more time in grade than did I; but it seemed pretty certain that Mitchell did not like blacks and even though Roger was one of the hardest working guys, his chances looked slim. Mitchell had submitted a list of six men to be promoted. Two were promoted to E-5, which really pissed me off. My date of rank was the same day as one of those promoted and was prior to that of the other grunt. Mitchell did not appear to be an intelligent individual, and he had a propensity for booze. He was so off the wall that we all wondered how he had ever made the rank of major. Several of the lieutenant colonels in the Mess had given Mitchell the nickname of "Hawk." Because a hawk is considered to be a smart bird he took to this name like a duck does to water. We all knew, however, why he had been given that appellation because at various times we had overheard several of the LTCs talking about him. They were always cracking jokes about his lack of intelligence. As an ironic epithet for his less than stellar mental acuity, they had started calling him "Hawk" rather than something more obvious like "Dodo," a derogative term for a now extinct bird. Personally, I could not stand the man. I knew Roger and I probably would not get our E-5 stripes, but I hoped Roger would — somehow — because he really was a hard worker and deserved them more than the other guys.

The month of March blew in and brought with it three new waiters. One, Bill Bellman from Winona, Minnesota, turned out to be a really super guy. I was relieved. I knew that the addition of these new waiters would enable me to get more time off and I could sleep. One good thing about being a waiter was that, the shorter one got, the less work he had to do, unless the Mess was shorthanded. I guess that's what increased our boredom level.

March also brought good news. I passed the GRE, even though I did not do a spectacular job on it — 490 out of 900 on the verbal and 530 out of 900 on the quantitative for a total of 1020. On the Advanced Anthropology exam, I scored 350, which was not good. Naively, I was sure this low score would not count against me after what the people at UT had written me.

Bill Bellman (left) serenades Mike Blair (right), two of the CG's Mess waiters.

On March 5, I received my orders for a seven-day leave to Bangkok, for March 25–31. I was extremely excited as I needed to get out of PV again, if only for a little while. I would have to fly standby, and, if not, I would have to pay for a round-trip ticket, but that did not matter.

About this time, Roger and I almost staged a revolt. Mitchell had really fucked over us. After I had been fired from the sergeant-majors' Mess, another grunt took over as their waiter. He turned out to be a real ass kisser and he buttered up those SOBs so much it was unbelievable. He had less than half the time in grade as a Spec. 4 than did either Roger or myself, but he had become the head sergeant-major's pet, and had all those SMs sitting pretty as pigs in slops. The head SM told Mitchell to put him in for Sergeant E-5, and, low and behold, the asshole got promoted to E-5! Roger and I seethed in suppressed rage. This was just too much for us to take. We had been fucked over once too often. When we learned the news, we went directly to our Mess sergeant and demanded he take us to see Colonel Kingston. The Mess sergeant, an E-7, knew we were pissed. We told him we wanted to bring the matter of our promotion directly to Colonel Kingston's attention as we had been royally fucked by both Mitchell and the head SM. I cannot remember whether or not we actually talked to

E. Tayloe Wise — Finally made Sgt. (E-5)!

Colonel Kingston about this matter. The stink Roger and I raised about the SMs' waiter stirred up a lot of dust. We wanted justice, and we were going to get it or there would be hell to pay. We got it. On March 15, both Roger and I were promoted to Sergeant E-5. I was really happy at this turn of events because, on March 22, 1969, I had been kicked out of INCOC School at Fort Benning. I had proved to myself that I could fight for and receive sergeant's stripes despite the stigma of failing in NCO School.

Two days after my promotion, on the night of March 17, an amusing incident took place, which just went to prove that we could not trust the South Vietnamese. The head KP was a mama-san who had been in the kitchen for as long as I had been a member of the CG's Mess. That evening she decided to go to the latrine and left the kitchen. She always used the lieutenant colonel's latrine, which not only was located about fifty meters from the kitchen but also was off-limits to South Vietnamese. She was supposed to use the South Vietnamese latrine, which was located some fifty meters past the LTC's latrine. We were cleaning up the Mess Hall and kitchen when the MPs marched in with her in tow. They had picked her up loitering around the rear of TOC, the Cav's nerve center, where all the brass worked. Even we waiters, who had access to almost every place in the compound, were not allowed in that restricted area, which was a good 200 meters away from the Mess Hall and at least 150 meters from the South Vietnamese latrine.

She was held for questioning until the CID men could arrive the next morning. We all hoped they would nail her ass but good. We later learned that she vehemently denied she was a spy. She even told her interrogators she did not understand English. The MPs, however, returned to the kitchen to verify her statements, and we told them she did understand English. So, she was caught in a lie. Her replacement, probably another NVA/VC sympathizer, arrived soon afterward. I never did learn what happened to her, but she was probably barred from the base. This whole incident only reinforced our beliefs about the South Vietnamese — they would sell their soul to the devil, if necessary. Then again, they did not have much choice because the NVA and VC controlled the village at night and could easily punish, or kill, anyone who did not cooperate in finding out and divulging much-needed information.

The 17th also brought me some other good news. The University of Texas accepted me into graduate school. I was elated. Now, I had to keep my fingers crossed and pray that I would receive the $3,000.00 teaching assistantship. I had already begun to worry about graduate school. I knew I had a good chance of being admitted. Mentally, I just did not know if I was ready for school again. I had been out in the world for two years, and Nam was deeply etched in my mind. I was beginning to have a lot of self-doubt as to the wisdom of returning to school because I was too emotionally crippled by Nam. I did not know whether or not it would be wise for me to leave one pressure cooker and enter another. The strain of Nam could easily be carried over into my forthcoming marriage and my return to school. All of a sudden, I wasn't so sure of myself, and what I really wanted to do with my life.

All of us knew about the 50,000 troop withdrawal that was to take place prior to April 15. On March 18, we received word that people who DEROSed in April (my DEROS date was April 29) would be eligible for drops. A drop was a cut in the amount of time that one had to serve in Nam. We received word that, if a person DEROSed on April 23, he would DEROS on April 8, which was a fifteen-day drop. To go home two weeks earlier was a dream come true. We were also told that starting April 1, drops of seventeen days would be automatic. I was elated! The reason for these drops was, of course, understandable. Men were needed so that they could be included in the 50,000 troop withdrawal. Not enough grunts DEROSed prior to April 15. So, any grunt who DEROSed within a couple weeks after that date was given a big drop.

Good news seemed to be following me. Without warning, one day several of us were ordered to assemble at the grassy area in front of the flagpole by the entrance to the Cav compound. Fourteen of us were awarded a Bronze Star for Meritorious Service (being members of the CG's Mess). I was flabbergasted as I never expected to get another medal, especially while in the CG's Mess. So, now I had my third Bronze Star.

The time for me to go on leave approached rapidly. Grunts were getting drops of up to eighteen days, which meant that when I returned from my seven-day leave to Bangkok I would be eligible to leave almost immediately from Nam. I went to the LTC in charge of drops for the Cav to find out the real story. I had thought about the possibility of going on leave and then not having to return to PV to clear battalion. I told him what was on my mind and asked him if it would be possible for me to clear battalion, go on leave, come back to Bien Hoa and DEROS. He said yes. God, I was so relieved! On March 23, I started clearing Headquarters Company. What a perfect ending to my stay in Nam. I was headed home!

By March 24, I had cleared HHC, bid my fellow waiters and cooks adieu, and caught a C-130 to Bien Hoa. That day in Bien Hoa, as I was running around getting some paperwork straightened out, I saw an approaching first lieutenant and saluted him. He said, "Hey, don't I know you? What school did you go to? TCU?" To which I replied, "Yep!"

Well, I did indeed know him. His name was Salvador Rodriguez. He had graduated from TCU in 1967. At TCU he had lived on the same floor of Clark dorm with me. I remembered him well, and we chatted about ten minutes. I felt this was the strangest coincidence—just out of the blue. He knew another friend of mine from TCU who was also stationed in Nam, and told me about him. I was surprised he had recognized me because I was a good 10–15 feet away and was turned sideways when I had saluted him. He was going to DEROS in May, and I told him I was going on leave and then would DEROS. Our chance encounter made my day. What a small world it was!

The 24th proved to be a hectic day. I shuttled back and forth between offices to check my records and make sure everything was in proper order so that I might process out of Nam smoothly when I returned from my leave to Bangkok. I learned that someone had screwed up on awarding me the Air Medal, so I had to get that straightened out. Since they had no paperwork on it, they had to resubmit it, and they told me that I would receive it upon return from Thailand.

I sat around most of the 25th, not doing much of anything. I learned that a bus would take us to Camp Alpha the next day. I was finally getting closer to leaving Nam. What a great feeling that was! That night, I got stoned out of my tree.

I stayed in Camp Alpha one night and caught a flight, as a standby, to Bangkok on the 27th. I was indeed looking forward to some good times. Upon arriving in Bangkok we were given a short orientation along with information as to the best hotels to use. A couple of other guys and I chose the World Hotel on New Petchburi Road.

On the way over to the hotel, our taxi driver, Mr. Nit, asked us if we wanted any girls. The other two guys said yes, but I hesitated and then told him I was there to tour and see the sights. Besides, I was engaged. Upon arrival at the hotel, Mr. Nit made arrangements with the other guys for the girls. He gave me his card and told me that, if I needed anything, to please let him know. I thanked him and went on up to my hotel room.

It took me about half an hour, alone in my room, to realize that I was not going to have any fun for three days before staying at Ted and Mary Stewart Ruhnke's unless I had someone to share in it. I called the desk and asked them to get in touch with Mr. Nit, who met me in the lobby. I told him that I wanted a girl. He drove me to the Bovorn Turkish Bath and Massage on Sukhuvit Road where I was introduced to a lovely young girl by the name of Kit. We agreed on a price of $25.00 per day for her companionship and then returned to my hotel, where I proceeded to avail myself of her services as quickly as possible. I did not realize I was so horny, but I made frequent use of her services that first night in Bangkok. I also found out that she was a clean girl. Each time, after we made love, she made me get out of bed and take a bath with her. She took great care to wash my genitals each time we had intercourse, even if it was two o'clock in the morning. She also took great care in washing herself. This reassured me, in that I felt I was getting a clean girl who was not taking any chances about contracting VD. Sometimes, during the three days we were together, I didn't want to get up and bathe, but she scolded the hell out of me and forced me to bathe with her, which was, after all, kind of fun.

I had told Kit that I wanted to take some tours around Bangkok, so we went down to the hotel lobby on the morning of the 28th, and I signed up for four tours. That morning, we went to see a group of temples that were located in a central area of Bangkok. I was absolutely fascinated by the skillful artistry of the Thais. Their temples were magnificent and the idols of Buddha that they contained were most impressive. I saw one Buddha, about ten feet tall, that was made of solid gold. I was awed by its beauty. That afternoon we went to Timland, which was both an amusement park and a zoo. I saw cobras for the first time in my life. An attendant actually got into a pit with cobras. I watched in rapt fascination as he teased these deadly vipers to rise up and strike. I shuddered to think about how fatal their bite would be. After the snakes, we watched a Thai boxing match that I found to be interesting because the combatants could use their feet to kick each other. After the show, which I thoroughly enjoyed, Kit and I returned to the hotel for fun and games. That evening Kit and I went out to a nightclub to dance and drink. I was tired, so we did not stay long.

The next day, Sunday, was one of the most memorable days of my life. I had signed up to see the Royal Summer Palace and the extensive ruins of Thailand's ancient capital of Ayudhya. We traveled by motorboat up the Chao Phraya River for about two hours. I watched the changing shoreline the whole way and chatted with Kit. Having majored in anthropology, I

E. Tayloe Wise on leave in Bangkok.

was excited about seeing Ayudhya. Our first stop was the lovely Royal Summer Palace, which I found interesting because one of the lawns had topiary shaped into various animal forms. I had never seen sculptured bushes and found this quite novel. After a quick tour of the summer palace, we proceeded upriver to the ancient ruins. Buses awaited us at the landing and took us through parts of Ayudhya. I was overcome with awe by this once magnificent civilization and wondered why it had disappeared. Never, in my wildest imagination, had I believed this area of the ancient world would be capable of such great feats of construction. We toured many ruins and finally ended up at a temple that rose high above the surrounding plain. Climbing the steep steps of this temple, we came to a wide terrace and walked around the temple. One could see for miles and I loved it. On our last stop, we viewed a huge reclining white Buddha, which was magnificently preserved.

Late that afternoon, back in the city, Kit took me to her beauty parlor. While I waited for her to be made up, one of the parlor girls gave me a manicure. I had never been in a beauty shop — much less one frequented by prostitutes! I was intrigued to see these girls have all their makeup stripped off their faces and then have it reapplied. Having never before seen how a woman applies makeup, I watched in fascination as these plain Janes were turned into beautiful women.

That evening, Kit and I ate at a little hole-in-the-wall. The food was delicious after such a long day.

On Monday, she and I went to the floating market where I purchased seven yards of silk so that Abby could make a dress. Later on, we went to a zoo that I enjoyed immensely.

Prior to my arrival in Bangkok, I had been in touch with Ted and Mary Stewart Ruhnke and had made arrangements to stay with them during my last two days in Bangkok. On the way, Kit, not believing I was leaving to visit friends, escorted me in the taxi to Ted's place. Mary Stewart met me, gave Kit the once-over, and didn't believe me when I told her I had just picked Kit up for the ride. My last two days with the Ruhnkes were uneventful, and I left Bangkok on April 2 for Saigon. My long journey was coming to a close.

I was tense after landing in Saigon and being transported by bus to Long Binh. In a few short days, I would be out of Nam. My long year's journey into hell was drawing to a close. I spent the next five days (April 3–7) processing for DEROS and ETS and was sent to Camp Alpha on the 7th. That wait at Camp Alpha on April 7–8 was the longest wait of my life. I was so keyed up that I don't even remember boarding the Freedom Bird on April 8, 1970. I know we stopped somewhere in Japan to refuel, but I cannot even remember landing in Oakland on April 8. I was home, on U.S. soil, once again. I had served 342 days in purgatory and now I was free! My terrible ordeal was over. I had survived. It took thirty-one hours, during which I got little sleep, to process out of the Army. But at 1530 hours on April 9, 1970, I was handed my walking papers. Free at last!

I got a taxi to the San Francisco airport and caught the next plane to Dallas. Abby met me at the airport, and we partied for two days. One of those days is a complete blank. I got so drunk I don't remember a thing.

On April 12, I flew to my hometown of Charlottesville, Virginia, took a cab home, walked into my parents' house, and surprised both of them. The first thing my mother said to me was, "Don't squeeze me!" A few years earlier I had squeezed her so hard that I broke one of her ribs. This time, I just hugged her tightly.

God, it was good to be home! I was no longer a grunt.

Afterword

When asked what he did during the French Revolution's Reign of Terror, the Count of Sieyès replied — "I survived."

Emmanuel Joseph Sieyès (1748–1806)

Well, I made it. Or did I? Perhaps I only survived Nam. The scars are still deep within me — hidden, but always present. The heat, the dust, the blood, the smell of decomposing flesh, and screams of "Medic!" are all there. They have been entombed in my mind. I can march them out at any time. I was lucky. I made it — physically. Emotionally, I will never know if I really survived Nam. It branded me with an indelible and invisible stamp. I am marked — nay, permanently tattooed — by what I saw and experienced. There are thousands like me out there in the jungle we call America. We are the walking wounded — the forgotten warriors. We gave our lives and our blood for this country only to be repudiated by our friends, neighbors, employers, and our government, upon our return to the World. Nothing could have been more devastatingly disillusioning. Truly, we made the supreme sacrifice — we fought in the first war that our country resoundingly lost. We will live with those stigmata forever, because Nam made us grow old before our time.

I had never really been out on my own before joining the Army. My childhood and adolescence were pretty much lived inside a glass bottle — an ivory tower. My surroundings were safe and secure, and I took a lot for granted because I was so sheltered. Yet, our great land and its leaders made Vietnam more of a lower-class war. Most of the sons of the rich and powerful sat back on the sidelines and drank their martinis as poor men, black and white, writhed on the humid jungle floor, drooled blood from their mouths, and died in vain, screaming "Mother!" I still wonder to this day what I could have done to avoid the trauma of it all, because I certainly don't need the emotional scars that are indelibly etched upon my psyche.

As a child, I had been raised on the concepts of "right" versus "wrong," and "good" versus "evil." I was inculcated with the firm belief that my country could do no wrong, and that it was an honor and a privilege to be born and raised in the greatest nation of modern times. Now, I wonder because that nation sent us out to kill ruthlessly and mindlessly. We killed just to kill, not to win. It was all a game for big boys—a grown-up cops and robbers or cowboys and Indians. We were forced to participate in insane body count games as an inane measure of quantitative success. In Nam, body counts only put pressure on us to kill for the sole purpose of racking up as high a human score as possible, thus making a firefight a fleeting step on the road to pointlessness. Yes, we were well taught in the art of killing. We were like the Harlem Globetrotters who continuously blow out the Washington Generals by 50–60 points every game. Our generation marched to the tune of a false drumroll—one that led us down a path of horror and betrayal. I firmly believe that the older World War II generation really duped the Baby Boomer generation.

I was raised to believe that those who died for their country were heroes. Maybe some of them were, but the rest were sold a shabby bill of goods. We didn't die in Vietnam to perpetuate the American dream, or to ensure that the United States would remain a healthy entity, so the old traditions would be continued. We died because *someone fucked up.* Someone without enough courage or guts to say no simply let us become entangled in the morass that became known as the Vietnam War. Ultimately, the blame lies with our Presidents, but they cannot take all the blame. It was as much their fault as it was that of both Congress and the military. Neither one of those institutions had the guts to say "NO!" Besides, the American economy—the multinational corporations—also needed an economic boost. The Vietnam War was an excellent way to do it.

I went and did my bit in Nam for the "good old U. S. of A." I received medals for heroism, but I didn't feel like a hero. I felt defiled, raped, dirty. My wonderful country had let me down. I had believed so faithfully in it. Now I find it extremely difficult to trust people. I just don't believe anyone—except a fellow Vietnam vet—can really understand, or even begin to comprehend, what happened to me. I guess that's why I have no close friends. I don't want to be close to anyone, because I am afraid I will lose them as I lost almost all of my buddies in Nam. Yet, sadly, I miss not having friends.

The sense of frustration and loss I felt upon returning to America was overpowering. I hadn't accomplished anything for my country. I had merely managed to survive for 342 days. True, I had saved human life. But was that helping my country or merely helping mankind? I was a survivor. All that useless fighting, just to survive. It made no sense. I had run the gauntlet and endured the whips of war. Inwardly, my wounds still bleed. I hate authority. I despise people who say we must obey orders because it's good for the country, or the economy, or the big corporations. Bullshit! Those people are incompetent nabobs who are seeking nothing more than political and economic power. Such individuals need to be toppled from their lofty positions of authority before they become scurrilous demagogues.

After I returned home in 1970, no one ever talked to me about Nam for almost twenty years. No one ever took an interest in what I did over there. Because of my country's betrayal of me and the rest of my generation, I still have a lot of bottled-up anger just waiting to be uncorked. I want to talk about it, because I enjoy telling others what I did. I want to be proud of what I did — not dirty. But no one wants to listen. They all feel culpable and want to make us feel guilty for participating in such insanity. I'm not guilty! Neither are the rest of us! After all that, how the hell could we not help but feel guilty by association? It's a wonder that we, who went, continued to fight. We were nothing more than lemmings. We need to throw off this yoke of collective guilt from our shoulders and place the blame on those who deserve it — our political, military and corporate leaders. Greed does strange things. Perhaps it's time for Vietnam vets to flex our muscles and prevent greed from ruining our nation.

What did I gain for all this? I honestly don't know. I think one of the most important things that I learned was that we can **never** trust our political leaders. They are whores, who will not only put their own selfish interests first, but will also advance them at all costs at the expense of sacrificing human life. They follow false gods — power, rank, authority, political gain, etc. If we cannot trust our leaders, who can we trust? The coins of our nation say, "In God We Trust" but, unfortunately, we can't even trust God to pull us out of the quicksands of time. Those who follow their traitorous idols will always drag us down into the dirt with them. I believe that we have a duty to prevent this by whatever means possible.

Never again should we be forced to fight in a war we cannot win! Our country cannot be permitted to ship its citizens off to unseen lands to die in obscurity. The blood of our young men and women must never again be permitted to run upon the beaches, jungles, or deserts of some two-bit nation, hell bent on self-destruction, regardless of who intervenes to help it out. Let there be no more Vietnams! Woe be unto the military and political leaders who attempt to involve us in hopeless causes! Our leaders should beware lest the uncaged tiger turns upon its master. For they will be the ones we will be looking at through the crosshairs of our rifle scopes.

We live in a great land. There is no reason why it cannot be greater if we have competent leaders at the helm who have enough common sense to keep us out of the quagmires of useless wars. Unfortunately, a bad apple sneaks in every once in a while and does far more damage than the electorate ever anticipated. Ruthless leaders, who believe in sacrificing people to achieve ambiguous goals or to advance their political and military careers, need to be replaced, or eliminated. Our politicians and multinational corporations cannot be permitted to dictate to America's youth as to where they will fight and for how long. I love my country but, when my country places itself in an unjust position, where it can assert a right to decide the fate of its youth in a hopeless and lost cause, such as Vietnam or what we are presently facing in Iraq, it must be stopped by *whatever means necessary.*

Our system of government must change. It must respond more quickly to injustice and unfair laws. If it cannot change or respond, then it must be forced into change by whatever means are necessary. Terrorism and violence cannot, *must not*, be ruled out. We must not be forced to kowtow to some "nebulous" societal dictates handed down from on high. It is time for us to stop thinking about society, or government, as a monolithic entity that cannot be overruled. Of course, it can be, and we should not be forced to do things because that is "what is expected of us." That is poppycock! The system can be, and is oftentimes, wrong. If the system will not adapt itself, then we must change the system by whatever means to ensure it is a better, more workable mechanism. Like an old car that needs new parts, we must throw out the old and begin anew. We have a duty to ourselves, and the society in which we live, to disobey any law when it is wrong or endangers our lives. Just because a legislative body enacts a law, does not make that law right. Laws must be questioned, and, if wrong, discarded as, finally, Prohibition was, much to everyone's delight. People point out that society makes the laws and therefore knows what is best for us, but they are quick to forget that they are part of that same society and responsible for what it does in enacting its laws. As far as protecting our lives is concerned, we should be allowed to do as we choose with the minimum amount of social restraint placed upon our actions. Some would say that terrorism and other means of violence would lead to anarchy and discord. Perhaps it might, but, if it can change our government and laws for the better, then we have achieved a modicum of success.

The Germans and the Japanese had formidable military might and power in World War II. Standing toe to toe we stood up to their threats and slugged it out with them both in the trenches of Europe and on the islands of the Pacific. We crushed them. We won. We emerged victorious. Yet, in Nam, there were no front lines. The local peasant was your friend by day — your enemy by night. In the boonies, we never saw Charlie. Or, if we did, he was already dead. The only bodies we ever saw were those friends who fell in various poses of the macabre and the grotesque. It was so mentally frightening ... fighting someone you never saw. A ghost ... a ... will-o'-the-wisp. Invisible. We fired hundreds of rounds in firefights and dropped thousands of pounds of artillery on top of enemy positions and never saw a soul, but the gooks were always there, watching, waiting ... and so goddamn frustratingly invisible.

People danced in the streets and sailors kissed pretty girls when World War II drew to a close. No military bands played for us. Not even the Army would welcome us home. We were flown to Oakland, California, and disembarked from our Freedom Birds with little or no fanfare. We were clandestinely infiltrated back into the mainstream of America, like a heroin addict shooting up on the sidewalk, right in the middle of downtown Manhattan. We found our nation hostile and bitter. No one wanted to kiss us. No one wanted to buy us a drink at the corner bar. After all, we were killers. We were drug users. Baby killers. Rapists. Mass murderers. We had lost. For the first time, the U.S. had met its match like David and Goliath, and had been humbled by a tiny enclave halfway around the world. It was embarrassing. No, it was humiliating.

Vietnam is a small country, approximately the size of New Mexico. Yet, with all our advanced technology, with all our air and artillery power, we couldn't beat the NVA into submission. Col. Harry G. Summers recounted a most apropos conversation:

> "You know you never defeated us on the battlefield," said the American colonel.
> The North Vietnamese colonel pondered this remark a moment. "That may be so," he replied, "but it is also irrelevant."*

Our nation felt guilty, and it took its wrath out on the losers — its returning servicemen. No one wants to talk about Vietnam. No one wants to understand us. We veterans are put on the back shelf, closed up in a closet out of sight and out of mind. We bore, and still bear, the brunt of our national disgrace. We are pariahs. Like lepers from Biblical times, we

---

*Harry G. Summers, Jr., *On Strategy — A Critical Analysis of the Vietnam War* (Novato, CA: Presidio Press, 1982), 1.

are shunned and pushed aside. After all, we were expendable — reminders of a shame no one wanted to face. Never mind that we had to fight with one arm tied behind our backs. Never mind that the Pentagon was fettered by Congress and the Presidency. No, never mind. The tune was the same all over the country —"Hey, GI, you lost! You fuckin' lost. You lousy son of a bitch!" People spat on us— made us ashamed to wear our country's uniform. Something was wrong, and we didn't know what. At first, when I returned, I felt lost without carrying a rifle. Naked. Vulnerable. Well, maybe that's OK. Because if I had walked around with a loaded rifle, I'd have been tempted, so sorely tempted, to strike back … to blow someone away with little or no feelings whatsoever. In many ways I still miss my trusty M-16.

During the Vietnam War, America suffered from an internal rot. Dishonesty permeated the highest corridors of political power and then filtered down into the lower echelons of the military. We also found the South Vietnamese Army and government — our allies— to be corrupt. Now our eyes have really been opened, and we can see the degeneracy in our own land that was the result of power-hungry politicos and greedy profit-minded corporate executives and stockholders. Profits at the expense of dead young men are inexcusable. Sacrificing soldiers to prevent a nation from reunifying, after having been illegally divided, is wrong. Our national security was not threatened. There was no excuse for us to have our young men die so needlessly. The leaders of our country, from the President and Congress on down, sold the American soldier down the drain. The big corporations seized on Vietnam to bolster employment and make a fast buck, at the expense of young men who were gullible enough to fight for a lost cause. Both the legislative and financial forces in our country betrayed its Vietnam veterans. This is a crime that should not have been tolerated. Our country owes us much more than betrayal! It owes us more than an apology. We can never, *never* be repaid for the sacrifices we were forced to make.

The American dream was dead. It died when Saigon fell, rather easily, to the advancing armies of the North on April 30, 1975. You cannot take a country such as Germany, or Korea, or Vietnam, divide it, and expect the two halves to operate independently. It just doesn't work. Sooner or later, reunification will occur through peaceful solutions— such as Germany — or violent means as in Vietnam. America the beautiful was not a bird in a gilded cage. Good versus evil, right versus wrong took on newer, more subtle overtones. Now things weren't black or white, they were gray. Fifty-eight thousand of our young men and women lie rotting in their graves. I would hate to think they died in vain, but it now appears they did. The

Spirit of 1776 is dead. The drum and fife corps will not beat so loudly, so patriotically, or so inspiring now, as it marches down hometown streets in July 4th parades. The American spirit is dead. At least it is for my generation. All we have left is a tomb-like black granite wall with 58,193 names carved upon it, to remind us of those who gave us their blood and their lives.

Therefore, we must ensure that our country pays for the wrongs and injustices it deliberately foisted upon us by preventing further fiascos such as Vietnam. The legacy we Vietnam veterans owe future generations is to prevent war. We cannot — we must not — bow to the politicos who follow the false gods of greed and power or avaricious corporate leaders who strive to make the bottom line insanely profitable. They must be made to accede to our will and wishes. We can have a strong nation, militarily, without involving ourselves in war, without committing our youth to future experiments in dubious "nation-building" schemes. Vietnam was an experiment in sanctioned violence gone awry and American young men were egregiously used as unwilling guinea pigs. It is time for the guinea pigs to turn the tables.

Today, I am more disillusioned with my country than I was in 1970. We still haven't learned our lesson. Because of my all-expense-paid trip to Vietnam, courtesy of the U.S. government, I learned that what I had been raised to believe in as a youngster was wrong. I had been taught to follow false gods, which were traitors to me and thousands of other young men. The stark reality of the American dream was brought home to me most graphically in Vietnam. It brought out the absolute worst in us as a nation. The military strategy, the tactics employed, were so convoluted. We took an unknown piece of earth by day and conquered it. Then, we'd call in the slicks and CA to another LZ and lose by nightfall what we'd fought so hard to gain during the day. It was tragic. Earth shattering. So ultimately disillusioning.

We owe it to ourselves, and our nation, to prevent future Vietnams. If we cannot throw the powers that be out of office by use of the ballot box, then they must be forced to resign or, if they refuse, they need to be removed from their position of authority by being recalled or impeached (politically), relieved of command (militarily), or, as a last resort — our ace in the hole — assassinated. Such people pose a threat to the orderly stability of American life and need to be exterminated like bugs. Let us hope we can prevent future Vietnams by the wise use of the ballot box and not by force, or terror. We also cannot rule out sabotage against the manufacturing plants of the giant corporations to prevent the manufacture of military matériel. If our nation persists in attempting to involve itself in backyard conflicts to achieve glory and multinational corporate profits, then it must be forced to pay the price for such involvement.

There has to be a way for inept leaders to be removed from office, or military command, more quickly than our present system permits. While I do not advocate the frequent use of assassination, it should only be used sparingly to accomplish whatever ends are necessary. After all, it is not a new concept to Americans. It has occurred in our own political spectrum a few times, in our national life some, and we have condoned and sanctioned its use by our CIA for covert operations for God only knows how long.

I am fully aware that certain thoughts I have voiced in this book go counter to our democratic ideals. But, having participated in sanctioned violence, is it not logical that I would then advocate the use of violence? Sometimes the system fails and, when it does, I believe that radical and controversial measures must be taken to ensure the continuance of that system. I am not advocating the overthrow of our system of government. Sometimes the ballot box is not enough, because there are too many Americans who refuse to vote, so the political winner is not always the choice of the majority. The 2000 presidential election is a case in point. Sometimes, the majority must have its nose tweaked so that the true desires of the populace can become manifest.

In sum, Vietnam made no sense at all. Looking back, I know I loved the action intensely. I was viscerally alive under fire — conscious of every second. I experienced a certain pleasure in the fighting … and killing … and healing. It made everything else that I thought was important in my life such a comedown. A firefight became the *deus ex machina* of our days, by warding off the inevitable boredom and ever-present weariness that dogged our every step.

Time heals and binds up wounds, or so we are led to believe. Perhaps this is true. The wounds, however, are deeply embedded within us. They can resurface at almost any time in a sudden outburst of rage or violence. We cannot tame our souls or minds. The hurt is still there. The guilt is still deep within us. We shall not forget the sarcastic, flippant way in which our nation welcomed us home.

Vietnam taught us an important lesson. It also taught us violence. Which tool — the dove of peace or the sword of violence — will we be forced to use to ensure our country never errs this way again?

Yet, just below the surface is always that one thought — that one basic, eternal truth that you will always remember — You don't win a war by dying for your country — only by making the other guy die for his country.

Glossary

Agent Orange   Highly toxic herbicide widely used to defoliate the jungle; sprayed from airplanes and named after the color-coded stripe painted around the barrels in which it was stored.

Air Mobile   Helicopter-borne, or those who jump from helicopters without parachutes.

AIT   Advanced Infantry Training; specialized training taken after Basic Training.

AK-47   a.k.a. a Kalashnikov AK-47. A Soviet-produced semi-automatic or automatic 7.62-mm assault rifle, which was also manufactured in China. AK is for Automat Kalashnikov after its designer. This is the most widely used assault rifle in the world. It is characterized by an explosive popping sound, and was the standard infantry piece of the North Vietnamese and Viet Cong soldier.

AO   Area of operations for a military unit.

ARA   Aerial rocket artillery; *see also* **Cobra**.

Arc Light   A B-52 bomber strike, shaking the earth and trees for at least ten miles away from the target area.

Article 15   Non-judicial punishment, meted out by an officer to enlisted personnel.

Arty   Short for artillery.

ARVN   Army of the Republic of Vietnam (South Vietnam); also a South Vietnamese soldier; pronounced "Arvin."

Ass Kicker   A piece of military equipment that was so heavy, or cumbersome, that it earned the name "ass kicker" because GIs dreaded having to carry it on their backs.

AWOL Absent without leave, leaving a post or position without official permission.

Azimuth A direction in degrees from north, a bearing.

B-40 A shoulder-fired, 82-mm rocket-propelled antitank grenade launcher, similar to the American-made LAW with an effective range of 150 yards; carried by the Viet Cong and North Vietnamese soldiers and most effective against bunkers.

B-52 A U.S. high-altitude heavy bomber; the mainstay of heavy bombardment support for U.S. ground troops in Vietnam.

Bandoleers Belts of M-60 machine gun ammunition.

Base Camp An administrative and logistical camp for a unit, a.k.a. the **Rear Area**, or **Rear**, usually semi-permanent, which contains the unit's support elements. It is a resupply base for field units and a location for headquarters units, artillery batteries, and airfields.

Beaucoup French for "many." Usually pronounced "BOO-KOO."

Beehive Rounds An explosive artillery shell, or recoilless rifle round, which delivered thousands of small arrow-like projectiles, or fléchettes; a.k.a. "nails with fins," instead of shrapnel.

Ben Casey A medic.

BEQ Bachelor Enlisted Quarters; place for enlisted men to live or sleep.

Berm An earthen perimeter line of a fortification; usually raised above the surrounding area.

Big Red One Nickname for the 1st Infantry Division.

Bird Slang for any aircraft, but usually a helicopter.

Bird Dog An FAC, or forward air controller, usually in a small, maneuverable, single-engine fixed-wing prop plane.

Birddog *see* LOH.

Blood Trail A trail of blood on the ground left by a fleeing man who has been wounded.

Blooper *see* M-79.

Blue Max *see* **Cobra** gunship.

Boo-Coo, or **Boo-Koo** *see* **Beaucoup.**

Boonie Hat A soft olive drab or camouflage-colored cotton hat which matched army fatigues, but was not part of the official uniform. It was worn by the infantry soldier in the **Boonies.**

Boonies Short for boondocks, or "out in the sticks"—the field, the bush, the jungle. Any place the infantry operates outside of a firebase, base camp, etc.

Breaking Bush   Moving forward through the elephant grass or jungle and not using a pre-established path or **Trotter.**

Breaking Starch   To put on a clean or newly starched uniform.

BS   Bullshit. Also BSing; bullshitting, as in chewing the fat, telling tall tales, or telling lies.

Bummer   A bad occurrence.

Bush   The outer field areas, or jungle, where infantry units operated in nonpermanent positions.

C-4   Plastic putty-textured explosive, carried in one-pound bars, or sticks. Burned like Sterno, so was often used for heating water and cooking as well as detonating.

C-130   a.k.a. Lockheed C-130; a medium cargo airplane also used as a troop carrier and a gunship.

C's   *see*   **C-Rations.**

CA   Combat Assault, or Charley Alpha.

C & C   Command and Control; *see also* **Command Bird.**

CAV   Cavalry; shortened term for the 1st Air Cavalry Division (Air Mobile).

CG   Commanding General.

CH-47   a.k.a. Boeing-Vertol CH-47 Chinook helicopter; a large twin-rotor helicopter used to transport troops, equipment, and supplies, for medical evacuation, and aircraft retrieval. An external sling could be used to transport heavy objects. It could also carry about 30 men with combat gear; a.k.a. "**Chinook**" and, derogatorily, often referred to as the "**Shithook**" because of the discomfort caused by the rotor wash to anyone in the vicinity of its landing.

CH-54   a.k.a. Sikorsky CH-54 Tarhe; the largest of all American helicopters, strictly for lifting and transporting heavy equipment and cargo up to 12½ tons; a.k.a. the **Flying Crane,** or "**Skycrane.**"

Charlie   The NVA or VC.

Cherry   A new troop, especially one who has not seen combat. *See also* **FNG.**

Chicom   Chinese communist. A Chinese-manufactured hand grenade.

Chieu Hoi (Vietnamese for "open arms")   A South Vietnamese program whereby enemy soldiers were encouraged to surrender, or defect, without penalty; an enemy soldier who so surrendered. NVA and VC shouted it to mean "I surrender."

Chinook   *see*   **CH-47.**

Chopper   Helicopter.

CIB   Combat Infantryman's Badge, awarded to Army infantrymen who have been under fire in a combat zone.

CID   Criminal Investigation Division.

Claymore   Curved antipersonnel mine with a one-pound charge of C-4 behind 600–700 steel miniballs which are thrown out in a fan-shaped pattern with a 60–80° arc. Lethal range is about 50 meters. The name is derived from the name of a huge Scottish broadsword which was used to cut a swath through enemy ranks.

Cloverleaf Patrol   A squad of 12 to 15-men patrols out from a main body of troops in a looping pattern which, when seen from the air, or diagrammed, looks like a cloverleaf.

CMH   The Congressional Medal of Honor; the highest U.S. military decoration, awarded for conspicuous gallantry to one who risked his life in action above and beyond the call of duty.

CO   Commanding Officer or Conscientious Objector.

Cobra   a.k.a. **Blue Max**; a Bell AH-1 Huey Cobra assault helicopter with 4 XM-159C 19 Rocket (2¾"-rocket) pods. It also fired M-79 grenade rounds, and had an electric 7.62-mm Gatling-type gun, which was capable of firing 6000 rounds/minute. *See also* **Mini-Gun**.

Colt .45-Caliber   *See* **.45**.

Command Bird   Aircraft in which a troop-unit commander circles a battle area to observe and direct his troops; a.k.a. C & C (Command and Control, or Charley-Charley).

Concertina Wire   Barbed wire that is rolled out along the ground to impede the progress of ground troops, or **Sappers**.

Contact   A **firefight**, or engaging in rifle fire with the enemy.

Coordinates   Numbers that indicate a specific place in the field when a unit needs to identify its exact location over the radio; used when calling in artillery, helicopters, mortars, medevacs, etc.

CP   Command post. Platoon-sized units or larger established command posts which coordinated the unit's activities from a central position.

Crash   To sleep.

C-rations   a.k.a. **C-Rats**, or **C's**. These were the standard meals eaten in the bush. They came in cartons containing 12 different meals, complete with extras such as coffee and cigarettes. Each meal consisted of a can of some basic course, a can of fruit, a packet of some type of dessert, a packet of powdered cocoa, and some chewing gum.

CS Grenade   Tear gas grenade.

Dee-Dee   *see* "**Didi**."

Deros   Date Eligible Return from Overseas. The day a soldier is scheduled to go home, or the act of going home.

Det Cord   Detonating cord used for explosives.

Diddy-Bopping   Walking carelessly; not paying attention.

Didi   Vietnamese for "to run," also "**dee-dee,**" or get the hell out of here.

Didi Mau   Also **Didi Mow.** Vietnamese for "to run quickly," or "go, go, quickly."

Dinky Dau (Vietnamese *dien cai dau*)   To be crazy, off the wall.

Dinks   A derogatory expression meaning or referring to the enemy.

Doughnut Dollies   Red Cross Girls.

Drop   A cut in the amount of time one had to serve on his tour of duty in Vietnam.

Duper   *see*   **M-79.**

Dust-Off; Dust-Off Chopper   Evacuation of casualties and the helicopter used for it; the term refers to the huge amounts of dust thrown up by the rotors of the chopper as it descended.

DX   To get out of, or take off.

81   Short for U.S. .81-mm mortar round.

Early-Outs   A drop, or a reduction in time in service. A soldier with 150 days or less remaining on his active duty commitment when he DEROSed from Vietnam also ETSed from the Army under the early-out program.

Eleven Bravo   Also 11-B, or 11B10 — the MOS for infantryman.

EM   Enlisted man.

ETS   Estimated Termination of Service. The scheduled date for getting out of the Army.

51   Short for a communist .51-mm heavy machine gun.

FAC   Forward air controller; an officer of the air control team who, from a forward position aloft, directs the action of aircraft engaged in close support of ground troops.

File   Line of march in the jungle.

Fire Base   A temporary artillery encampment used for fire support of forward ground operations.

Firefight   An brief and often violent exchange of small-arms fire with the enemy.

Flak Jacket   A heavy fiberglass-filled vest worn for protection from shrapnel on FSBs — it was extremely hot, heavy and cumbersome, so most troops refused to wear them.

Flare   An illumination projectile, hand-fired, or shot from artillery, mortars, or air; a.k.a. **Illumination.**

Fléchette   Antipersonal rounds which burst after traveling a certain distance, saturating the immediate area with arrow-like "nails and fins" projectiles.

Flying Crane   *see*   **CH-54.**

FNG   Fucking new guy; a **Cherry.**

FO   Forward Observer; usually an artilleryman, he accompanies infantry in the field and observes and adjusts artillery or mortar fire by radio, or other means.

.45   Colt .45-caliber pistol; standard sidearm issued to U.S. forces.

Frag   A fragmentation hand grenade.

Fragging   The use of a grenade by a man of lower rank to wound or kill an officer or NCO, especially a "**Lifer.**"

Freedom Bird   Passenger airliner returning troops from Nam to the World.

Free-Fire Zone   Territory designated by the government of South Vietnam that was deemed completely under enemy control; an area cleared of civilians within which artillery and aircraft could fire without having to obtain clearance. Anyone — men, women, and children — found within the free-fire zone were considered to be enemy and could be shot.

FSB   Fire support base; a.k.a. an "LZ"; it was established to provide artillery support for Allied units operating within range of the base.

GI   Term applied to the American soldier, carried over from World War II; GI = Government Issue.

Gook   Korean slang for "person," passed down by Korean War veterans and others who served in Korea. It is also a generic term for any oriental human being, especially an enemy.

Green Line   Outermost ring of bunkers surrounding a defensive position.

Ground Pounder   *see*   **Grunt.**

Grunt   An infantryman; supposedly derived from the sound made by an infantryman when he stood up with his rucksack in place on his back.

Gung Ho   Enthusiastic.

Gunship   Early in the war this meant an extra heavily armed helicopter used primarily to support infantry troops. Later, it referred to a Cobra AH-1G equipped with ARA, 40-mm cannons, mini-guns, and rockets.

HE   High-explosive, usually with reference to artillery and mortar shells.

Heat Tabs   An inflammable stick tablet used to heat **C-Rations,** or water for **Lurps.** They were always in short supply, so C-4 was used in their place.

Hippie   Combat engineer.

Hooch or **Hootch**   Any dwelling, whether temporary, as in an Army poncho hooch, or reasonably permanent, as in a bunker.

Hot LZ   A landing zone under enemy fire.

HQ   Headquarters.

Hueys   Bell UH-1H Iroquois helicopters. It was the primary troop insertion/extraction aircraft of the 1st Air Cavalry Division (Air Mobile) and the most widely used helicopter of the Vietnam War; a.k.a. **Slicks**. It usually carried a pilot, copilot, 1–2 M-60 machine gunners, and up to 8 troops with **gear**.

Hump   To patrol, or walk, carrying a heavy weight, usually a fully loaded rucksack.

IG   Inspector General.

Illumination   *see*   **Flare**.

INCOC   Infantry Noncommissioned Officer Course; an accelerated program during the Vietnam War designed to produce NCOs (usually Sergeant E-5 or E-6).

Incoming   Enemy artillery, mortars, rockets, or grenades fired into a troop location. Used as a shouted warning—"Incoming!"—to take cover.

In Country   In Vietnam.

Insert or **Insertion**   To be deployed into a tactical area by helicopter.

I & I   Intercourse and Intoxication. Derogatory term for **R & R**.

Joint   Marijuana.

Jungle Boots   Specially designed Army footgear for Vietnam, of lightweight canvas construction, with vent holes to let water out, and metal plates in the soles to resist **Punji Stakes**. The canvas speeded drying after stream and rice paddy crossings.

Jungle Penetrator   An elongated basket lowered by helicopter through thick jungle canopy so as to extract wounded men.

KIA   Killed in action.

Killing Zone   The area within an ambush where everyone is either killed or wounded.

Kit Carson Scout   Former enemy soldier who defected and actively aided American infantry forces.

Klick   A soldier's term for kilometer, or one thousand meters, or .6214 of a mile.

KP   Kitchen Police, or to work in an army kitchen.

LAAW   Light antiarmor assault weapon or light antitank assault weapon; *see also* **LAW**.

LAW   M-72 light antitank weapon; successor to the bazooka. It was a shoulder-fired, 66-mm rocket, similar in effect to a 3½" rocket, except that the launcher is made of fiberglass, and is disposable after one shot. Most effective against enemy bunkers.

Lai Day   Vietnamese for "Come here!"

Lancing   Cutting into the skin with a scalpel.

Lid   Marijuana cigarette.

Lifer   Career military personnel, often used derogatorily.

Lift   Helicopter trip to and from an infantry position.

Line One   American KIA.

Log   Resupply of ammunition, clothing, food, and water in the jungle. Sometimes we got sodas and beer.

Log Bird   Logistical (resupply) helicopter that brought the **Grunts** their C-Rations.

LOH   Hughes OH-6A Cayuse; light observation helicopter (pronounced "Loach"). These were mainly used to draw enemy fire. When fired upon they would swing away so the **Cobras** following them could strafe the enemy positions; a.k.a. "Scouts" and "Birddogs."

LP   Listening post; a fire team consisting of 2–3 men who traveled outside a fixed perimeter at night and set up in position so as to detect enemy movement or activity and give advance warning of any probe or attack; considered a suicide duty in Nam.

LRRP   Long range reconnaissance patrol; an elite team of 5–7 men who were inserted deep into enemy territory to observe NVA, or VC, activity without initiating contact.

LTC   Lieutenant colonel, usually a battalion commander.

Lurps   Members of a LRRP, or meals. The meals were usually freeze-dried food which, when mixed with water, was delicious. Prized by the grunts when issued to them.

LZ   A landing zone. Anyplace a helicopter could land troops or supplies. Also used to refer to FSBs.

M-16   A gas-operated, air-cooled automatic/semi-automatic assault rifle, 5.56-mm caliber, weighing 7.6 pounds with a 20-round magazine. Maximum range was 2350 meters. Maximum effective range was 460 meters. Automatic firing rate was 650–700 rounds/minute, sustained automatic firing rate 100–200 rounds/minute. Standard rifle carried by American soldiers.

M-60   The standard U.S. caliber 7.62-mm American light machine gun which was a gas-operated, air-cooled, belt-fed weapon; with a weight of 23 pounds and an effective range of 1100 yards.

M-72   *see*   **Law.**

M-79   An American single-shot 40-mm grenade launcher. It is a shotgun-like weapon that shoots spin-armed "balls," or small grenades with an effective range of 30–400 yards; a.k.a. **Blooper, Duper,** or **Thumper.**

MACV   Military Assistance Command, Vietnam, 1964–1973; U.S. command for all U.S. military activities in Vietnam.

Mad Minute   A weapons free-fire practice and test session. Usually held on LZ's at night to disconcert any enemy soldiers who might be lurking nearby.

Mama-San   Mature Vietnamese woman.

Mars   Military Affiliate Radio Station; used by soldiers to call home via Signal Corps and ham radio equipment.

Medevac   To medically evacuate a wounded or ill person; also refers to the helicopter doing the evacuation.

Medic   Medical Aid Man.

Meter   39.37 inches, or 1.09 yards.

MIA   Missing in action.

Million-Dollar Wound   A non-crippling wound serious enough to warrant evacuation to the United States.

Mini-Gun   An electric 7.62-mm Gatling-type gun, which was capable of firing 6000 rounds/minute. Usually found on **Cobras**.

MOS   Military Occupational Specialty; job title code.

MP   Military Police.

MPC   Military Payment Certificates; these were used in lieu of American green currency in war zones to discourage black marketeering.

Napalm   A jelly-like incendiary used in flame throwers and fire bombs; it adheres while it burns at about 2000 degrees Fahrenheit and can "deoxygenate" the air, causing death by asphyxiation.

NCO   Non-Commissioned Officer; usually E-5 rank and above.

Night Log   Overnight position in the jungle.

NLF   Communist National Liberation Front in Vietnam; founded December 12, 1960.

No-Fire Zone   An area occupied by Vietnamese civilians into which U.S. forces were not permitted to direct small arms, or artillery, fire.

Non-Com   *see*   NCO.

Number 1   The very best, first place, the highest. Also "**Numba 1,**" or "**Numbah 1.**"

Number 10   The very worst, a loser, the lowest. Also "**Numba 10,**" or "**Numbah 10.**"

NVA   The North Vietnamese Army, or a North Vietnamese soldier; a.k.a. People's Army of Vietnam (PAVN).

101   One-O-One; cellophane packet containing candies, toiletries, writing papers and pens, cigarettes, and other sundries, which came with **C-Rations**.

105   One-O-Five; short for U.S.-fired 105-mm howitzer; range 11,500 meters.

122   One Twenty-Two; 122-mm communist rocket capable of traveling, with booster, 22 kilometers.

155   One-Five-Five; short for U.S.-fired 155-mm howitzer; its shell weighed 95 pounds and its range was over 9 miles.

175   One-Seven-Five; short for U.S.-fired 175-mm howitzer; its shell weighed 175 pounds and its range was 20–23 miles.

OCS   Officer Candidate School.

OD   Olive drab; the color of military uniforms.

OJT   On Job Training.

Old-Timer   An infantryman who has survived his first 3–4 months in the jungle or who has been in numerous firefights.

On-Line Assault   A squad, or platoon, stands up and, walking abreast toward an enemy position, fires at the enemy; a highly dangerous maneuver that can lead to severe loss of life and limb.

OP   Observation post; an outpost, manned during daylight hours by 2–3 men to watch for enemy movement.

P-38   A small, 1½" long, collapsible metal can opener used to open **C-Rations**.

Papa-San   Any older Vietnamese man.

PAVN   *see*   **NVA**.

Platoon   A subdivision or a company-sized military unit, normally consisting of two or more squads or sections. Our platoons in Nam were supposed to contain 40–45 men, or 3 squads. We rarely had more than 20–25 men in a platoon.

Point, or **Point Man**   The soldier, or team of men, out front of a unit traveling in single file. It was the most exposed position and the **Point** was responsible for **Breaking Bush**.

Poncho Liner   Lightweight nylon insert to the military rain poncho, used as a blanket.

Pop Smoke   To ignite a **Smoke Grenade** to signal a helicopter.

Post-Traumatic Stress Disorder   *see*   **PTSD**.

Pot   Marijuana; also refers to the steel helmet infantrymen wore.

POW   Prisoner of war.

PRC-25, or **Prick-25**   Portable Radio Communications, Model 25. A backpacked FM receiver-transmitter used for short-distance communications. The range of the radio was 5–10 kilometers, depending on the weather, unless attached to a special, non-portable antenna which could extend the range to 20–30 kilometers. It was the standard radio used in Vietnam by the infantry. Carried by **RTOs**, it was so heavy, it was considered an **Ass Kicker.**

Profile   A prohibition from certain types of military duty due to an injury or disability.

PSYOPS   Psychological Warfare Operations.

PTSD   Post-traumatic stress disorder; term used to describe stress disorders in Vietnam veterans.

Puff or **Puff the Magic Dragon**   A Douglas C-47 cargo plane mounted with 3 General Electric 7.62-mm Gatling-type mini-guns and illumination flares. It provided intensive ground fire support for U.S. troops under attack; a.k.a. "**Spooky.**"

Punji Stake   A sharpened bamboo stake covered with feces and placed in the bottom of a pit or just underneath the water of a rice paddy alongside a well-used path.

Purple Heart   A military decoration awarded to any member of the U.S. military for any wound acquired in combat conditions. The awarding of the Purple Heart was much abused in Vietnam.

PV   Phuoc Vinh; headquarters of the 1st Air Cav Division (Air Mobile) in 1969–1970; located in south central Binh Phuoc Province.

PX   Post Exchange; department, grocery, or small general stores where GIs could buy necessities and personal-use items at a lower cost than available in civilian stores.

PZ   Pickup zone, where infantry troops waited for **Hueys** to pick them up.

RA   Regular Army, prefix to serial number of enlistees.

Rack   Bed, or cot.

Rack Time   Sleeping.

Rake   To fire an M-16 on full automatic.

R & R   Rest and Relaxation leave. A one-week vacation to an exotic place, allowed once during the 12-month tour; *see also* **I & I.**

Rear, or **Rear Area**   *see*   **Base Camp.**

Recon   Reconnaissance.

Recoilless RIFLE   A portable heavy weapon similar to a bazooka that fires **Fléchette** rounds.

Redlegs   Slang for artillerymen. In the Civil War, the Union artillerymen had red stripes on their pants.

REMF   Rear-Echelon Mother Fucker — someone who worked in a rear area and never saw combat.

Rock 'n' Roll   Firing an M-16, or M-60, on full automatic.

Roger   In radio language: "OK," or "I understand," or "Will do."

Rotate   To return to the States at the end of a one-year tour of duty in Vietnam.

RPG   Rocket-propelled grenade; *see also* **B-40**.

RTO   Radio-telephone operator, or the man assigned to carry the **Prick 25** radio while out in the jungle.

Ruck or **Rucksack**   Backpack issued to the infantrymen in Vietnam.

60   U.S. 60-mm mortar round.

Saddle Up   To put on one's rucksack and prepare to march. Also can be an order to do this.

Sappers   Enemy demolition, or assault, teams who were adept at crawling deftly through many strands of concertina wire, or mine fields, and penetrating defenses; usually armed with explosive **Satchel Charges**.

Satchel Charge   Explosive package fitted with a handle for easy handling or throwing. So called because of its resemblance to a satchel.

Shake 'n' Bake   A sergeant who attended INCOC School and earned the rank of E-5 or E-6 after a very short time in uniform.

Shammer   One who goofs off, or tries to get by with as little effort as possible.

Shamming   Goofing off, or getting by with as little effort as possible.

Shit Burning   The kerosene incineration of excrement for sanitizing latrines; the most dreaded duty in Vietnam as stirring of the contents was often required.

Shithook   Derogatory term for a **CH-47**.

Short   *see*   **Short-Timer**.

Short-Timer   Soldier nearing the end of his tour in Vietnam; usually a person with 100 days or less left in country; a.k.a. "**Short**."

Shrapnel   Pieces of metal sent flying by an explosion.

Sitrep   A situation report.

SKS   Soviet 7.62-mm carbine.

Skycrane   *see*   **CH-54**.

Skytrooper   An infantryman with the 1st Air Cavalry Division (Air Mobile).

Slicks   *see*   **Hueys**.

SM, or **SMs**   Sergeant-major(s), the highest enlisted rank (E-9) in the U.S. Army.

Smoke Grenade, or **Smokes**   A grenade that releases brightly colored smoke; used for signaling.

SOP   Standard Operating Procedure.

Soul Brother   A black soldier.

Spooky   *see*   **Puff.**

Starlight Scope   An image intensifier using reflected light from the stars and moon to identify targets at night.

Steel Pot   A GI helmet; rarely worn in the jungle due to its weight.

Step-On   An enemy soldier killed by U.S. forces.

Strobe   A hand-held strobe light for marking LZ's, or a military position, such as LP, at night.

Syrette   A collapsible morphine tube attached to a hypodermic needle. The contents of the tube were injected by squeezing it like a toothpaste tube.

Tee-Tee (Vietnamese *titi*)   Very small.

Tet   Vietnamese Lunar New Year holiday; usually in January–February; the most important Vietnamese holiday.

III Corps, or **Three Corps**   The 3rd Allied combat tactical zone covering the area from the northern Mekong River delta to the southern Central Highlands of Vietnam.

Thumper   *see*   **Blooper.**

TIG   Time in grade; the length of time one has held a specific rank in the military such as Sergeant E-5 or Captain.

TOC   Tactical Operations Center; an LZ's main communications center.

Top Sergeant   An E-9, highest NCO grade in the Army; *see also* **SM**; more familiarly "Top."

Tracer   A bullet, or artillery round, designed to provide a visual path, usually red, along its trajectory. Used at night to mark locations and fire zones. In M-16s the tracer bullet was usually spaced every fifth shot. The NVA used green tracers.

Trip Flare or **Trips**   A ground flare triggered by a trip wire used to signal and illuminate the approach of an enemy at night.

Trip Wire   A wire or string, placed across a path or trail, which would set off either an explosive charge or a **Trip Flare.**

Trotter   A jungle trail made by the VC/NVA.

201 File   A U.S. Army personnel file.

Two Digit Midget   Term used to refer to a soldier who had 99 days or less to serve in Vietnam.

UH-1H   A Huey.

VC Viet Cong; a reference to a member of the NLF; a derogatory contraction of Vietnam Cong San, or Vietnamese Communist.

Wake-Up The last day of a soldier's Vietnam tour. For example, "10 days and a wake-up."

Waste To kill.

Weed Marijuana.

WIA Wounded in action.

Willie Peter or **WP** A white phosphorus artillery or mortar round, used for adjusting onto targets, for marking targets, for incendiary effects, and for smoke screens.

Wimp Weak incompetent malingering pussy.

Wood Line A row of trees at the edge of a field or rice paddy.

The World The United States.

Xin Loi A Vietnamese idiom meaning "Sorry about that."

XO Executive Officer; the second in command of a military unit.

Zap To kill or wound.

Bibliography

Vietnam-Related Sources

Baker, Mark. *Nam: The Vietnam War in the Words of the Men and Women Who Fought There.* New York: William Morrow and Company, 1981.

Boettcher, Thomas D. *Vietnam — The Valor and the Sorrow: From the Home Front to the Front Lines in Words and Pictures.* Boston: Little, Brown and Company, 1985.

Davidson, Phillip B. *Vietnam at War — The History: 1946–1975.* Novato, CA: Presidio Press, 1988; New York and Oxford: Oxford University Press, 1991.

Donovan, David. *Once a Warrior King: Memories of an Officer in Vietnam.* New York: McGraw-Hill, 1985.

Downs, Frederick. *The Killing Zone: My Life in the Vietnam War.* New York: W. W. Norton & Company, 1978; New York: Berkley Books, 1983.

Edelman, Bernard, ed. *Dear America: Letters Home from Vietnam.* New York: W. W. Norton & Company, 1985; New York: Pocket Books, 1985.

Glasser, Ronald J., MD. *365 Days.* New York: George Braziller, 1971.

Hackworth, David H., Colonel, and Julie Sherman. *About Face: The Odyssey of an American Warrior.* New York: Simon and Schuster, 1989.

The Library of America. *Reporting Vietnam: American Journalism, 1959–1975*, 2 vols. New York: The Library of America, 1998; New York: Penguin Putnam, 2000.

MacPherson, Myra. *Long Time Passing: Vietnam and the Haunted Generation.* Garden City, NY: Doubleday and Company, 1984.

Marshall, S. L. A. *Vietnam: Three Battles.* New York: Da Capo Press, 1983.

Maurer, Harry. *Strange Ground: An Oral History of Americans in Vietnam, 1945–1975.* New York: Henry Holt and Company, 1988; Avon Books, 1990.

McMahon, Robert C., ed., *Major Problems in the History of the Vietnam War.* Lexington, MA: D. C. Heath and Company, 1990.

Nolan, Keith William. *Battle for Hue: Tet, 1968.* Novato, CA: Presidio Press, 1983.

O'Nan, Stewart, ed. *The Vietnam Reader: The Definitive Collection of American Fiction and Nonfiction on the War.* New York: Anchor Books, 1998.

Salisbury, Harrison E. *Behind the Lines: Hanoi December 23, 1966–January 7, 1967.* New York: Harper & Row, 1967.

Santoli, Al. *Everything We Had: An Oral History of the Vietnam War By Thirty-Three American Soldiers Who Fought It.* New York: Random House, 1981.

_____. *To Bear Any Burden: The Vietnam War and Its Aftermath in the Words of Americans and Southeast Asians.* New York: E. P. Dutton, 1984; Ballantine Books, 1989.

Summers, Harry G. Jr. *On Strategy: A Critical Analysis of the Vietnam War.* Novato, CA: Presidio Press, 1982.

Williams, Tom, ed. *Post-Traumatic Stress Disorders of the Vietnam Veteran: Observations and Recommendations for the Psychological Treatment of the Veteran and His Family.* Cincinnati, OH: Disabled American Veterans, 1980.

General Reference

Barnett, Alex. *Words That Changed America: Great Speeches That Inspired, Challenged, Healed, and Enlightened.* Guilford, CT: The Lyons Press, 2003.

Dunnigan, James F., and Albert A. Nofi. *Dirty Little Secrets of the Vietnam War.* New York: St. Martin's Press, 1999.

Editors of the Boston Publishing Company. *The Vietnam Experience.* 25 vols. Boston: Boston Publishing Company, 1981–1988.

Hudson, the Rev. H. N., A.M., ed. *The Works of Shakespeare — The Students' Handy Edition,* rev. ed., Vols. 4 and 12. Boston: Estes and Lauriat, 1871.

Tucker, Spencer C., ed. *Encyclopedia of the Vietnam War: A Political, Social, and Military History,* Vols. 1–3. Santa Barbara, CA: ABC-CLIO, 1998.

Williams, Oscar, ed. *Immortal Poems of the English Language.* New York: Washington Square Press, 1963.

Newspapers

Arnett, Peter, and Horst Faas. "Draftees Receive 'Bull's-Eye' Baptism." *Richmond (VA) Times Dispatch,* 7 September 1969, sec. A, p. 1.

Salisbury, Harrison E. "Hanoi Premier Tells View; Some in U.S. Detect a Shift." *New York Times,* 4 January 1967, p. 2, column 4.

The Skiff (Texas Christian University), 21 November 1969, p. 4.

Government Documents

"Command Message," *The Stony Mountain Work Horse 2/8 Command Newsletter,* Vol. 2, No. 2, 26 September 1969.

Index